SHAKESPEARE
BEHIND BARS

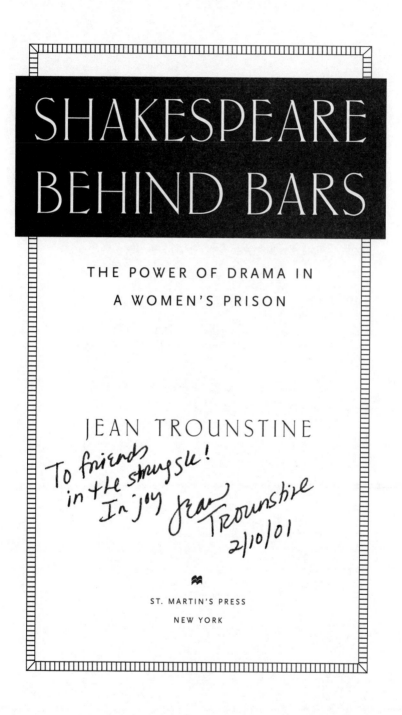

SHAKESPEARE
BEHIND BARS

THE POWER OF DRAMA IN
A WOMEN'S PRISON

JEAN TROUNSTINE

To friends in the struggle! Injoy Jean Trounstine 2/10/01

ST. MARTIN'S PRESS

NEW YORK

www.stmartins.com

Book design by Michelle McMillian

Some passages in this book have appeared, in slightly different form, in articles in *The Southwest Review*, *Writing Work: Writers on Working-Class Writing*, and *The Boston Globe Magazine*.

Library of Congress Cataloging-in-Publication Data

Trounstine, Jean R.
 Shakespeare behind bars : the power of drama in a women's prison / Jean Trounstine—1st ed.
 p. cm.
 ISBN 0-312-24660-9
 1. Prison theatre—Massachusetts—Case studies. 2. Women prisoners—Massachusetts—Case studies. 3. Women prisoners—Education—Massachusetts—Case studies. 4. Shakespeare, William, 1564–1616—Study and teaching—Massachusetts—Case studies. 5. Drama—Study and teaching—Massachusetts—Case studies. I. Title.

HV8861 .T76 2001
365'.66—dc21   00-047041

First Edition: February 2001

10 9 8 7 6 5 4 3 2 1

In memory of my parents,
Amy and Henry,
and dedicated to the women
at Framingham Prison

Contents

The quality of mercy is not strain'd;
It droppeth as the gentle rain from heaven
Upon the place beneath. It is twice blest—
It blesseth him that gives, and him that takes.
'Tis mightiest in the mightiest; it becomes
The throned monarch better than his crown;
His sceptre shows the force of temporal power,
The attribute to awe and majesty,
Wherein doth sit the dread and fear of kings;
But mercy is above this sceptred sway;
It is enthroned in the hearts of kings,
It is an attribute to God himself;
And earthly power doth then show likest God's
When mercy seasons justice.

THE MERCHANT OF VENICE, IV.i.184

SHAKESPEARE
BEHIND BARS

Prologue

In 1988 I was given a tentative go-ahead to teach acting and to re-hearse a play with a volunteer group of inmates at Framingham Women's Prison, the most secure facility for female offenders in Massachusetts. I first focused on Shakespeare's *The Merchant of Venice*, filled with conflicts about love and law and peopled with fascinating characters I hoped would engage the prisoners and their audience. I believed that if my students tackled Shakespeare, a writer they thought was beyond reach, they would also be learning to take on what was most difficult in life.

The six women who form the nucleus of this book, and the hundreds I met throughout my ten years at the prison, came to classes partly out of the desire to make time pass more quickly and partly out of the desire to become someone who wasn't considered a criminal. The women yearned for change and growth.

When at last the prisoners gathered for the performance of the play, we all had gone through changes that none of us could have imagined

1

before we began. What started as an experiment—creating theatre behind bars—had gradually grown into a program. Eventually the program took on a philosophy: art has the power to redeem lives. That philosophy, often challenged and at odds with Corrections, was in part, what drove me to write this book.

It took me five years to begin writing *Shakespeare Behind Bars* because the women touched me so deeply that it was difficult to find the words that would do them justice. There were nights when I would drive home from the prison, crying about something deeply personal that one of the women had revealed in class, or shaking my head in wonder at an insight another had unearthed about a text. I came to realize that most women in prison are not dangerous. The majority do not engage in physical assaults or sit in cells making weapons. Female inmates may form alliances against one another, and certainly they can be ruthless, but what characterizes them more than anything else is their heartache. Instead of frightening me they seemed lost, with tragic lives—lives like those of Shakespeare's characters, complete with flaws, comic mishaps, and ironic endings.

I began to understand that female prisoners are not "damaged goods," and to recognize that most of these women had toughed it out in a society that favors others—by gender, class, or race. They are Desdemonas suffering because of jealous men, Lady Macbeths craving the power of their spouses, Portias disguised as men in order to get ahead, and Shylocks, who, being betrayed, take the law into their own hands.

Certainly I'd heard of abuse behind bars, was curious about the crimes that women commit, and guessed that many inmates are immersed in poverty and hopelessness and have no avenues out, but I knew nothing of the fellowship that exists in prison. Women inmates seek relationship, thrive on it. Alone, without their children, ignored by lovers or husbands, they ultimately came to my classes to ward off loneliness and to find connection with others and themselves. It is this prison community that sustains women who do time, cut off, often abandoned by loved ones and forgotten in their home towns. This sisterhood offered me comfort when my mother died, celebration when I married. It is this community that taught me to value the prisoners' lives, to like and respect them, and to understand that they are more than news stories tucked away on a back page in our local papers.

Thus, when I began to write about teaching behind bars, I wanted to let the women's quirks and habits, their humor and insight, their beauty and bullishness, and their sense of community shine through my story. And since what also engulfed me was the power of art in a repressive environment, I wanted this book to focus on the creative world that I experienced with the inmates. It was their words on paper and their improvisations onstage that I witnessed, and it was in their work that they revealed their deepest needs and secrets, their struggles with the system, devotion to and despair over children, rage at spouses, insights on survival, and relationships with one another.

When people ask me what inspired me to teach in a prison, I tell them that what kept me going was not simply my love for literature and theatre. While it is true that prison is a repressive environment, the one who offers hope in the classroom has the potential to effect change. For many of the women I encountered, education offered hope; and drama, freedom. But, more important, as I watched personnel leave, restrictions broaden, and inmates run amok, the women offered revelations about their world. I felt a chemistry, a link between their lives and mine, a connection partly due to gender and partly due to yearning. The women of Framingham sought a way out, and their struggles gave them dignity. My heart went out to them, and as I wrote about our work I could hear their voices, as actors and as women, speaking out of the darkness.

ENTRANCES

O that I were as great
As is my grief, or lesser than my name!
Or that I could forget what I have been!
Or not remember what I must be now!
KING RICHARD II, III.III.136

B ertie swings elegantly into my classroom wearing a multicol-
ored striped hat of African design, perfectly pressed white
pants, and a crisp sleeveless orange shirt tied at the waist. It is 1986,
and she is dressed more for a rendezvous at a café on Boston's posh
Newbury Street than for a stay in prison. There is a sheen of sweat
on her muscled brown arms, a tautness that I associate with cheer-
leaders and athletes, and a grace that often comes from years of ballet.
I imagine her sipping a glass of red wine, a man hanging on her every
gesture. Suddenly she yells loudly at the recreation officer down the
hall, saunters in, and tosses me a smile as if we've known each other
for years.

I like her immediately but can't get over how young she is, nineteen,
twenty, twenty-one at most. I'm a high school teacher, and the last
place I ever expected to be was teaching in Framingham Prison, Massachusetts's most secure facility for female offenders. But there's something about a woman who dares to get in trouble that has always been

4

close to my heart. As a sixties rebel, I lived in a commune, had unsafe sex, and moved in with someone I'd known for only twenty-four hours. And now, as a dedicated teacher who has difficulty knowing where the classroom ends and home life begins, I've taught drug-addicted city kids in residential treatment centers, girls who've run away, and troubled teens who've come back to visit me long after they've left my classes. But all that aside, I never expected to be teaching college in a women's prison; and like most people, I am filled with prejudices, fears, and garbled TV images about the community of women living behind bars.

Two inmates seated at the long table look over at Bertie and whisper to each other. The tone of their sighs and phony coughs lets me know something is up. The one who calls herself Kit pulls a Camel out of her jeans jacket pocket and taps it at least ten times on the tabletop. She wears her hair up in a tight ponytail with strands of hair straggling out, making her look bedraggled and old. I notice that she has purplish rings under her eyes and no teeth. I overhear her complain, "They think my false teeth are a goddamn weapon."

I can feel how much she dislikes Bertie, and at first, I assume it's about race. Kit is white, and at this point, before the rest of the writing class has arrived, so are the others who sit around the table. I remember reading stories about race riots at Attica and conjure up frightening pictures of criminals beating one another with sticks.

Bertie seems unfazed by Kit's grousing. She hands me a slip of green paper that has the words, "Permission to Enter" at the top and a scrawled signature at the bottom. When I look at my attendance sheet, she says, "Hi, I'm Ber-tie. You won't find me on your list." I like her accent, the way she trips over her words with a lilt. I figure she might be from the Caribbean, although no one has mentioned much about these women. "It's policy," the program coordinator told me. "You're better off not knowing their crimes, so don't ask. Just do your job and leave. We only run into trouble with instructors who try to get too close."

Bertie moves gracefully toward me, the books under her arm almost sliding onto the table. We are in Program Room 2—a small room in which a blackboard covered with chalk dust, its tray without chalk, teeters in the corner. Everything about Bertie is youthful petulance: her sense of style, the flamboyant hat even though she has nowhere to go, an actor's sense of timing, a way of talking with her whole body. No lines on her smooth face. An arched neck drawn from a Modigliani painting, so that her chin juts out triumphantly. Her hands are dotted with rings—these are the days before jewelry and clothing privileges are taken away—and her nails painted a flamingo hot pink, a color that inspires salsa music. I want to know why someone this young is sitting in my prison English class. I want to know what she's in for.

" 'Bertie' must be short for something," I say, trying to sound experienced. I don't want to let on that every moment is extremely dramatic for me, filled with people who seem larger than life but who are nonetheless confined and controlled at every turn. Yet, in an odd way, prison also seems ordinary. Walking to my classroom, down a dingy white corridor painted too many times so that the paint is peeling and cracked on the ceiling, I could be in any aging institution. Posters on the walls advertise evening activities; there's a mop sink tucked into a hallway nook; a few tissues are strewn along floorboards. More than anything I am struck by the amount of noise I hear: women's voices mixed with raucous laughter; some low rumbling over a loudspeaker and announcements for visits, packages or medication lines; the shuffle of shoes on a floor above me blended with singing and church music; yelling and cheering and basketballs reverberating off backboards in a gym; rock music filtering down from somewhere; the sounds of Spanish, as women call out to one another from corners or from dinner lines; and incessantly, women's whispers hovering in hallways.

But at this moment, with all eyes focused on Bertie, who has brought tension into the room with her, I put on my detached voice: "Did you add this class?"

Bertie places one hand on her hip and another casually on my shoulder and shakes her head: "Girl, I didn't have much of a choice. This is prison. It was ESL or you."

A middle-aged prisoner who is knitting a white baby bunting bursts into a throaty laugh. She has a pug nose and pockmarked face, and her blond beehive reminds me of a racetrack bookie's. I figure large breasts and pale coloring have earned her the nickname "Dolly," after Dolly Parton. She turns her palm up, and Bertie sashays over to her. "Give me five," Dolly says as Bertie slaps her hand.

Bertie turns back to me. "My real name's Jasmine, but everyone calls me Bertie."

Kit sneers, muttering something about Bertie's crime to another woman across the room, who shakes her head. This one I don't know yet, but she's got the name "Ana Lou" tattooed on her biceps and wears a baseball cap backwards. Later I find out that her name is Cody and her mother's a schoolteacher, a "grammar fanatic" with what she calls "red-pen mentality." Cody guffaws a lot and keeps cigarettes tucked in the turned-up sleeve of her T-shirt like James Dean. She's in cahoots with Kit in some way I can't figure out.

Suddenly the room is dead quiet. I look at Kit, who is still muttering under her breath. She's crossed her arms and stonewalls Dolly and Bertie, refusing to smile at the warm humor between the two. Cody shoots a nasty look in their direction. She seems to be angry, but it's all silence and chill, as though words would hold less weight.

Dolly beckons Bertie to sit down next to her, patting the chair, and gives the hostile two a nod that signals them to back off. "She belongs with us," Dolly pipes up in my direction. Her tone has shifted. She's serious now. "ESL won't get her anywhere. She needs to learn to write, right?"

"Thanks, Ma," Bertie replies casually to Dolly. I sense that Bertie is in for more than prostitution or drugs, but I don't ask, and in some way, as much as I want answers, I am afraid that knowing would prejudice me, make it harder to teach. I smile politely at Bertie, adding her name to my roster, and wonder why she calls Dolly "Ma."

Bertie sits as though she was made for the chair, giving the orange tie on her sleek tummy a little pull and crossing her legs. The hostile two are about to make a comment, but Dolly shushes them. I'm wondering if I should abandon all lesson plans and let the women write nonstop for two hours. At least that way they wouldn't have to talk to each other.

There's some argument in the hall, and Kit and Cody rush to the door. Connors, the correction officer who led me down the hallway earlier tonight, appears at the doorway. "Cool your jets, ladies. You aren't going anywhere," she spouts at Kit and Cody. While Kit and Cody disgruntledly head back to their chairs, Connors turns to me. She points out names on my roster. "They're at basketball. Cross them off your list."

Connors looks about twenty-six and, like most correction officers, had barely ten weeks' training before becoming a CO. She chews gum, "contraband" for the prisoners or contract employees like myself, and she doesn't crack a smile. "Turn around and face the wall," she said tonight with this deadpan voice after she cornered me in the tiny room off the main entrance where everyone has to be pat-searched before they set foot in Framingham. These are the days before high-tech scanners and computers that open and shut doors, before a new brick gateway with its antiseptic cleanliness makes entering Framingham almost effortless. Then she said, "Hands out to your side. Spread your legs. That's it. All right, take off your shoes. Show me the bottoms of your feet. Good. Head forward. Hair. Behind the ears. Good. Stick out your tongue. Okay, open your mouth wide." I mumbled something in response, knowing why she had to search me but wanting to hurl something at her, angry words, a punch, anything to offset this invasion of my body. Somehow I rose above anger and tried to make her laugh, but that didn't work with Connors. She's a follow-all-orders type who insists that she be called only by her last name. When I asked her what it was like to search people, she gave me an indifferent look. "College teacher or not, you have to follow rules. Prisons," Connors reminded me, "model themselves on the military."

I give Connors a nod and start to ask her more about the students who are absent, but she's off, talking to a few other inmates in the hallway. A big black woman with a thick neck and arms of hammered steel comes in moments later, huffing and puffing as if she's climbed up two flights of stairs. She stops in the doorway and scans the room before she enters. I guess that she senses the energy, which, from where I sit, seems kinetic, almost dangerous. But if she does, she doesn't show it. She walks slowly around the chairs toward Bertie, measuring her steps. She has a limp and drags a leg behind her, which makes her look older than her fortyish years, but I like her slow gait, the solid ankles that support a frame made for work, contrasting with her delicate long fingers and tiny eyes. She has bifocals on a red string draped around her neck. "I'm Mamie," she says, a polite nod in my direction.

Kit and Cody give her the cold shoulder, but Mamie couldn't care less. She says she's looking forward to our writing class, and when

Cody and Kit snicker, she says it again, only this time louder and pointedly at them. Then she seats herself next to Bertie, whose face immediately lights up when Mamie says, "I got some plant cuttings for your room. Purple mums. Prettiest flowers I rescued this week."

"Mamie's the prison gardener," Dolly says, aiming a knitting needle in my direction. "Brings the girls greenery. Real nice." Kit makes some kind of coughing sound and Cody chuckles, but Mamie is unruffled. She has a stack of greeting cards in her hand, one of which she shows to Bertie. It's clear that even in a women's prison there is a pecking order, and that Mamie and Dolly have taken Bertie under their wing to protect her from women who sling slurs at her.

When Mamie sees me leaning over to look at her artwork, she says, "I make poems." She holds up a card. It's filled with handwriting and bits of pressed dried flowers. I smile at her and check her name off my attendance list.

"I spend my days in the greenhouse," Mamie continues, "but I was a nurse in the free world." As she pulls her chair into the table, she looks straight at Cody and then at Kit, "We must be about ready to start this class, right, ladies?" And as the women turn to me, I know opening night's begun.

It will be weeks before I feel that I know these women and months before we begin producing a play at Framingham. After all, this is only my first class. I am meeting my students.

DOLLY

By heaven, I do love, and it hath taught me
to rhyme, and to be melancholy.

LOVE'S LABOUR'S LOST, IV.III.13

D olly is the one who gets me thinking about putting on plays at Framingham. And frankly, I'm surprised by the hold she has on me. Maybe it's the fact that people have given up on her that pulls me in, or the challenge when she says, "No one in the free world cares about women in prison." Maybe it's the fighter instinct we have in common that makes us click. But as I get to know Dolly, something about her won't let go.

It's late March 1987, an Introduction to Literature class that focuses on reading and writing, our second semester together. Dolly has been in a foul mood all evening, dark circles under her eyes; she says that this month she's had little sleep. She's come to class after a trip to Shattuck, Boston's hospital for the homeless and the incarcerated, stomping in the door, furious about trekking to get a breast exam that never occurred. Before any of us can speak, she hurls us into how she spent the day in a holding cell, waist-chained and cuffed.

"Over ten hours, packed in with women. They strip-searched us twice—twice fer Chrissakes—transported us like dogs in one of those dogcatcher's wagons, and kept us in a very small cell with a one-way glass mirror and only a hole in the ceiling for ventilation. Fed us like animals—with one handcuff on while we ate. And to top it all I never got to see the doctor. Can you believe it?"

The women are nodding sympathetically. I worry that Dolly might be sick but she waves away my concern with, "It's just a regular breast exam, every two years, but I'll be damned if I'm going again, even if I have to die of cancer in this hellhole." She tosses her notebook on the table and sits, everything about her now heavy, slowed down. "Sorry for the outburst. I know I should be grateful we get breast exams and all, but I'm fed up with this place."

At first I hesitate to speak. Dolly's demeanor seems to say, "Don't push me." But as I watch her turn to the other students, stirring up the room, I break in, "Let's take this energy to the page. Everyone grab a pen, some paper." There's some groaning, but only for a moment as I coax them to find blank pages in their notebooks. I take up my pen as well. In minutes we're into free-writing, all seated around the wobbly table. Dolly settles down while we write nonstop, pens scratching into paper. "Writing to discover," I call it. "Go wherever your pen takes you." They know the routine by now. We write without looking up. We write to find out what we are feeling. It's a chance to "wash out the crap," the women tell me, and it's true. With free-writing they often dredge up the inexpressible: anger at guards or at a family member who refuses to visit; regrets about something that happened the last time they saw their kids; frustration at pipes that clang all night; or the kind of loneliness that comes when a train goes by the prison, its long, low whistle reminding them that they aren't going anywhere.

Dolly drafts a poem she doesn't want to read aloud, and I chalk it up to her lousy day, but at the close of class, as inmates drift out of the room, she waits, pulling the cap on and off her pen. I'm expecting something simple. Maybe she'll ask for an extension on the next assignment or complain about not liking the book we're reading. Maybe she'll ask me to look at a photograph from home or an article she's found in the newspaper about her housing project in Chelsea. Perhaps she'll tell me all about the long-termers' group—those sentenced for more than a few years—or about the family picnic that they're planning this spring. All these things have happened before, so I'm prepared for them.

"I bet the men get more than three classes in their prisons," she says. Not an odd comment, considering the almost ballistic way she entered the classroom and her contentious attitude tonight. But I can't tell where she's heading.

"We only have three classes at the women's prison," I say, "one English, one math, and one history or science—biology this term, with no lab—because of funding issues."

She scoffs at me. "I'm an English major, Jean," and Dolly looks away, "but not exactly by choice."

There's some longing on Dolly's face that I can't name, but something also tells me that Dolly has lived with more heartbreak than she admits. Kit, who lags behind, stacking chairs, turns to her, laughing as she speaks. "Hey, Doll, this is jail, not Yale." By now I've learned that Kit considers Dolly a "friend," having known her on the street. She looks disappointed when Dolly doesn't respond to her joke. Dolly puts on a shaggy wool sweater, too heavy for the season, and walks toward the small window.

"What's on your mind?" I ask, watching Dolly walk across the room. She stares outside. The evening sky is lit up with a full moon and streetlamps dot the landscape, light catching the tips of purple weeds in the marsh beyond the barbed wire. Soon it will be spring in New England, where even on a night in prison you can see trees bloom, feel the air rush by you, and breathe in forsythia. The stillness of evening pervades and softens us. Sounds from the poolroom across the hall punctuate the quiet.

Dolly looks over at me as though she has just lighted on a thought. "If we get more students, we can do it."

"Do what?" I ask. I'm helping Kit straighten up.

"A play." I pause. Dolly says it again. "I want us to put on a play. Here."

From the side of the room, Kit says, "Some of these girls are excellent cons." I laugh.

"Well, whaddaya think?" Dolly looks over at me, catching me squarely in the eyes.

"I think it's a great concept," and I fold up a metal chair, avoiding her gaze. It's not that I haven't thought about theatre at Framingham. It's just that I've never considered it seriously. I'm flooded with obstacles—my full-time teaching schedule outside of prison; the idea of dealing with temperamental actresses, props and costumes, rehearsals and rules. "We should probably start with a something smaller, maybe a class." I pick up my briefcase.

Dolly pulls out a pack of Camels, tilting the pack so that one cigarette spills into her hand. As she lights it Kit cuts in, "You know we have to be outta here pronto."

Dolly sits on the sill, lost in thought, alternately blowing puffs of smoke out through the side of her mouth and taking in breaths of night air. "The men have an inmate council. They can buy fresh meat, fruit by the bagful when in season. But that's only a part of it." By now Kit and I have packed away all the chairs, and we're standing by the door, watching Dolly. She keeps on smoking and talking. "They have a very active lifers' group that tours with their theatre program. They came to Framingham a few years ago and put on a production."

"Hey, I saw that!" Kit blurts out. "It was about an old man or something. No, it was about dreams—"

Dolly interrupts, the cigarette at her lips. "It was *Man of La Mancha*, that's what. And the men designed their own set and they ran the lights. They have real carpentry and electrical shops in their prisons. If they can do it, so can we. So can I."

I look hard at Dolly. She spends her sentence making flags and creating microfiche. She worries about her family, works toward her degree, takes part in groups, and counsels other inmates. She's even founded a battered women's group, based, she says, on her own experience. But here in the loneliest place I know, I can feel her wanting to stretch, to be more than she is.

"We could tour," Dolly continues. Now she's got a glimmer in her eye and is gesturing with her cigarette. "You know, go to other institutions. Show our talent."

I'm thinking how inmates who get paroled or transferred could quit in the middle. I'm imagining canceled rehearsals for visits, dentist appointments, and bad behavior. It is too much. No, not a play, not in prison. But still . . . and I notice Dolly's hands, the painted mauve nails gracefully curving past the ends of her fingers.

"All right," I say. "I'll think about it."

"All right," she says. "And so will I."

. . .

Even before Dolly gets me to consider putting on plays, her aspirations catch me off guard, and I discover her desire to be part of something that takes her outside of daily prison life. The first night we meet, in September 1986, I'm in Program Room 2, waiting for my students and thinking how strange it is to be locked in, how unsafe it feels to say what I think to an officer. Even though a few weeks ago I spent three hours listening to an officer talk about prisoners' scams and watched a video of simulated scenes—inmates trying to con volunteers by forging passes or by faking IDs—I'm hardly aware of what a prisoner does all day, much less what she thinks or feels. I'm reflecting on Connors, the female guard who's escorted me down the corridor.

On our way past No-Man's Land, the area between the glass entranceway and the iron door that is the official door to the prison, Connors told me, "Remember, you're not here to be their friend." I wanted to ask her if she'd ever been a teacher, but I didn't, instead following her diligently, watching her from behind, keys on a metal ring hooked into her belt. They jangled when she walked. Connors is short, maybe five foot three, but she has a big man's attitude, a stride to her step, always heading down the corridor like there's no stopping her, heels hitting the floor heavily in black police shoes. She often carries a bottle of Pepsi and a brown bag that smells like pickles, and says nothing to prisoners we pass who mop the floor, a bucket of sudsy water by their sides.

"Where is everyone?" I asked as we arrived at the door marked "Program Room 2."

"At dinner," Connors replied. "The Upward's in fifteen."

"Upward?" I said.

Connors looked bored. "It's called an Upward. When the women come up from their cottages, you know, for dinner, activities."

"Oh."

Connors unlocked the door and turned to go. I looked into the room, barren, with a blackboard and chairs scattered here and there. There was no table.

"Do we have to write on our laps?" I could feel myself wanting to keep her there.

"If you have any questions, you'll have to talk to the recreation officer. No one's in Education after three." Connors shrugged. "I don't know why they didn't put you upstairs. But they didn't." She disappeared, leaving the door open behind her.

Now I wish I were upstairs, imagining what I'm missing in Education: maybe desks, a real wall blackboard, the kind of classrooms that look like public school resource rooms, with dictionaries and bookshelves, a pull-down map, or a globe on a stand. Everything feels uncomfortable in this small room. It's overheated and stuffy. A piece of track lighting hangs loose from the ceiling, and a fluorescent light flickers on and off. A broken piece of electrical cord sticks out of the wall socket. I head over to the single window in the corner and push it up to where it locks. On the top half of the window behind the glass there is an iron grating that functions like bars. You can only open the window an arm's width. I gaze outside at a scrawny tree in the yard.

"Won't make it till Sunday," a gravelly voice says behind me. I turn around, half expecting the recreation officer, whom I've seen darting around the halls in her shiny blue trousers and white T-shirt, a whistle hanging from a string around her neck, like a camp counselor's. Instead, there's a woman in the doorway who looks a little like a gangster moll, a middle-aged Bonnie from *Bonnie and Clyde*. She's blue eyed and ash blond, someone who might have been a real knockout when she was younger but who's spreading out now. There's something about her that's sweet too, a dimple in her cheek, a pouffiness to her hair, like cotton candy.

"What are you talking about?" I'm thinking she's an inmate, but I'm not sure. She's close to fifty and wearing gold button earrings and a blazer that looks like a patchwork quilt over black jeans. But the blazer's not new, and the jeans are faded.

She crosses over to the window and points at the tree. "Lookit."

"At what?" I ask, staring intently at the trunk of the leafless tree. I have no clue what she's getting at. I notice a dark streak stretching from the base of a branch to the ground, almost as if a part of the tree has been burned. "Was there a fire or something?" I look closer, above the tree, and see a dead bird crucified on a wire that crosses the prison yard. The bird is brown, perhaps a pigeon, although by now it has decayed and appears to have only one wing. "Was that bird electrocuted?"

"Who knows? That bird's been there forever." The woman comes closer. "Look in the tree." She points to a bird's nest hidden by the longest tree branch. There are three speckled eggs. "Poor suckers," she sighs. "No way to save those eggs. That area's out of bounds. No one's allowed in there. And the mama seems to be gone." She points again, this time to a sign that says, AREA OFF LIMITS and at yellow plastic tape strung all around the space. The tape has the words CRIME SCENE in black letters printed every twelve inches.

"Was a crime committed there?" I ask.

The woman laughs. "No crime. Just off limits. It's prison talk for 'stay out.'" She reaches out to shake my hand. "You must be the English teacher."

"Jean. Jean Trounstine." I smile and try to look tough at the same time. "And you?"

"I'm Dolly." She turns to go out the door. "See you in a few. Gotta go find you a table."

When I step outside to look for the recreation officer, Dolly's been distracted. She's directing a tall redheaded inmate with a scar down her left arm next door to the room where haircuts take place. "It's the beauty parlor," Dolly says to the prisoner, who trails her. "Even though people are inside, the door is kept locked. Bernice will let you in."

Suddenly there's a flurry. The tall one begins to knock, complaining that she set her haircut appointment weeks ago. Through the glass wall I see a prisoner with her head in the sink and another, the barber, standing over her. The barber, a chunky shorter woman with loopy earrings and a lot of eye makeup, yells back that she'd cut hair all night if they'd let her. "It's not my fuckin' fault they curfew us at nine P.M." Dolly soothes and coos until Bernice, the recreation officer, rescues her. The haircutters then begin to badger Bernice, who maintains a cool demeanor through all their demands. In her detached calm, I see the role that non-inmates are expected to take: Don't get rattled. Don't get involved. Be neutral, and when the women bounce like Ping-Pong balls around you, be a strong post but not the net to catch them.

Dolly becomes animated when she sees me standing in the doorway. "I know where we can get a table," she announces. "Cheap." She seems in charge of everything, waving her hands around, interrupting the troublemakers. "Hey, Bernice, we need that table in Storage. It wobbles," she apologizes to me, "but it's a table."

More women stream into the halls, while Dolly and Bernice head off to another room a few doors down. I follow along the spotless floor, past a poster of a middle-aged woman and her daughter seated on a couch, with the caption ANYONE CAN GET AIDS. We pass a bulletin board with a photo display of inmates at what looks like a party with their kids in the gym. Bernice unlocks the door.

"This is the English teacher, Jean," Dolly says. "I don't remember your last name."

"Trounstine." I feel awkward and just stand there until Bernice smiles hello. We enter a room that smells of mildew. An old TV on a stand is crowded into a corner near a broken lamp. A dusty rectangular table, clearly out of commission, sits stored on its side, next to stacks of magazines and old pieces of broken pottery.

"I used to teach," Bernice tells me almost confidentially, "high school arts and crafts, but when Proposition Two and a Half came around and schools all over the state cut teachers, I lost my job. I've been here ever since." We move boxes out of the way, and the three of us pick up the table and file out, pausing while Bernice locks the door behind us.

"I have bad luck, a bad back, too, but you'd never know it. Bernice always forces me to move furniture," Dolly says.

"She makes great money," Bernice teases as we round the corner into the English room. "Takes home a lot too." We set the table down in the center of the room, and Dolly puts a piece of folded-up paper under the wobbly leg. Bernice exits, talking on her walkie-talkie. It is time for the Upward.

"I've done some writing," Dolly says. "A short story or two. Some poems. In the free world. You know, I'm in your class."

I nod and tell her that's great, glad to have her, and although that first night I am mostly concerned with logistics, I can't help wondering—where's the chink, Dolly? Why are you here if you seem so together? I open my briefcase and pull out tablets of lined paper and a bunch of blue pens. I place them on the table.

"What else do you teach?" she asks.

"You mean besides English?" She gives me an uh-huh while we arrange folding chairs around the table. I scoop up two small pieces of chalk from the floor. The longest one is red. "Sometimes drama." Dolly's eyes widen and she smiles.

"You mean plays," she says. "I was in one of them. In school. Community theatre too. A long time ago," she adds, and laughing, "before I came to this place. You shoulda seen me then. I was a star."

. . .

One fall evening that first October, I begin to learn more about what drives Dolly. I arrive a few minutes before class, and unfortunately, Kojack's not on. Kojack's the bald-headed officer who considers me a "regular" and lets me skip the pat-search. At 6:00 P.M., just before Visits, he is usually eating a sub and sitting on a stool in the glassed-in guard station, which looks like a small cage inside the prison's entrance. He's a master at dealing with the crowded visiting room, where everything reeks of smoke. Even well-dressed lawyers look seedy in that setting. He's friendly to the few men waiting to see their wives and girlfriends. Occasionally he directs inmate workers to pick up trash from a floor littered with pop cans and scraps of paper.

But tonight, without Kojack, getting in is endlessly long. There's a wait while Connors hands out entry slips to mothers whose children play tag or climb on the wooden hard-backed seats that once were church pews. There's a delay when she "processes" my forms.

By the time I get to Program Room 2, Dolly is next to the windowsill, puffing away on a Camel. It's not unusual to find her in the main institution while other inmates are still in their units. As one of Bernice's assistants, she often comes straight from dinner to help set up chairs for AA meetings, clean up the gym for volleyball, or do paperwork. Tonight she's placed chairs all around the table, but she barely moves when I hurry in. She has a dark sweater wrapped tight around her shoulders, and the way she angles her head, the loose strands of hair around her neck and face, signal some kind of weariness.

"You're late," she says, a distinct wavering in her voice. She takes a drag on her cigarette.

"You're right. I'm usually inside a good twenty minutes before the Upward, getting ready for class."

"I know. I have no choice. I have to wait." Dolly crosses over to the table and sits, still not looking at me. When she wraps a tuft of hair around her finger, I notice a little raw spot on top of her head where she's pulled out hairs. She tilts her head away from me, but with her puffed-up eyes and blotchy cheeks, I can tell she's been crying.

"You're early," I cajole. "Must be that great job you have, coming up before the rest of the compound." Assisting the recreation officer does have special privileges, like eating dinner early, input into movie night, listening to music on a boom box in the recreation office. But tonight Dolly's not interested in my humor. She doesn't react.

"Sorry, I'm late," I try again. "Connors couldn't find my admission form. Kojack isn't on tonight." He's the inmates' favorite guard and bound to get a smile out of Dolly. But no such luck. "With Connors at the front," I say, "it's always, 'Lift up your hair, take off your boots, and empty out every scrap of paper that's in your pockets.' "

Dolly sighs. "Connors is a ball buster, all right." She slides a photo out of her Middlesex Community College notebook and looks up. "I want to talk to you." Tears begin to well in her eyes. "It's about my daughter, Elizabeth."

I sit down in the chair next to Dolly.

"I don't know what I can do for her. She says she's afraid all the time, even to visit me. Her husband, you know, hurts her." Dolly pulls a tissue from her pants pocket. "Like mother, like daughter."

"Have you talked to her?" I'm not sure how to address this, or if I should.

"Talk?" Dolly gulps in air. She dabs her eyes with the tissue, trying not to cry. "Beth loves to talk. She promises to leave, swears she'll do it, just walk away from him, but Jean, I'm afraid for her. And she has his baby."

She passes me the photo, ripped almost in half and taped back together again, of Elizabeth, her husband, and Dolly's granddaughter, a bright-eyed one-year-old with bows in her hair. They are all smiling.

"Beautiful girl," I say. "Looks like you."

Dolly takes another deep breath. "What really gets to me is I was just like Beth, you know, with Frank. He used to beat the hell outta me. Emotionally." When I stare at her blankly, she says, "Frank, my codefendant. I loved him, but people say I went to jail because of him. Sometimes I think that's true."

"I remember now. You wrote about him." I think of one of the first pieces of writing Dolly shared with the writing class, a poem, with the line, "A love so deep, you hurt when your love hurts." And then there was the poem Frank sent her from prison—"Like a lily among thorny weeds you are / Like an apple tree among the trees of the forest."

"Beth keeps saying that she needs me," Dolly goes on. "I'd do anything I could for her. But what can I do from here? It breaks my heart." I hand her another tissue, this one from my briefcase, and that starts her crying again. She dabs her eyes. "Just sit with me, Jean," she says, and I do, silently, the truth of Dolly's pain suspended between us like stale air.

Suddenly the room is filled with women and noise. Cody takes hold of a metal chair and swings her leg over the seat, straddling it, pushing it backward into the table. She is chewing something and tips her baseball cap toward me. I've heard she got in a fight recently over some woman in her cottage.

Dolly tucks the photo into her notebook. Bertie crosses over to her, and the two of them put their heads together, whispering. Dolly hands

Bertie a fireball candy and delightedly, Bertie pops the red-hot in her mouth. Cody says loudly in their direction, "What's the scoop on Jackson? Don't hold out. Where's she housing?"

Bertie and Dolly don't answer Cody, who continues to press them about Jackson. From the way Cody says the name "Jackson," almost biting out the syllables, I get that she must be Cody's former lover, someone who'd do well not to come anywhere near Cody tonight.

An announcement booms over the loudspeaker informing prisoners who need meds to report to the medical office immediately. Dolly says she needs water and almost collides with Kit, who enters the classroom just as Dolly exits. Bertie opens her notebook and turns to a page filled with doodling. She shades in the cheeks on one of her women's heads. Other inmates find chairs, tossing comments around the room, sounding more like they're in a cafeteria than a college classroom.

After Dolly returns with a pitcher filled with water and paper cups for everyone, Bertie asks if we can get the class going and not wait for latecomers.

Kit pours herself a quick cup of water and says, "Cody, you always complain that you're the last to get picked to read. Just do it." She chugs the water like it's a beer. Tonight Cody's not on her good side.

We all look at Cody. "You sound like that Nike ad," Cody says to Kit, getting a little laugh out of the room. "But okay." She grudgingly pulls a scrunched-up piece of paper out of her jeans jacket. "I don't think it's much of anything." She whips through the writing, a story about getting a bike for her eighth birthday. The only catch, she tells us, is that to keep the bike, she has to prove to her father she can ride it; since her birthday is in December, she has to ride over ice. When she finishes, Cody yanks at her cap and breaks into a smile. "Had bikes all my life. All kinds, some with ribbons off the basket, even a few Harleys. But not any bike like the one my dad gave me."

"Yeah," sighs Bertie. "I wish my father had taught me how to ride a bike." She cups her head in her hands, resting her elbows on the table. Dolly pats Bertie's forearm and then joins in while we praise Cody.

Just as we finish the discussion, Dolly says, "You're gonna kill me, Jean." She shoots a look at me. "I don't have a story."

The class is all eyes, waiting to see how I'll respond. Even though I know Dolly's been upset about her daughter, I don't want to play favorites. "So why did you need water, if you're not going to read?"

"Ouch," Kit says, pouring herself another glass.

"Sorry, bad joke. Dolly, can you get something together for next class?"

"Ma," Bertie says, under her breath. I now notice whenever she calls Dolly "Ma," she's aiming to connect with her friend, the care-taker. "You have something to read, don't you?" Bertie asks.

Dolly shrugs and turns away, gazing out the window at the barren tree. It is early October, and the desolate tree is surrounded by other leafy ones, all in various states of yellow and ocher. Someone sighs. Bertie and Kit look at Dolly. "Ma?" Bertie asks again.

"I do have something I wrote." Dolly thumbs through her folder. "It's a letter to a lawyer. I want her to take my case." She pulls out a couple of typed pages. Since in 1986 there are few computers, and no typewriters except in offices, I know she has put a lot of work into this.

"Read away," I say, and relax into my chair. I'm expecting "To whom it may concern."

Dolly's eyes dart around the room. She's hesitating. "I want you to help me decide if this letter is good enough to send. It's more than important. It could get me a new sentence." Suddenly the texture of the class is different. The air is thick, palpable. We're listening to words that can change a life. The women nod or mutter, "Yeah," "Go girl," or, "Do it."

Dolly decides to stand up while she reads. She takes hold of the back of the chair with one hand. I notice that the hand holding the letter is shaking. When she reads the name, I realize that she's writing to a well-known female lawyer in the Boston area, someone who later will be instrumental in a famous battered women's case involving one of the Framingham Eight, women convicted for killing their abusers. Some earned a commutation from the governor or a reduced sentence once their case gained national attention.

Dolly wants a chance to be heard. She starts off forcefully by telling the lawyer that her codefendant, Frank, stabbed a man who died eighteen months later. She says that she was convicted on the theory of "joint enterprise," and although she doesn't define it, I'm sure that must mean she's been found guilty of being equally involved in Frank's crime.

Kit, who's slumped in her chair, sits up. She nudges the woman next to her to get her head off the table.

Dolly is lost in her letter. She paces the room. It's not often that the women mention their crimes, and we are watching her almost as if she's onstage. She explains that she lived with Frank in an apartment in the projects, that she was cochairperson of the tenants' council and got along with everyone. For a minute I see Dolly and Frank sitting on the stoop, listening to country music, Johnny Cash and Patsy Cline.

Dolly then walks toward the blackboard and takes hold of its frame with her free hand. She slows down, describing the events of the day of the crime, telling how another man in her unit, Luciano, a known troublemaker, got into a fight outside her building with her sixteen-year-old son. When she tried to intervene, Luciano threatened her with his fists. She reads: " 'Go ahead, hit me,' I told him. 'That's just your style, bullying women and children.' Lou yelled at me, patting his pocket, saying, 'I've got something here that's going to put you in a box.' He was raving he was going to kill my mother, father, my kids, my whole family."

Dolly heads toward Bertie and falters over her words. But even in her stumbling, she's got everyone's attention. She seems fragile and scared when she tells us that she ran upstairs to call the police. She can't understand why Frank yelled, "Put the phone down or I'll break your fucking legs!" but she was afraid to do anything he didn't want her to, so she didn't make the call. Frank headed out the door, she says, and he and Luciano began arguing. As she ran downstairs to try and stop this fight too, Lou's sister-in-law accused her of getting Frank to beat up Luciano. Dolly looks up from the letter and searches our eyes, "What, was she crazy? I didn't go upstairs to get Frank. I meant to call the police."

Kit mutters under her breath as though the story were hers; Cody massages the knuckles of her left hand with her right. Bertie pulls on an earring that dangles from her pierced ear and lets out a sound of shock mixed with disapproval. Perhaps this is the first time she's hearing details about Dolly's crime. I realize Dolly is trying to tell us something that I can't quite piece together. I know the court thinks she had a part in instigating the fight.

Dolly pauses, takes a breath and leans in, bracing herself on the back of the empty chair next to Bertie. Then her voice gains volume in spite of its shakiness. "All hell broke loose. Lou's sister-in-law was yelling, 'He stabbed Luciano!' I saw Lou take three steps backwards, holding his stomach, turn, and walk to his brother's car. I didn't see any knife. It was awful."

Dolly wipes her brow with the back of her sleeve; a moment of defeat seems to immobilize her. "Frank," she says to us, "I know he has a temper . . . ," and her voice trails off. "I shoulda known he'd go crazy, but I never knew he'd get a knife outta his truck."

"Shit," Kit says. "Bastard. You were framed."

Bertie looks up at Dolly. "You were, Ma." A few of the others shift in their seats.

Without another word Dolly begins pacing again, now with anger in her voice as she recounts the circus of a trial with a lawyer she said didn't call any witnesses for her, a lie detector test she passed that was ignored, and an appeal without new evidence. She says that she first received a sentence in 1983—assault with intent to kill, armed—and was given nine to ten years. I look around the room, wondering if we are all thinking the same thing. Armed? Dolly, were you armed? But no one asks Dolly that question, and it seems clear to me that in the melee of the day, witnesses might not have seen where Frank got the weapon.

Dolly then tells us that in January 1984, after Luciano died, she was sentenced again, this time for life. She pauses and looks up for a moment at the stunned faces of the women around her. "I didn't kill anyone," she says emphatically to us. "I'm afraid I might have been what is known as a 'trade-off.' "

As Dolly breaks from her letter and pauses, shutting her eyes tight for a moment while she gathers herself up, I'm wondering if, on appeal, Frank told the court that Dolly got him to stab Luciano. Maybe the reason she's doing so much time is because of his testimony. Frank gets off easy, but Dolly gets nailed.

"I haven't got a previous record." Her voice has sunk. She's barely audible. She heads toward the chair next to Bertie. "I think the only thing I'm guilty of is a crime of the heart, of loving the wrong man."

As she says the word "man," she slowly lowers herself onto the metal seat.

I sit transfixed. Dolly is in for life. They say she's a murderer.

"Well, whaddaya think?" Dolly asks us softly, breaking the quiet that fills the room. She's skimming through the pages of her letter, barely looking up. "I know, I'm responsible for my associations. That's what one of my lawyers told me."

"Instead of jail you should've been given probation," someone says.

"Yeah," Kit says, "and told to stay away from Frank. That scumbag made you pay, and he offed Luciano. But what do I know? I think most men are bums."

A titter from across the room. "You had a lousy lawyer," Cody says quietly.

"That is a good letter, Ma." Bertie is snuggled up in her shawl. "I think you have nothing to lose by sending it." She leans in closer to Dolly. "This was hard. I didn't know you went to prison for Frank."

"Forget Frank," Kit says. She takes her pack of Pall Malls out of her flannel shirt pocket and taps a cigarette on the table. A few of the women laugh.

"I don't know if I have enough guts to go through any more of this," Dolly is saying, still sifting through her papers. "But I gotta do it for my family. And to get rid of this crazy life sentence the court's making me serve. This lawyer's helped a lot of women." She turns to me. "Will she take my case?"

Kit edges over to the window to smoke, sitting on the sill. Cody joins her, leaning against the wall. She gets a light from Kit's cigarette. I notice that one or two of the women look at the floor or out the window. They probably think Dolly is guilty.

Dolly stares at me. It amazes me how much the prisoners expect me to know about things I know nothing about, like the law. I want to ask Dolly what detail I might have missed that led a judge to sentence her to life in prison. I want to say how I sense that she is telling the truth but that it's difficult to be sure. I know that a man lost his life, but I am also moved by her story, even though it is fragmented; the passion of her reading pulls me toward her. What I do tell her is that I'm not sure what a lawyer might say, but she's written a powerful letter and she should send it. I add, "I want you to believe in yourself."

She says, "Don't make me cry. You know the day I've had." Then she turns to Bertie. "Besides everything else, my daughter, the one with the new baby, is talking about leaving. That bastard will kill her if he finds out."

. . .

Months later, I am back for my second year and have managed to get permission from the college to run a play-reading class. I've also applied for a grant from the Massachusetts Foundation for the Humanities to study and put on a Shakespeare play in late spring. I'm in Program Room 2, busily filling in the attendance sheet for the new class, noting that a few of the old-timers have a big *W* for "withdrawn" next to their names. I figure Intro to Drama has sent some of them packing.

Inmates are scattered around the table, old along with new; others sit in desk chairs, all with open books. Students are finishing a writing assignment about the play we've read in class and seen on film, Shakespeare's *The Taming of the Shrew*. I've picked *Shrew* because it deals with love and war between the sexes. Petruchio, who thinks he's always right, engages Dolly. "He's a macho stud with problems," she's said, "trying to win Miss Wildcat Kate by 'taming' her, showing up late for their wedding, starving her when she gets to his house."

Last week we talked about what problems Kate has being open to love, since she is slighted by her father for her younger sister, and known around town as a shrew. I asked the women to write about Kate and to decide if she really needs all that "punishment" to come around, as she does eventually, to loving Petruchio. But Dolly's comments have given me the idea of having them consider the Petruchios in their lives, so tonight, I ask them to write about what it means to be "tamed."

I get up and walk around, checking out the assignments. "I'd go anywhere when I first met Dave," Kit writes. "He led. I followed. And then kaboom. It was over. Forget men. The only subject I'm really any good at is lunch."

Bertie's scribbling fast, and I can barely make out what she scrawls, something about how Kate gets herself into trouble and has to learn to get herself out. I ask her what she means. "Kate's known for her 'scolding tongue,' right?" Bertie says, looking up at me. "My mother always told me you get more bees with honey. Kate needs to step off."

I move behind Dolly. She writes about a dream that reminds her of a scene from the movie we saw with Elizabeth Taylor and Richard Burton, in which Petruchio lords his power over Kate. In the film Petruchio is at the top of the stairs in his stark mansion, refusing to spend his wedding night with his new bride. Kate's in the kitchen below, sullen and alone. I read over Dolly's shoulder as she describes her dream:

> It starts off with a very large home with a very large winding staircase. As I start climbing, it goes on higher and higher. When it seems to me that I have reached the top, an ape—a very large white ape—appears, beating his chest and scream-ing. The light catches his canine teeth. They are so large, so

31

white. The light hits them and they gleam. A thick glob of saliva is dripping from his mouth. His black eyes are wild, and they sparkle like fine diamonds. I stand a long time on that spot. I feel like Kate, frozen.

"That's powerful," I whisper to her.

"Kate's a wimp," Dolly whispers back. "I still can't understand why she doesn't ditch Petruchio after he knocks her around." Bertie gives her a look as if to say that she of all people should understand.

Rhonda turns to Dolly. "I like Kate. She's got spunk." Rhonda's a statuesque black woman and the prison education secretary who answers the phone, assists the school principal, and is anything but what she calls, "your average Joe, earning a degree from Street University." She's decided this semester "to make school a priority." She's also, Bertie says, one of the best cons, "so slick she could talk Mother Teresa into partying," and "ready for anything," meaning both volleyball, which Rhonda plays feverishly, and cruising the halls for any kind of action, which Rhonda does routinely. She and Bertie joke with each other about who gets the most come-ons from other inmates.

She straddles a chair next to Dolly. Rhonda plays down her model looks by wearing sweats, but tonight she's decked out in a silky warm-up suit. "Kate might not leave Petruchio, but she fights back. She beats him up with words."

"Yeah, well, whatever," Dolly says.

"And she scores the guy in the end," Rhonda adds.

Cody guffaws. "She's fulla piss and vinegar, but then so is her dude. Now, Bianca—there's a useless broad."

Bertie gets up and does a little dance around her chair, high-fiving Cody. "Gotcha, girl."

"You are so damn dramatic," Dolly says to Bertie. "See?" she says, cocking her head at me. "See what I mean about these women doing a play?" I pick up the writing assignments while the women banter about the characters.

Mamie shakes her head, *tsk-tsk*ing the others. "If everyone acted like Kate, beatin' up on people when the mood hits, the world would be a sorry place." Mamie's been in and out of classes and has deep creases in her brow, cracked hands from greenhouse work. She's aged a lot in a year. She goes on, "Less heat woulda saved a lot of heartache for my roommate, you know, Gloria, the one who shot her husband."

I remember seeing Gloria on the news, talking about killing her husband in self-defense, soon after I started teaching at Framingham. A middle-aged dark-skinned woman, Gloria could've been my third-grade teacher. She was the picture of suburban success, a neatly coiffed and well-dressed mom. Her seven-year-old son stood outside the prison, a microphone in hand, newscaster at his side and said sadly, "Mama, I wish I could have done it for you."

"Anyway," Mamie is saying, picking up some dried flowers she's brought with her for cards, "I hope Gloria makes it in here. She goes off on me about the man she killed every day. Keeps his picture on her wall. She's got a red wall. She calls it 'the color of the blood I shed.' Talk about Shakespeare." Mamie glues a few flowers onto a piece of green construction paper folded in quarters. Someone sighs heavily from across the room.

Dolly turns to me. "Can we do something theatrical, now, here?"

Kit makes a face and mouths words at me, "No way."

I glance around the room and see that it's not only Dolly who needs a break from this discussion. A few others look like they've had the wind knocked out of them. "Okay. Let's move the chairs out of the way, fold up the table."

Soon most of the women are up. Cody's not moving. She complains that reading plays is one thing but that she's not interested in a damn acting class. Kit's excuse is that her feet hurt; she doesn't want to be on them for long.

"Form a circle," I say, ignoring them both. "This is just an exercise to take your minds off whatever. Throwing vowels, I call it." I push and pull, teasing the laggards with my cheerfulness, and in no time I get everyone into something resembling an oval. "All together," I say, and begin inhaling, winding up, ready for the throw. A few make noises of protest, but their bodies imitate mine and soon, they're all winding up and inhaling. I exhale with sound, yelling, "Ah, aie, ee, aw, oo," extending the vowels so they seem to be "thrown" across the room. Women break out in laughter, but they are into it, using their best pitching arms, throwing sounds across the circle. "Don't throw like a girl," I yell, and vowels whiz into the air. "Louder," I insist, and a cacophony of sound fills the room. I place myself in the center and yell, "Hit me, come on! Think Red Sox."

By the end of the exercise, it's as if I'd given them all shots of adrenaline. Mamie and Rhonda are talking about how crazy we white folks are. Kit's babbling that she was in a play once in elementary school where they had to be witches—we shoulda seen it—and by God, the cackling could've filled two of these rooms. Dolly tells Bertie it feels good to throw something. The women make me promise we'll do this again.

At the end of class Dolly approaches me. "Had a visit from Beth over the weekend." She pulls out an off-white handkerchief, embroidered with blue initials. "They let me keep this with my package. It was my mother's. Did you know I lost her this past summer?"

I nod. "I'm sorry. By the way, Dolly, you were great in that exercise."

Dolly smiles and then shrugs off my compliment. "Funny girl, that

Beth. Loves me to death, but when it comes to herself, she can't give two cents." Dolly places the handkerchief in my hands. "She brought this up for me, from home."

I hesitate, turning it over. It's soft and smells like something familiar—Ivory Snow, a hope chest filled with antique linens. I think about how Dolly didn't get to go to her mother's funeral. "Maybe it will take her more time, Dolly, to be strong. Is it . . . okay that she came to visit?"

"Yeah, she thinks she's safe. She takes it one day at a time. I can only pray. You know, when I started that battered women's group, the women all thought it was their fault. A man beats you up, and it's your fault. You know the redhead who follows Bernice around? Two black eyes a week. And Alexandra, the tiny black girl who moved into Laurel last week? Almost killed herself before she told. Anybody ever hit you?"

"Well, maybe once," I say, and then, catching myself, "but then, 'hit' is a relative term, isn't it?"

Dolly laughs at my unintended pun, but she doesn't press me, and we pause for a moment, silent, understanding something about each other we don't say. She folds up the handkerchief and slips it in her notebook pocket, next to her photos.

"What about that play?" Dolly asks. "Have you thought about it?"

"Beat you to it. I applied for a grant."

"Good," Dolly says, "because I'm not going anywhere. That lawyer who believes in justice for women wouldn't take my case."

• • •

"A few of the ladies say they're interested," Rhonda announces, standing in the classroom doorway. She's chewing gum, contraband for prisoners, and seems out of breath, as if she ran here from her unit. "But they want to come to our class first, to check us out."

It's almost Thanksgiving, and there's a paper turkey in Rhonda's hand, some sort of sign-up sheet for volleyball. Rhonda waits for me to say something, but I'm hesitating, worried that acting too sure might jinx the foundation grant. Dolly might be getting her hopes up for nothing.

"Well," Rhonda says, "I'm waiting." I look at her. We both know that inviting prisoners to sit in on a class they're not enrolled in is against policy. Rhonda tapes the sheet to the outside of the classroom door. "Look, I volunteered to find new bodies for the play-to-be, but hey, my offer doesn't last all year. Some of these lawbreakers want an answer."

I look at Dolly, a half smile forming on my face, but Dolly shakes her head. Ever since I told her about the grant possibility, she's decided she's the keeper of the code. She's moving the table for our first improvisational evening, a break from the plays we've been reading. Already she's put a row of chairs facing the door, the "stage" being the bare end of the room.

"I'm not gonna make an idiot of myself in front of strangers," Dolly says. "Who knows what they'll tell the big cheeses upstairs about what we do in here. No, sir." She eyes Rhonda suspiciously. "Anyway, this room is too small for a crowd."

"I know, buddy, but hey, didn't you say we'd do well with more students? Jean too?"

"I don't think you should get me involved in this, Rhonda," I say from a chair, where I'm copying down the names of the three inmates Rhonda's invited, noting that Gloria is among them. I figure Dolly's annoyed that Rhonda's put herself in charge and that the invited guests are not Dolly's friends.

36

Rhonda joins Dolly, pushing the blackboard behind the row of metal chairs. "You really look like Bette Midler tonight, Jean, with that new do. Doesn't she, Dolly?" Dolly rolls her eyes.

"Thanks, I guess."

Rhonda has found a broom in the corner and holds it out to me, "Hey, how 'bout this. A prop." Dolly makes a kind of grunt and sits. There are sounds over the loudspeaker, a torrent of footsteps, and women's voices in the hallway. Bertie's the next in, and the others follow, including the three Rhonda calls "potential new blood."

"Welcome," I say, deliberately avoiding Dolly's eyes. While the women introduce themselves, Dolly grunts and groans. Before Dolly gets too testy, I decide to let the old-timers lead off. "I need you on your feet—Dolly, Bertie, Rhonda. You're learning improvisation to-night." They're up, Dolly more reluctant than the other two.

"Dolly, you're a shop owner." I begin to make up an improv. "You own an ice-cream store, and you're planning a special night with your husband. So you have to leave the store at exactly five o'clock to go out; you decide where."

Dolly says "Jee-sus," and grabs the broom that Rhonda placed by the door. "Could this be any stupider?"

"Come on, Ma," Bertie says.

"Bertie, you're seven, and Rhonda's your big sister." Rhonda turns to her, amusedly. "In fact, it's your birthday, Bertie, and you love ice cream. You've bicycled with your sister to this shop to get some special cone you can't find anywhere else."

"Mint marble swirl," Bertie says. "No—coffee fudge."

"You can decide when you arrive," I say. "The point is, it's impor-tant that you, Rhonda, get this cone for your sister. It was a promise." Dolly is arranging the shop, somewhat halfheartedly, placing a chair here and there, getting others to help her move the table so it looks like a countertop. "You two make an entrance from the door, but give Dolly a minute to get started." Bertie and Rhonda go outside the classroom into the hall, leaving the door open a crack so they can see Dolly.

The improv begins. Dolly sweeps, keeping her back to the door. Bertie and Rhonda bang three times, and Dolly ignores them. They bang again, and Dolly ignores them again. I whisper, "Say something to them, Dolly."

"Sorry girls, ice cream's finished for the day and that's that!" Dolly yells, sweeping away. She is so resolved to ignore them and close her shop at five o'clock that the scene is over before it begins.

"That sucked," Kit calls out from her seat. The three guests mutter to one another. Kit takes off her sneaker and tries to pull something out of the rubber sole.

I am up out of my seat. "I won't go that far. But yes, it didn't work." Dolly glares at Kit. Bertie and Rhonda stand against the doorframe, annoyed.

"Look," I say, "we've never done this before. You don't have to know it all at once. But acting is like life. You have to take it seriously, and there's listening as well as talking. Dolly, let's imagine that your character likes kids; in fact, she loves them. She would never want to disappoint a child. What would that do to the way you play the scene?" Dolly looks at me, slightly interested. "Begin again," I say.

Dolly starts sweeping, and when the banging begins, she tries to ignore it. I fidget in my seat, thinking she's about to blow the improv again, but this time, when she opens the door, she peeks around it and is almost charming. "Hi, girls." She stands poised, the broom at her side.

Rhonda puts one foot in the door. "Hi. My sister and I want to get ice cream." Bertie stands on tiptoes behind Rhonda, looking over her shoulder, pulling on her shirt. Kit belly-laughs at their characterizations.

"Uh, I'm sorry, girls, but my store is closed now. It's five o'clock. Come back tomorrow." Dolly's pushing the door closed. Behind the door Bertie is muttering the names of ice cream, changing flavors over and over, "mint marble swirl," "coffee fudge," "pecans 'n' cream."

"We rode our bikes all the way from Fremont Circle and we just want two cones." Rhonda firmly pushes the door open. "It's my sister's birthday."

Dolly's insistent. "I'm really sorry, but I have to lock up. I have to get downtown—and, you know, traffic." Bertie hangs her head. "You girls can go down the road to Steve's. They're open 'til eleven."

"Noooo!" Bertie cries out. "We came here last year. I want an ice-cream cone from here."

Now Rhonda is flustered. "Couldn't you let us stay, please, lady, for only five minutes? Please?"

Dolly's voice is strained. "Five minutes, and that's it." She heads behind the counter and fervently starts to scoop ice cream.

With perfect timing Bertie blurts out, "Not the marble one, the mint marble." Dolly looks up midscoop. I think for a moment that she might throw imaginary ice cream in Bertie's face.

"She'll take whatever you've got," Rhonda pulls Bertie back with a jerk to her arm.

Dolly scoops and scoops, producing two cones, telling Bertie to hush up, it'll be fine, and everyone's going to get ice cream. She hands the girls the cones, takes Rhonda's money, and tosses her imaginary apron on the counter. "Now out," she says. Bertie and Rhonda exit.

Kit whistles, and the rest of us applaud wildly. The class breaks into conversation about the scene, reenacting it, as though they were a TV show on instant replay. "We were awesome," Rhonda says to me.

"Yes," I say, "you negotiated a solution. There was give-and-take." They're beaming, Dolly especially.

Eventually others get up, create new scenarios. Kit sets up a scene in which she and her friend, played by Cody, get stuck changing a tire and have to call the cops to help them out. When Bertie enters the scene, trying to play an American cop with her Jamaican accent, no one can stop laughing long enough for the scene to work. Mamie decides to play a mother whose daughter forbids her to visit her granddaughter. Gloria volunteers to be the daughter. This scene takes place on the phone. Mamie gets it in her head to be really old, and she crunches herself up like an elderly person with arthritis. Even her voice sounds different, pinched and high as she scolds daughter Gloria. Gloria tells Mamie what an unfit grandmother she is, smoking, drinking, and who knows what in front of her granddaughter, and she ends the scene by hanging up on Mamie. "This is a downer," Dolly says, and at that Bertie grabs Rhonda and we set up a restaurant scene in which a woman breaks up with her man. Rhonda slings herself into a chair and leans back, using her notebook as a menu. She crosses one leg over another in her attempt to be the callous girlfriend, forcing Bertie to play the dumped lover, whom Rhonda calls "pet." Kit keeps interrupting as a waitress who can't get the order right, and her clumsiness is as engaging as the rest of the scenario. After every scene the inmates cheer for one another.

Before the class ends Dolly says to me, "I told you we'd be good. What's the next play we're reading?" She's energized now, color in her cheeks.

"*Lysistrata,*" I reply. "It's a play about women who keep their husbands from going to war."

Bertie moans from across the room, "I hate history."

"By withholding sex," I add. That gets a huge round of laughter. The women make jokes about improvising on that theme. Rhonda thumbs rapidly through her literature book to find the play. She reads aloud, pretending to have eyeglasses and holding her textbook in the air with one hand, as if she's performing. "Lysistrata: she who disbands armies. A natural peacemaker . . ."

Kit interrupts, "Peace in prison. Now there's a good one."

"I like that," Bertie says first to Rhonda, then to Dolly. "I do."

"Lysistrata sounds better than that Kate character." Dolly's relaxed now after our improv, and her smile is easy, full of confidence, a smile that spreads over her entire face. It's a smile I haven't seen for a while. It's the same smile she sports in *Lysistrata*, two years later, as the lead in our updated production of the Greek classic, in which a political activist convinces her compatriots to protest war. In her long, billowy white dress, Dolly's a suffragette protesting U.S. involvement in World War I, and she charges across the yard in a sash that reads NO SEX and carries a flag of peace and a bullhorn. We rehearse that play outside in the late afternoon sun when trees are in bloom. Officers and inmates alike pass us on their way to the cottages. One actress tries to get me to bring in insect repellent, and Dolly fusses about having to carry chairs outside for the set. But in that production Dolly's her best self, standing on top of a platform, winding up and thrusting her fist into the air, summoning the audience to be ready for peace.

At 8:30, as our improv evening winds to a close, an officer enters the room, announcing the Downward. He looks around, and then, checking a list of names, he informs me coolly, "You've been here over a year, Trounstine. No one's allowed in classes without permission. I'm sending a warning to the education director." He

41

turns to the three guests and says, "Let's go." They follow. He slams the door.

"If he thinks we're finished," Dolly says, "he's in for a surprise."

. . .

"Never take gifts, or else inmates expect something in return," Ron Zullo, the coordinator of Inmate Services, tells me when I see him a few months later for permission to put on a play in Framingham. "I've heard you're not one to follow rules, Jean." He motions for me to sit and wait while he thumbs through a stack of papers, calls in his secretary for a brief consult, and hands her some typing. I cross and uncross my legs uncomfortably, knowing that my tenure at the prison depends in large part on what he thinks and does.

Ron's been a mystery to me, friendly when I see him alone in the halls, but ice cold when he's walking around with the deputy. I can't decide if he's here to help the prisoners or just likes being in charge. "He's a criminal justice type," Cody has warned. "You know, crew cut, chews gum, blank face."

Sitting across from him in his office, I am trying to judge how accurate Cody's description is. Ron is short and feisty, what my high schoolers would call "buff" because of his muscles, reminding me of a boxer. He's young for such a big job, maybe thirty, and he looks a little like a TV cop. I wonder if he got here by being part of the Boston in-crowd. Rumor has it that his predecessor went to Alaska "to chill," after failing to get support for therapeutic art programs. She was "soft," the women gossip, and "the prison knocked her out."

Ron puts a big grin on his face, but something doesn't seem right and I'm nervous. He's not wearing a suit, only a plain blue shirt and a striped tie, and he loosens it at the collar. He seems distracted but focused on something I can't name. He turns around to adjust the only air-conditioner I've seen at Framingham. It whirs noisily, the fan turned on in winter to circulate air in this cramped space. To the right of huge piles of papers on his desk is a photo of Ron with his wife and kids. He fiddles with the picture frame.

"Employees taking gifts . . . ," he continues without finishing his sentence. "They've been my undoing." I look away. I don't know what he wants, but being here feels slippery. I could make a mistake, say the wrong thing any minute.

I am aware of Dolly, whom I see through the window behind Ron, standing by a tree outside in the yard. She appears to be alone, and smoke from her cigarette curls up into the air.

Ron leans across the desk and folds his hands. "I'm not trying to scare you, Jean, but we always have to be on the lookout for people who bring their personal lives into the prison. They cause trouble." I nod.

Ron begins rummaging through a stack of papers. "I've seen your grant proposal and it's good. We see you've received full support from the Massachusetts Foundation for the Humanities . . ." He pauses, thumbing through what look like letters, and he looks up at me. Behind him Dolly now appears to be talking to someone. She's bundled up in a coat, gesturing with her hands.

"Yes," I say quickly. "The prison won't need to pay for a thing." Immediately I regret my glibness. But Ron doesn't seem to notice. He's focused on pulling open a stuck drawer.

"You'll have to sign these papers and talk to my assistant, Florence, to work out details." He stands up, and it startles me. The office seems smaller and I can't figure out why he is walking around his desk. He sits in a leather chair next to mine, reaches over and rests his hand briefly on my arm. "I hear you're getting married."

His touch surprises me and I swallow, hard. "In the spring," I reply, carefully pulling my arm away. "Probably the same week as the play. Just kidding."

"That's good. We like stability here."

"Do you want to know what play I'll be doing, which women will perform?"

"No, no, that's all here. And I hear you're doing good work with the women." He waves his hand at his desk, and absently picks up a fancy ballpoint pen, clicking the point in and out. "That's good. I like to hear that, because I think programs like yours are good for the inmates. But no matter what, you have to do what we say."

"Are you referring to something—" I begin, but he cuts me off.

"I don't want to get into particulars, but I know everything that happens here, and Jean, I have to tell you, this theatre stuff has caused us a lot of problems in the past."

"What kind of problems?"

"Big ones." Ron is on his feet now, moving toward the door, the window. He pauses. Something outside in the yard seems to catch his eye.

"Excuse me a moment." He goes over to the windowsill, turns off the air-conditioner, and raps furiously against the glass. He waves his hands and says loudly to the glass. *I don't want smoking by this office. Get it? Not by the building!*" He raps again and then, seeming calmed down, makes his way back to the chair.

"Before your time two women screwed up, and I took the rap. They were supposed to be doing a play and taking photos of rehearsals. But they bent the rules. You drama types are all alike."

He smiles again, that eerie grin from ear to ear, and I laugh a little, in a phony way, to appease him. He rambles on about how the two sneaked into places they weren't supposed to, snapping pictures without approval. "They wanted them for a book or something," he isn't sure, but he knows from reports that they "used the prisoners" and were asked to leave soon after, terminating their relationship with Framingham. "I'm going to give you a chance, but I'm not going to let that happen twice."

I think about Dolly outside, six feet from Ron's window. Who knows how close she is to getting a disciplinary report, known as a D, for such a seemingly small infraction: smoking in the wrong place? D reports can keep an inmate from activities; too many can get her locked for weeks; some can keep her from parole. I think about cases of staff violations: the nun who carried aspirin in her pocket, contraband for prison workers; a teacher who wrote a novel based on the prison; the recreation officer who came on to inmates and another who sold them drugs. All were kicked out.

"I don't want any hassles with this project, Jean." He stands, beckoning me to do the same. "Do you understand? No hassles on my watch."

I nod, aware that undertaking anything in prison is like entering a country that doesn't really want visitors. I am in by the skin of my teeth.

. . .

"Shakespeare is white man's theatre," grumbles Gloria. It's winter 1988, and Gloria's joined the acting class. Even though she's bound for pre-release in a few months, and has no intention of being in the play we plan for early summer, she thinks it'll be a good distraction. She throws her bulky coat on a chair.

"Not if we do it," I counter to Gloria.

She looks at me sideways. I notice what a handsome woman Gloria is, even in her sweats and headband, and think about what Kojack said to me earlier this evening when I saw him at the entrance. "I hear you've got Gloria in your class. Ron Zullo tell you about Gloria?" I shook my head no as I passed through the metal detector and the glass doors. "She loves the camera. Can't get enough of herself on air." I disappeared into No-Man's Land.

Now I think how I keep narrowly escaping from serious reprimands and hope Gloria won't mean trouble. The women are coming into the room one by one, and staring at the stack of *The Merchant of Venice* scripts on the table. They tentatively pick up texts, flipping through them. Dolly mutters that the play looks a little long. Bertie turns to Dolly and makes wisecracks, like no way is she saying words such as "thou" and "hast" on stage. Rhonda tells everyone she is sick of their lousy attitudes, don't they realize they are in a damn prison? "Anything free is a privilege." She drops into a chair, and the other women follow.

I know that I have to get them interested in this story if the play's to work. I tell them I picked *Merchant* because it explores issues that I think will intrigue them: how women get power, racism, the ambiguity of love and crime, and the nature of justice. I don't tell them how much they remind me of Shakespeare's women or that the challenge might be just what they need. Kit asks if we're going to get dictionaries any time soon.

"Let's start with the story," I say. I decide to stay standing and walk around the table, talking a little louder than usual. I throw a hand into the air. "Picture Italy, four, five hundred years ago, before cars, before electric lights—"

"Before prisons?" interrupts Bertie, who's been whispering to Mamie and not paying attention. Now she's smirking.

"Cut the crap, Bertie," Rhonda says, in her macho guy voice. I watch her take a piece of gum out of her pocket.

"Not before all prisons," I continue, "but before Framingham." I walk around the table. "A man borrows say, in today's terms, two million dollars from a moneylender, loaning money to his best friend who desperately needs it. To ensure the bond, the borrower agrees to pay it back or else . . ." A few women are glued to me like children listening to a bedtime story. "If the borrower reneges, he'll pay with a pound of his own flesh."

"A pound of flesh?" Bertie echoes. "That's disgusting." She's doodling heads as usual, women with high cheekbones and no bodies.

"Wouldn't he die?" Rhonda asks. "This borrower?"

"One would think so."

"Well then, why does he do it?" Dolly presses. "What's his name, anyhow, this mister moneybags?"

"Antonio," I say, sweeping back around the table. "And you can read the part when we begin. Then you can tell us why."

Dolly smiles at me, a slow smile, deep and warm. "Go ahead," I say. "Read a little."

Dolly opens up the script and looks for Antonio's first line. She reads aloud, "In sooth, I know not why I am so sad." "I understand that," she says. "Something's up with him." The others pick parts, and Dolly jumps into the reading, stopping to make sure she puts all the lines she doesn't understand into her own words.

Turning to Bertie, who sits next to her and seems delighted to be addressed, she reads, "I hold the world, but as the world, Gratiano— / A stage, where every man must play a part, / And mine a sad one."

"He's just not getting anywhere fast," Dolly says. "He's held back by something inside him." Then, in a voice thick with a Boston accent, she says to Bertie, "Antonio's in trouble, or so they say."

Bertie says, "You sound like that old merchant from Chelsea." Bertie starts calling Dolly "Antonio."

Kit gestures at Dolly and then says to us, "Antonio from Chelsea. Another Eye-tal gambler." She's laughing at her own joke.

Gloria asks, "This is the play we're going to do, that Shakespeare wrote?"

"Yes. I mean, not exactly. We'll do our own version."

"Well, call me stupid," Gloria says, "but I never would've guessed *The Merchant of Venice* was this down to earth—you know—real." She sits in front of the blackboard, the word "Angel" scrawled over her head, writing left behind from another activity in Program Room 2. She looks over at Mamie. "What do you think of this play?"

"I suggested it," Mamie says, smiling wryly at Gloria. Mamie tosses her book on the table and exits to get meds.

"Hey, Kit," Dolly says, "read this part with me. Bassanio and Antonio—you and me on the streets."

Kit laughs again, toothless as ever, and slaps her pants leg with an open palm. "Nah."

"Here," Rhonda says, coming out of her seat and around the table. "I'll be Portia. You be Antonio." They flip to the trial scene, the part of the play where Antonio, having lost his ships at sea, must give Shylock, the moneylender, a pound of his flesh, unless someone can find a loophole in the law.

Rhonda stands over Dolly, book in hand. She reads in a crisp, clear voice, "Do you confess the bond?" Then she says, "Do you admit you signed a contract stipulating a pound of flesh?" She's improvising on the line.

Dolly looks up and paraphrases back, "I admit to that."

Then Rhonda lets the script drop to her side and goes off on her own, as if trying to understand what Shakespeare had in mind. "Why would you agree to such terms? That's barbaric. A pound of flesh? He can hold you to that."

Dolly turns and looks across the table at Kit, pointing her script at Kit as if she were Bassanio. "My friend Bassanio was in trouble financially." Kit smiles. Others have their heads together, whispering, enjoying the surprise of this improvised scene.

For a moment I imagine Dolly onstage, in a suit and tie, a fedora on her head. She's in the Mafia, I decide, a red carnation in her lapel, a silk hanky in her pocket, wearing shiny black shoes, and Frank, her codefendant, is sitting next to her.

"Bassanio needed a great deal of money. I signed the contract," Dolly continues.

"Including the pound of flesh?" Rhonda asks.

Dolly sighs and places her hand on Bertie's shoulder. Dolly's eyes are downcast as she says, "I would die for my friend."

BERTIE

Grief fills the room up of my absent child:
Lies in his bed, walks up and down with me,
Puts on his pretty looks, repeats his words,
Remembers me of all his gracious parts,
Stuffs out his vacant garments with his form.
KING JOHN, III.iv.93

Before the inmates arrive for class, it is often quiet, early evening, with dusk pouring in through the small window that looks out on a courtyard. Past the prison is the auto plant, lit up with a neon sign, a field of purple weeds to its right, dried-up ponds nearby. It could be late September, that famous time for remembrance, when leaves are about to turn in New England, or early April, before the scrawny tree in the yard has all its new buds. It's always a time of reflection—jobs I've had without proper credentials, all the symbolic lights I've run without looking back—and how thankful I am to be teaching in a place where people want to learn. "A captive audience," I joke with my friends.

This particular night I'm alone, reading and rereading their papers, still new, still recovering from "that damn search machine" as the inmates call Connors. I'm thinking about Bertie.

It's been two months or so since I met her, and she hasn't wanted to share much of her writing out loud. In fact, in spite of her flamboyance, she only reads bits and pieces to Dolly and has asked me not to discuss what she writes in class. So far she's handed me her papers folded up, hiding her writing, filled with tight little letters that slant too far to the right and verb tenses that jangle pleasantly. "I want to have faith in God but no one support me," she wrote in a free-write early on. Sometimes she makes comments that are cryptic, almost like she's talking in code, and I wonder if she's aware that her words often seem to have deeper meanings. "I'm writing for my life," she mentioned one night. Another evening, when most of the trees outside our classroom seemed to burst into fall hues overnight, Bertie was the one to say it was a comfort to see color, even though she hated losing summer to the change of seasons. "Must be the Jamaican in you," Mamie had replied sympathetically. Bertie just nodded her head and stared off sadly, as though she could find herself in the trees.

I turn to a piece of writing and think about what Bertie did a few weeks ago when Kit and Cody were the first two students to arrive. As soon as Bertie came in, she saw no Dolly, no Mamie; immediately seating herself as far away from Cody and Kit as possible, she acted the bitch, not even saying hello to me. On her way out she announced loudly, "You have to be cold in here, Jean. People take kindness for weakness." After that night Kit and Cody seemed to let up on Bertie, at least in our classroom. But it's clear from their whispers and caustic glances that they know some terrible secret about her. Since it's Bertie's night to read, I'm uneasy about how the women will respond.

Suddenly "the ladies," as the officers call them, arrive, and it's a party. Dolly whooshes into the room, followed by Kit. Kit's talking a mile a minute about how her unit's been turned upside down for some damned "ho." This "whore" apparently did an officer for extra phone privileges. It's more theatrical than soldierly, the way they round corners as if they're onstage, throw themselves into chairs, gesticulating with notebooks and hands. Kit and Dolly seem to be on good terms tonight, one-upping each other. I imagine them together "on the street," wheeling babies in carriages past shop windows in Boston's working-class neighborhood of Chelsea.

Mamie comes in moments later, griping about not getting to do her laundry, much less my writing assignment, with all the room changes and whatnot in the cottage. I've learned that "cottage" is Framingham's euphemism for a large group of cells. Definitely not Jane Austen bungalows with thatched roofs, Dolly says, more like army barracks where you live four to six, in pint-size rooms. The cottages have ironic names like Laurel and Pioneer, and some are better than others because they're newer or cleaner or less filled with "the mental health types."

Mamie may spend her days in the prison's greenhouse, pruning shrubs, but the scoop is that she set a woman on fire, a fact Kit blurts out in class one night, moments before Dolly slams her fist down on the table to cool the conversation. It's not okay to discuss another's crime. "Do your own time" is the mantra. But that doesn't seem to stop the whispering about Bertie. Now Mamie settles in, greets the others with waves, and lumbers over to a chair.

Bertie enters. Kit and Cody don't even look in her direction. Bertie's eyes dart around the room for a safe place to sit. She tightens her shawl around her shoulders, bits of gold and red metallic threads shimmering in the early evening light. She places herself next to Mamie, and the two exchange niceties under their breath. The room fills up with women.

I'm watching Bertie, waiting for her to say something before I begin the class, but she's gabbing with Mamie, trying to ignore that tonight she's on. Even though I'm uneasy, I know that it would be my undoing to give in to her fears. She pulls out a nail file and a bottle of coral nail polish from her pants pocket, fortifying herself for the evening. An officer sticks his head into the room and announces that one of the prisoners has a visit. Commotion. An exit. Silence.

"So, whose turn is it to read?" Bertie asks, all innocence. I watch the other women look from face to face. They know Bertie is playing dumb.

"It's yours," I say simply.

Kit kicks her feet up on the table and folds her arms over her chest, as if to say, *This isn't gonna be easy, babe*. Cody follows suit. Mamie sees their move and looks at Bertie through her specs. She's a rock of security. She couldn't be sitting any closer.

"My story isn't really finished," Bertie begins, a streak of coral landing more on her cuticle than on her nail. Somebody groans.

"That's okay," I say, diverting their criticism. "We'll help you. Where's your writing?"

Bertie points to her notebook. Kit shakes her head at Bertie's wet nails while I rifle through her folder to find three or four loose pages. Bertie glances quickly at Dolly, who pushes a glass of water across the table. "You might need this," Dolly advises.

"Thanks, Ma." Bertie's hesitating a little. She turns to me. There is fear in her eyes, but on the outside she's projecting cool. "I should read it . . . out loud?"

"Yes," I reply. "Yes, out loud," I repeat while she manages to put the papers in their proper order. Then, as Bertie readies herself for the task ahead, breathing, clearing her throat, drinking a few sips of water, I say quietly, with a steady voice, "You can do this."

"I come from a poor family. My mother was a good woman, taking care of her chicks. . . . She loved us all, teaching us to think with our hearts."

Bertie goes on to tell how in her elementary school in Jamaica she was asked to write a paper about the most important friend she had. The teacher called it "a contest," and Bertie, who had raised, fed, and loved her pet goat from its birth, entered, writing lovingly about her goat. She did not reveal his "animal nature" but instead, described him as "my childhood best friend."

Dolly smiles, and the other women, taking her lead, relax and laugh a little.

"Filled with joy," Bertie tells us, she won the contest, and when the teacher asked her to bring in her best friend to meet the class, Bertie brought in the pet goat for show-and-tell. Even though some of the students made fun of her, Bertie did not care. "I loved that goat with all my heart."

"You go, girl," Mamie says, and the others around the table titter.

Bertie suddenly sits up straight in her hardback chair, staring down fiercely at the paper. "One night my mother had a party, and I feel strange, something is happening. I go out behind the house and there it is, behind the house, in tall grass, my goat's head in a pot." We all gasp. "I could not stop crying for days."

When Bertie looks up from the paper, no one speaks. Surprisingly Cody breaks the silence, "I wish I could write like you." Others follow, carefully at first, praising the story and Bertie's courage in writing it. Even Kit, who keeps quiet, seems respectful. Bertie is smiling. None of us ask if the mother did it out of meanness or because she was in need of food. None of us talk about how we imagine what it must have been like for Bertie to be so betrayed by her mother, what deep sadness haunts her.

Too moved to be the one who's not supposed to get close, I look at Bertie with new eyes. I want to hug her, take the pain away. I want to yell at her mother, besiege Bertie with questions. It is the women who save me, saying, "Great job," or in the case of Dolly, who wipes tears from her eyes, "You blew my mind." I see how Bertie's words have softened the other women and how reading out loud has helped her transform fear. If writing earns respect and telling one's story builds connections, I realize the power theatre might have in this place.

Bertie turns to me. I haven't spoken. "Did I sound Jamaican—I mean my accent—could you understand me?" She's looking at me anxiously.

"You were fine, no, better than fine; what I mean is, you were perfect," I say. "No one else could have read it like you."

Bertie's face floods with relief. "I was perfect," she says, returning to the others, repeating my comment, like a cat, preening, her back arched, that chin up in the air proudly. They nod, chattering away. I've broken the ice with Bertie. She's all over me now, can't stop asking about our next assignment. Can she have it early? She wants to get started right away. At the end of class she walks me down the hall almost to the iron door a bit before No-Man's Land. She tells me to be sure and drive carefully. Before I exit I watch her walk through the hallway and stand with her back against the gym entrance, one knee tucked up under her. She holds her notebook across her chest like a coed.

At the end of the semester, just before Christmas, Dolly takes me aside and tells me, "Bertie can't do that take-home final you gave us." When I seem surprised—Bertie's been writing week after week, each assignment more developed than the last—Dolly tells me she's holed up in her cottage. "She can't concentrate on her homework. All she can think about is the baby she killed."

"What baby?" I ask. Dolly looks at me as though I should know. We are standing just outside the door of Program Room 2.

"Her baby," Dolly says. "Bertie's in prison for the unspeakable, Jean.

Jee-sus, I thought you knew. It's what they call a sin, even in prison. She killed her four-month-old daughter."

Some inmates and a male officer pass us in the hallway. I lower my voice. "Oh, my God! Bertie? She killed her child?" I think of her mother, the goat, the horrible betrayal, and then of Bertie's little girl. "Of course she can't concentrate," I say.

"I'll let her know you didn't have a clue," Dolly says. "It's tough in here, the girls, the holidays. She's pretty low."

"Tell her she can have an Incomplete," I say, sounding ridiculous to myself. "No, tell her to get through Christmas and New Year's and then write her heart out. I know it will help her." Dolly shrugs her shoulders as if to say, *Whatever.*

Bertie never turns in her final, but in spite of that I give her a B.

. . .

"Do you want a fireball?" Bertie asks one late fall evening while we are studying *The Doll's House* in an Introduction to Drama class. It is 1987, as cold as it gets in Massachusetts, and I've been worried about Bertie. She says she can't get out of her "funk," and although she drags herself to classes, she admits the weather doesn't help. She's not herself.

Snow arrived early this year, and the compound is covered with it, drifts of white pushing up against the barbed-wire fence that surrounds the yard. My rule is, *If I can come to class, so can you.* Tonight students sit hunched over in their coats, numb, they tell me. "No heat in the cottage this weekend. The pipes broke or something." Dolly is seething, ignoring my assignment to compare Nora to someone in their lives, and instead writing a letter of complaint to the superintendent. Bertie sinks into a chair next to Dolly, a row of candies lined up neatly alongside her notebook.

I hesitate. "I'm not supposed to take anything from an inmate." I notice how the insides of Bertie's lips are red from the sweets.

"No problem," Kit wisecracks. She reaches over and palms the candy, swooping it into her mouth, while I think about where to get fireballs on the way home that night.

The women spend the rest of the class discussing why Nora left her husband. Kit's opinion is "She was more immature than some of the girls in here, needing space, running away and all from her kids."

Someone says, "If my husband treated me like that, gushing all over me, I'd freak. How could she ditch him?"

Other women disagree and praise Nora. Dolly looks up from her letter and says, "Nora might have been selfish, but, hey, she was just lookin' for something she couldn't get at home." Mamie nods and chimes in, adding a few words about women needing to find their place in the world.

Even Cody joins the discussion. "Self-fulfillment, my ass. Who has time for that these days?" She's come to class with her sweats on, a kerchief around her neck, and wears a pair of Nikes that look two sizes too large. Her feet are on the table, and she leans back in her chair.

"I'd never leave my kids," Kit adds, turning to Cody. "Christ, I'd never have a man to leave." There's a chuckle throughout the room.

Bertie is noticeably silent on the subject of why Nora leaves her family. She sucks on her candy and hums to herself, sitting cross-legged in the one orange barrel-shaped chair so that she looks like a little Buddha. Kit tells her to stop humming, but Bertie ignores her. "There are enough rules in this place without yours," she snaps at Kit.

Kit takes this as an opportunity to recite as many rules as she can from memory. I ask her to cut it out, but some of the other women are laughing, and Kit always responds to encouragement. She pulls out a sheet of the sixty "Cottage Rules and Regulations" and reads aloud, entertaining her audience. "Number thirty-eight. Inmates are not allowed to put their feet on tables, chairs, sit on the arms or backs of furniture, sit on tables, lay on the couch, sit on another inmate's bed. Violators will be subject to disciplinary action."

"Bertie, get your feet off the floor," Cody orders without moving a muscle.

"Jean, I have to get out of here," Bertie says. She's up before I can stop her, grabbing her coat and slamming the door behind her.

It's not the first time a woman has stormed out of a class, nor will it be the last, but in the early days I have no idea what to do, and I tersely give students homework and tell Kit that there's no way we're going to do a play in here if she doesn't shape up. On my way out, when Bernice asks how the class was tonight, I say, "Fine."

. . .

The next week I see Bertie on my way into the institution, and she's smiling. "Guess what?" she says to me. We are on a cement path by the stone steps outside the yard's entrance to the main institution. It's just after Afternoon Count, one of the four times that women are stationed in their cottages to be accounted for each day. I've come to the prison early to see Ron Zullo, and I figure Bertie's on her way to her secretarial job.

"I'm in a hurry, Bertie," I say. "It's freezing." I shift from foot to foot, pulling my camel's hair coat close so no air gets on my neck.

"You have to hear this," Bertie says to me. "I made it, Teacher Jean." She holds out her gloved hand for me to slap and I do, although I have no idea what she means.

"What did you make?" I ask.

"You know, that group I was telling you about, the one that counsels teenage girls. Ron says I can be in it." Bertie seems changed, beaming, almost. "It's a chance to help kids stay out of prison. You know, a program like Scared Straight but without the fear. We just talk to the girls and tell them our stories."

"Oh. Great," I say. "That's terrific. I'm proud of you, Bertie. Let's go inside."

Bertie follows me up the stone steps and through the door. She takes off her gloves and pulls a cap off her head. She shakes out her hair, today a mass of curls. I start to give her a hug, but she pulls back.

"I hear you're going to see Ron," Bertie says offhandedly.

"How did you know that?"

She brushes off my question. "Anyway, it has to be something for you to be here in the day. Jean, if it's about the play, I'll do it!" She laughs and adds, "I'm doing everything I can to work on myself. I'm choreographer for the prison talent show too. No joke, Jean." She laughs again, and says, "Got to go ruin my lungs before work." I watch her disappear down the hallway.

A month or so later we are beginning classes for the play. I come to work to find a dance held in the gym, our rehearsal space. Bertie boogies by me with two of her cronies and disappears into the crowd. The room is packed with women bouncing and grooving, a sea of bodies. Onstage is a four-piece live band, men wearing matching pale green suits, and the lead singer has a microphone.

To my surprise Ron Zullo walks across the room to me. "Mondays aren't any different from Saturdays in a prison," he says, loudly, the sounds of a clarinet wailing behind us. "You'll have to hold your class in Program Room 2."

As if anyone would choose my class over this, I think. Ron's not wearing a tie, and his shirtsleeves are rolled up. Everything about him seems less calculating in this room full of dancers. He edges next to me by the side of the room, where he points out a few chairs set up for "wallflowers."

I try kidding him back. "Has anyone asked you to dance?"

"Four women," and, "yes," he says, tilting his head a little too close to mine, "I've refused." In a funny way I feel connected to him here in this crowded room of inmates. Besides the band, we are the only two who can leave tonight, and as I watch one woman spin another to a Marvin Gaye tune, I realize that we are also linked by our inhibitions. "They really wanted a dance," Ron confides. "They worked on this for months. All inmate-initiated." I am impressed. He's brought music to the prisoners.

We stand there near the gym doorway, as the blues surround us. I sway a little, restraining myself from the impulse to dive into the wave of women. Ron has crossed his arms and leans back, almost relaxed, against the wall. I am about to make a joke about "being chaperones" when a line dance begins. Twenty or so women, their arms in sync, swing themselves, *American Bandstand*–style, from the end of the floor where the basketball hoop stands to the rim of the stage. Others gather, commenting on the dance or trying out steps.

Bertie is at the head of the line, crossing one foot in front of the other, and leaning way back, while everyone imitates her. She is wearing a long white skirt with a purplish border around the hem. It sweeps the floor as she turns her head this way and that, swiveling her hips. Bertie brings a Caribbean twist to all things American, I think, wishing that we were allowed entrance whenever we chose and that I could come back in my off hours to see the jazzy steps she's choreographed for the prison talent show.

"Hey, Ron!" a woman yells from a few feet away. "Can I talk to you for a second?" Before Ron can uncross his arms, the inmate darts through the crowd, shouting to be heard over the drums. She goes on about her cottage and a roommate. At first Ron seems sympathetic, uh-huhing here and there. He even gives the prisoner this really concerned look, his brow furrowed. But then his voice turns harsh, insistent, filled with nos. I try to savor one last bit of music and back away from their conversation. After I slip out, I head for Program Room 2.

"I told you," Dolly calls after me. The door slams to the gym behind her. I turn around and see her following me down the hall. "Everyone wants the gym. How are we ever gonna put on a play?"

"I don't know," I yell back down the hall. "But why don't you try dragging Bertie out of that dance?"

. . .

By February 1988 Bertie is coming into her own in the prison community. She's become one of the long-termers who counsels high school kids. As the star of talent shows, she teaches dance steps, and while she works toward her associate's degree, manages her secretarial job in a prison office. This is better than many of the other jobs available to inmates. For a few dollars a week Dolly sews flags in a seedy shop that's been around since Betsy Ross, and others spend their time cleaning cottages. But Bertie's success seems less emblematic of her than does her sadness. More and more she reminds me of a young girl lost in a fog.

When we begin studying *The Merchant of Venice*, Bertie grasps the plot if we read aloud, but when I assign "homework," she tells me "regular" English is hard enough, much less this Shakespeare. She isn't one who personalizes the text quickly and, unlike some of the women, is not in tune with Shakespeare's wit. She laughs only when others retell Shakespeare's jokes or elbow her at his bawdy lines.

One night we are sitting around the table in Program Room 2, and

I ask the students to summarize the story of the play. Kit readily admits that she hasn't been able to read in the cottage, so she didn't do any homework. "There's a helluva lotta noise in the crib," she says. "It's easier when we read it in class."

I am bent over the book, trying to decipher words, and I look up, unfazed, used to Kit's grousing. "No problem," I say. "Bertie, you tell us. How does the play end?"

Bertie says, "There's just too much going on in my head."

"It's her son," Dolly tells me the night of the next class. "She misses him wicked awful."

"Her son?" I am caught off guard. It was a girl she killed, I thought, attempting to conjure up how and why the murder occurred, wishing, on my long drives home from the prison, it might have been an accident.

"Yep. The one who lives with his father, her boyfriend, in the States. He's not doing well without her." Suddenly Bertie's life has changed for me, taken a new twist. She's still a mother to a child who needs her.

"How old is he?" I ask, carefully placing Xeroxed sheets of Shakespearean lines on the table. I've been planning to lure the class into Shakespeare by showing them that his words have many meanings, that there is always more than one way to interpret a line.

"I don't know, four, maybe. She says he has her eyes." Dolly's putting her hair up into a twist while she talks. "She pastes all of his scribbles on the wall above her bed. It's a regular poster board."

A few weeks later Dolly and Bertie engineer a trip for me to their cottage, something unheard of even then in the liberal 1980s. But Mamie is in the hospital, sick, and she hasn't been in class. Bertie and Dolly want me to bring books for Mamie's return, but more than that, they want me to see where they live. The recreation officer puts the call through to get permission, and on a moonlit evening we find ourselves walking together down a stone path in prison.

"Do you know the names of any of the stars?" Bertie asks, looking up and pulling her denim jacket tight around her.

"No," I say. "I was never much good at remembering names."

"I always wish on stars," Bertie goes on. The compound, lit from what resemble tall streetlamps, looks more like a campus than a prison. It is cold, probably twenty degrees. The units seem miles away. "I used to have a favorite. I think you call it the Dipper?"

"Big or Little?" Dolly asks, walking alongside us. She is wearing a huge gray wool coat and has her hands in the pockets.

"I didn't know there were two dippers. The one with the brightest star." Bertie stands for a moment, pointing upward. "That one." We stop too, tipping our heads back.

In the cottage Bertie makes me tea, posing against the doorframe as she asks if I want one sugar or two. She snaps her fingers, clicking into the idea that I am "the Sweet 'n' Low type." We sit around a table in the center of the unit, drinking tea, while women in housecoats walk by and a male guard watches us from what looks like a small cage at the entrance to the cottage. We are ostensibly sorting books into piles, but really it feels more like a gathering of friends. Bertie and Dolly decide to show me their room, which they share with two other women. It is a bit larger than a king-size bed and holds four thin cots. "Jean, here, see my kids?" Dolly says, pointing out the collage of photos over her bed on the wall. She pulls out a stuffed doll she is making for her granddaughter; so far it has no head. Bertie points proudly to the letter display on her wall, and I assume the display of crayon scribbles and envelopes is from her son. "Nice drawings," I say. She does not respond.

After my cottage visit days pass without a mention of Bertie's son.

I hear rumors that Bertie is constantly in and out of court. By the time spring rolls around, she hardly notices the crocuses budding on the compound. Bertie is as downcast as I've ever seen her.

One April evening Bertie appears without any makeup at my classroom door. "They want to deport me," she says. "I'll get to see my mother but not my boy." I imagine some politician claiming we don't want any more foreigners than we already have in the United States, especially ones who are criminals. Bertie looks forlorn, and the class feels it. Cody rubs her sneaker into a dustball. Dolly makes a sort of sympathetic clucking sound in the back of her throat. I reach out and squeeze Bertie's hand, telling her that these things can take a long time, maybe years. She looks at me and nods. The sadness spreads over all of us.

"Okay," I say to the group, improvising. "On your feet." I want to help Bertie in whatever way I can; and as much as that, I want to convey to the class that acting a character can give words to our feelings, beauty to the darkest moments. They all are spiritless, but I coax them to move the table and get the blackboard out of the way. "We're going to try using Shakespeare's words tonight. Let's see if we can make scenes have meaning."

I send Cody to stand on a chair at one end of the room, and Kit, to the opposite corner. "You can do this," I say to the two actresses as I hand them each a Xeroxed sheet from *Macbeth*. It involves two men meeting in the dead of night. At first they read the lines, stumbling over words, but I surprise them when I ask them to shout. "Yes, shout," I say to their puzzled faces. "And when you shout the words to each other, pause between each line, like people far apart trying to reach each other."

Cody, who is fiddling with her baseball cap, shuffles a bit on the chair and then calls out, "How goes the night, boy?"

The rest of the inmates crack up, but Kit dutifully takes a beat and, cupping her hands around her mouth, yells back, "The moon is down; I have not heard the clock."

Cody replies with even more volume, "And she goes down at twelve."

"Hold, take my sword," Kit shouts back, throwing her arm into the air. "There's husbandry in heaven. Their candles are all out. Take thee that too."

Everyone but Bertie is into it. In fact, the room erupts with women yelling, "How goes the night, boy?" at one another from corner to corner. Bertie sits listlessly on the sidelines.

Cody and Kit tell me they feel charged up after the exercise, swelled up with power, "like kings," I say. It takes no time for others to figure out, on their own, what happens if they whisper the lines. The room hushes with secrecy, the whispering itself seeming to take us to midnight, fear, and illicit activity.

"It's Bertie's turn," Dolly says. She's already on top of a chair, raring to go.

"No," I counter, "not on the chair this time, Dolly. Stand next to Bertie."

Bertie is doodling heads on her notebook, the same women she always draws, but these are all without eyes. She sits cross-legged in her chair. The lines from *Macbeth* are on the floor.

I pick up the discarded paper and give it to Bertie, ignoring her heavy sigh. "Dolly, you try Lady Macduff. Bertie, you play her son." I tell them quickly, so as to avoid Bertie's quizzical look. "Lady Macduff," I say, in my businesslike tone, "fears that her husband's disappearance means death. Dolly, you speak only before or after you physically touch your son, Bertie. And Bertie, you respond to that touch each time."

The other students don't seem confused by this suggestion. They know by now that I throw in ideas. They seem farfetched at first but they eventually make sense. And touching in this way is not yet a problem at Framingham. It is a few months before embracing and many other forms of physical contact are "banned" throughout the institution, partially due to a teacher's posing inmates as nude models in an art class. But for now education feels valued, and risks seem possible, so I forge ahead, urging women to flop on the floor or in chairs as Dolly moves close and stands next to Bertie. "Begin," I say to Dolly.

"Sirrah, your father's dead; / And what will you do now? How will you live?" She gently places her hand on Bertie's shoulder.

Bertie, turning to look behind her into Dolly's eyes, replies, "As birds do, mother, and so shall I."

"What, with worms and flies?" Dolly moves behind Bertie and strokes her hair, which tonight is a bundle of loose braids punctuated by beads.

"With what I get, I mean; and so do they." Bertie's words are clipped and certain. She leans her head back against Dolly's legs.

"Poor bird!" soothes Dolly, bending forward, her hand grazing Bertie's cheek. Although it is not written she says it again, "Poor bird."

. . .

In late April a group of college students comes into the prison to talk to some of the long-termers and Bertie is asked to be in the group. I get permission to sit in. The meeting takes place in what the women call the People-to-People Room, across the hall from Program Room 2. It is twice the size of a living room, with two windows that look out onto the yard, and a dozen extra chairs stacked in corners for AA or NA meetings, outside speaker programs, religious groups, or movies. The students space themselves in the circle of metal chairs that the People-to-People program coordinator has set up.

I hear Bertie greet someone in the hall, her voice shrill and frenetic. Bertie is, as far as I can make out, complaining about an incident in the cafeteria. She backs into the room, gesturing with her hands. Her nails are crimson. Then she turns and, caught off guard by the students staring at her, puts her hand up to her mouth to stop sounds of surprise. Her eyes flash around the room until she finds me.

"Jean." She hedges over and sits next to me, taking a deep breath and leaning back in the chair. "I didn't realize there'd be so many."

"They're just students," I whisper.

"I think I'll do a relaxation exercise," she whispers back.

While Bertie is waiting for the other speakers to arrive, I look around the room at the college students. Two males, with caps on backwards, tilt their chairs back against the wall, trying to appear casual. Two women who sit across from us keep on their coats, as though they were still outside. One student who has a bad back has asked if she can stand, and she holds on to her chair, glancing at us periodically. The others stare at Bertie.

"I bet you can't believe you're actually sitting behind bars with a prisoner." Bertie says, sounding confident. "We're not so bad." A few titters and uncomfortable throat-clearing sounds.

"We've been to Lancaster," a young man announces.

"But they didn't have keys, did they? You could leave any time you wanted, right?" Bertie smiles at the student. He backs off, agreeing there is a real difference, hearing those doors clang behind you at Framingham. Lancaster Pre-Release is for those who have served hard time but are most likely on their way out. In 1987, before laws change and no one with a murder sentence can do any of his or her time outside the walls, someone like Bertie might be eligible.

"Sorry we're late," says a tall, serious-looking white woman, carrying a bunch of flowers and a paper folder. She rushes into the room followed by a black woman wearing a hat that looks like a crown. They both smile at me and sit in the circle of chairs next to one of the young men with caps.

"My boss gave me these flowers," the serious-looking one says to Bertie. "He's a gem." She has a scar above her right eye, and her jaw is overly square. Her dingy blond hair is held back with a rubber band, and her faded yellow shirt rolled up at the sleeves. Bertie tells her to begin.

"I was one of those women you read about." She speaks with an urgent voice. "A statistic. One of the women battered every day by a husband or boyfriend. I used to be just like you." The students shift uncomfortably in their seats. She then passes a picture around so they can see what she looked like before the beatings.

One female student gasps when the photo comes to her; she keeps looking up at the speaker and down at the picture. In the photograph the speaker is young, with unblemished skin and one of those smiles that belong to the undefeated. "I was lucky. I lived," she continues. "My husband raped me with a bottle and knocked my teeth in with a hammer. Other women aren't so fortunate. I never intended for my husband to die, but after the hammer incident, some friends of mine asked me if I wanted them to hurt him. I said yes. I enticed him to the woods, and he thought it was for sex. When they began beating him up, they didn't stop. The jury found me guilty of manslaughter."

"Christ almighty," someone says under his breath.

She continues. "I was the first woman in the state to use the battered-woman's defense, but I lost and got ten to fifteen years. I wrote a paper about having spent three years in the old awaiting-trial unit, an experience even worse than my abuse." She can't keep back tears as she recounts what it was like to count ceiling tiles in a locked room for twenty-three out of twenty-four hours, women around her screaming day and night. "That was before I was sentenced."

One of the young men has taken off his cap and crosses his arms tightly across his chest. The hat hangs from his hand like a limp rag.

The focus shifts to the twenty-four-year-old African American, who grew up in the projects but was never in trouble before she killed her boyfriend. She rocks back and forth in her chair as she recounts her tale of abuse. "I am not proud when I say I spent years afraid of Juan and experienced continued beatings, black eyes, and fear. I am sorry that I killed him, but it was either him or me." The students nod their heads as though they understand. She answers tough questions from the class, and says, yes, she did try to leave, and no, police were not able to stop the abuse. These are the days before shelters were known places of refuge, before women felt they could seek safety outside their homes. We all sit silently, and I wish my high-schoolers could be here, listening.

Bertie is the last to speak. "I'm not a victim," she tells the students, who sit close together. Sunlight forms a puddle in the center of the circle of chairs. "I'm what they call a baby killer. My sin was taking a life, not just any life, but the life of a four-month-old baby who was helpless and couldn't help herself from my hurting her." Some look at the floor. Even the students with the caps turn and twist in their seats. But Bertie keeps on, describing her life in Jamaica, her family, and her prison experiences.

"When I first came here," she says, "all the inmates called me names because of my crime, and they wouldn't give me a chance. I had to fight my way to prove myself to them. I take things very personal. Even when we read a book in class or I play a part on stage, I feel like her. I know what it is like to be judged and chastised by other people."

Bertie looks around the room and catches the eyes of the students. She does not back away. "No, I am not excusing what I did, and I have to live with this terrible crime for the rest of my life. I relive it every day, and I will continue to until I find some kind of peace with myself. I am not asking people to love or even to accept me; they shouldn't have to. I just want them to accept that I am a person. No one knows till they've been there. I don't know if I'll ever forgive myself."

At the end of the hour, after the students silently leave the room, on their way to tour the prison, Bertie comes up to me and says softly, "I think maybe they didn't hate me."

. . .

In a shot from the video of our *Merchant* production in 1988, I am standing in the middle of the cast, all of us with our arms around one another. We are smiling, squeezing not just our bodies but every last bit of our energy into the picture. The women have just talked to the camera, telling children, parents, and spouses how difficult and thrilling it is to put on a play in prison. They say: "This play was hard. This play brought up memories for me. Pops, I finished something! Hello, Leticia, Mary Lee, Big Michael. Hello, Bobby, Little Roy. Hello, Tommy, Carmen, Papi and Mami. I hope you enjoy this video."

It is a frozen moment captured in real time that makes one remember every sound and smell. The prison gymnasium, old and mildewy in any season, with a hardwood floor that buckles in places. Creaky wooden steps lead up to the stage. Light comes in through barred windows and gives a luster to the room, a sort of holy glow. Steam hisses from the pipes overhead.

I have my arms around as many as my arms can reach so that there is this snuggling-up quality, a slumber-party feeling, a gaggle of prisoners all dressed up in 1920 period costumes, gangster-style. Pimp hats and suits for the women who play men. A flapper outfit for our Portia. A flowing beard and earlocks for Shylock. Bertie as a youthful Gratiano stands next to me, dapper in her white suede shoes, a blue satin hanky sticking out of her pocket, a pencil moustache drawn across her upper lip. She calls me "Teacher Jean" and guides the others to crowd in close and to enunciate their words. "I am proud we finish this play," she tells the camera.

Five years later she has finished four plays. She balks when I ask her if she wants to join up again.

"Only if we do a show with music." Bertie tells me in the hallway one evening. "Sharine's known for her church singing, and she's got this girlfriend Angel who choreographs steps for the talent shows." Bertie leans against the wall near the open gym door; sounds of rap music from a boom box drift into the hall. "If we don't do it now, I'll never get the chance. I'll be gone next year."

"I like the idea of a musical, Bertie."

"Good." She snaps her fingers to the music, mouthing a few words I don't understand. "Salt 'n' Pepa," she says to my inquiring look. "They're a group. Later." Bertie swings past me through the gym door to join the volleyball game.

Six months later, she's a star in *Rapshrew*, our rap adaptation of Shakespeare's *The Taming of the Shrew*. She's the one who's gathered the Shrews, our rap group, turning them into dancers, while I coach them on diction. Their torsos bumping and grinding, arms swinging and heads wagging, they belt out, "Rollin', rollin', roll with the Shrews now, everybody sing!"

At our final performance staff, inmates' parents, spouses, relatives, and children clap and sing along with the Shrews. Bertie, who plays

Kate's spoiled sister, Bianca, is standing with me backstage, ready for an entrance, decked out in a teal satin dress, cut so it shows her shoulders. She has on long black gloves and her bare arms bend like swans' necks. "In the next play I want new shoes," she insists before taking a part in *Shrew*, and here she is, "stepping out," as the ladies like to call it, in new black high heels. They're not unlike the ones worn in three of the plays she's performed in, but still, it's clear she feels fancy in her costume, crowned with a cloche hat, topped off with a black feather.

She peeks out from behind the green curtain. Slowly I become aware that she is staring at two small children who sit with their grandmother in the front row. I'm reminded that no one from her family is here or has ever come to see her perform. One of the little ones in the front starts to cry, and the grandmother turns to her, mouthing words that the performer sings on stage, "I'm a shrew, I'm a shrew, she's a shrew, I'm, a shrew." The little girl's face brightens up. "This is a hoot," Bertie whispers to me.

After the cast breaks to eat cake and drink soda, the room is abuzz with family. Children with plates of food and glasses of ginger ale mingle with prisoners in costume. Bertie sits on the bare stage, seated so her feet dangle over the sign that reads STAGE OFF LIMITS. A mother and daughter sit next to her, eating chips. Two of the Shrews, holding the mikes that they used as rappers, ask if they can sing a song for their families. They spontaneously begin a hymn, joined almost immediately by Bertie, who finds a mike. The three sway and sing, "I remember Mama in a happy way," as cast and audience turn from wherever they are in the gym. Some hum softly, nodding away, eyes closed.

Later that evening Bertie sits alone after the families have gone and writes in her journal, "I know now I am somebody."

KIT

Motley's the only wear!
As You Like It, II.vii.34

In Shakespeare there is always a fool. Ours is Kit, who slouches in a chair, fidgeting with an earring. She's got a look on her face that reminds me of a mistreated dog's, eyes dark and aching. I should feel sorry for her: the toothless smile; the unpressed flannel shirt; the ratty sneakers she wears without socks; she can't make her greasy hair stay in a ponytail and settles for rivulets down her neck and around her ears. I should laugh off her attitude—the cryptic comments and snarls. But when she guffaws at others' mistakes and spits out the window if she thinks no one's looking, I think she's nasty, a sad little character about whom I would never want to write a story.

The first time I get a full dose of Kit's temperament is at the end of our first class in prison, 1986. We're winding down. Bertie and Dolly are lingering at the doorway, talking softly. Most of the night Kit's either been a joker or hostile to Bertie, and I won't be sorry to see her leave the room. But now she's glued to her chair. She stares at the pile of new blue ballpoint pens and clean pads of lined paper in the center of the table. I look up at her from my attendance sheet and smile weakly, but she doesn't seem to notice me.

At the door Bertie and Dolly have their heads together as Bertie softly reads her free-write to Dolly. "What was it like this morning when I get up—what did I feel?" it begins. "I look out my window and see nothing! Nothing! Not the beautiful day, not the lovely colors of the leaves turning, not the sounds of the birds. . . . I don't want to get out of bed, why, what for? That's when I remember I'm in prison." Dolly tells her to save everything she writes. Kit looks over but doesn't react.

An officer bellows, "Last meds!" into the room.

"Thanks, Kojack," Dolly calls back.

Snapping the metal chairs closed, Mamie arranges them against the wall, and then she stops to hang out by the door with Bertie and Dolly. Cody exits, yelling after friends she sees in the hallway, and they all carouse outside the room as if they're at a bar. An inmate passes by, humming something with the words "blessed Lord," most likely from the church service that's held upstairs. Someone else is complaining to a friend in rapid-fire Spanish.

Kit untucks her flannel shirt and loosens her belt. She lets out a deep sigh and stands up. I feel some relief as she starts out the door, and reach across the table to gather up the pens and pads, sweeping them into my briefcase. As though thinking twice about leaving, Kit turns around. "I hate these state-issued black pens. Can I have one of yours? One of the blue ones?" She moves back into the room. Bertie glances over at her.

I wonder if Kit's up to something. I remember how, earlier this evening, she was the one who held up her state-supplied red notebook and ballpoint, saying, "No one trusts a con. They make sure we don't do dope by giving us no-take-apart pens. They think we're all junkies." Dolly had turned to her and said, "Kit, you are a junkie."

I reach into my briefcase to retrieve the pens. I pull out a fistful; they're sleek and cobalt, each with a pointy top. "Sure, Kit, no problem. These pens were approved." I say it in a teasing way, but I want her to know I'm no dummy. I'd thought of these pens as ordinary, stood by while Connors checked them out, and felt relieved that my basic Bics could go with me into prison. Now Kit eyes them hungrily. I figure I can't lose anything and hand her a pen.

"Can I have two?" she asks, looking at me with those eyes.

I hesitate. One seems okay, somehow part of the package, but two? What if everyone asks for more?

Kit's not budging. Firmly planted by my side, she crosses her arms in front of her chest, her feet apart, as if she's a traffic cop.

"If I give you another, I might not have enough for next time." Blue, the color of sky, the color of hope, the color of freedom, I think as I start to zip up my briefcase. Kit gives me one last piercing look and turns back toward the door. Women exiting from chapel services are still passing by. Loud sounds burst in occasionally over speakers, ordering prisoners to units. Kit's hunched over now, older than her forty-odd years, a burned-out woman heading to her prison cell.

"Here Kit. Take two." I hand her another pen. She grabs it up, and immediately I regret it. Bertie and Dolly ask for blue pens, not just one each but two. Kit heads outside, talking to Cody, tossing the pens in the air, almost as if she's juggling. By the time I'm halfway down the hall, I've given away all the blue pens. When I look back over my shoulder, I hear Kit telling Cody, "Ed-u-ca-tion's good for something."

• • •

Weeks later, just before Halloween, Ron Zullo drops in on our class. "Happened to be here in the evening," he says to me. Almost in sync a few of the women sit up straight in their chairs. Kit's in the middle of picking at a scab on the back of her hand with a matchbook cover. She looks like someone who she hasn't slept in days. There are bags under her eyes, and a coat two sizes too big is thrown over her. Dark hair, half gray, sticks out in clumps under a knitted cap.

"Harrigan, can I speak with you, please," Ron says pointedly to Kit. It's not a question.

Kit, who's been trying to avoid Ron's eyes, looks down at the paper she's been reading aloud, a journal assignment that begins, "I really dislike my brain. I've seen pictures in books and it's terrible looking. Thank God we don't have to put clothes on it or even try to make it up to look good. The worst part of it is it completely controls you." She shrugs her shoulders as if she couldn't care less and cocks her head at Ron.

"Outside," he says in a harsh voice. Kit gets up out of her chair. She scoops up a half-smoked Pall Mall from the table and puts it back in the pack. Her fingers are long and skinny, yellowed around the nails. She shoves the cigarettes into her coat pocket and taps the pack as though she wants to make sure it's still there. No one says a thing until Kit's out the door.

"Do you think she'll get Iso?" Cody asks Dolly.

"At least." Dolly's gathering up Kit's class materials. One of the women whistles under her breath. I've learned that "Iso" means Isolation, a midweight punishment in prison: The inmate is locked in the unit for everything but meals.

"What's going on?" I ask the students. One week a prisoner arrives for class and the next she's transferred to pre-release, on a visit, or locked. In most cases I don't find out until it happens.

Rhonda says, "Bullshit, as usual." Rhonda's been a regular for a couple of months, although it's clear that she's torn between sports and school. She's in the process of borrowing Bertie's sweater-jacket, tying the sash around her waist. "Just for the evening, B," she says to Bertie. I know trading anything—clothes, cigarettes, supplies from the compound store—isn't allowed, but still the inmates thrive on barter. If they're caught they get a D report, and often have to reckon their version of events at a hearing with an officer. "Don't give it a second thought. Kit's screwed," Rhonda adds.

Someone's muttering that Kit is always in trouble for one thing or another. Bertie's being cool, carefully putting on nail polish with no expression on her face. Dolly starts to tell Rhonda not to talk about Kit.

"No, seriously, Dolly," Rhonda says. "Excuse my French, but some-one in Laurel got caught with—big deal—hooch in her room." She looks in my direction to explain. "Sorry, home brew. They put fruit from the cafeteria in Kool-Aid so it turns to alcohol, ferments. That's hooch." Then she returns to Dolly. "They think Kit's involved. And with her rep—"

"Kit's done with drugs," Dolly says. "And alcohol. She'll get blamed, but she didn't do it."

"Hey, I know, I know, but you've got to take into consideration how everything around here is a federal offense, and—" Before Rhonda can finish her sentence, Kit comes back into the room, slam-ming the door behind her. Her face is hard to read, mouth set in a tight line. She pulls her cap down tighter over her ears. I'm wondering what's going on.

"I don't wanna talk about it," Kit says to the room. To me she says, "I'd like to finish reading and be done with it." I nod. There's silence. Dolly hands Kit her notebook, and we settle into Kit's reading aloud.

For a few minutes we're engrossed in her story as she tells us about a summer day, with her daughter in a baby carriage:

> I couldn't afford to go shopping for real, so this was quite often a game I played with myself. I'd look in a window and then at my daughter in the carriage and say to her, "Mommy is going to buy that red coat next week. How do you like it?" Of course she wouldn't answer me. That was okay though, because Noreen the Bean didn't know how to talk yet. So I'd go to the next window and say, "I'll buy this black dress in a few weeks." I always kept in my mind that we were going shopping for real because it made our day more fun.

I try to tell her that her piece is touching, but she waves away my sentiment with a "Phooey," and keeps on reading.

> I was getting bored as hell with all this daydreaming and window-shopping, so I decided to go visit a friend of mine, Gina. Gina was all of five feet one inch tall, weighing a good two hundred pounds, with long black hair that needed washing badly. You could see her bust coming before you could see Gina.

The women laugh, and as they comment on how she puts her words together well, Kit's mood begins to improve. She starts into the tale of how, that day, Gina decided to do laundry in a ragged T-shirt, and got her shirt and then her breast caught in an old-fashioned washing machine, one with a wringer. Although it sounds painful, and at first we wince, Kit is reading in a monotone that strikes us as particularly funny, and every time she gets to a place in the story that seems

78

absolutely outrageous, she looks up, holds up her hand, and says, "Swear to God." Then she laughs at herself, a frog-in-the-throat sort of laugh.

She reads, "I really didn't want to laugh, but you had to see her, standing there, her black T-shirt a shirt no longer, her bust starting to enter the wringer, like a pancake looming, about to explode, swelling right in front of us, turning colors." Then she tells us that Gina too was laughing in spite of the pain, particularly when they had to call the police to take her to the hospital. She adds the kicker that doctors "did manage to fix Gina's tit and put it in a sling." By the time Kit finishes, she's got all of us in the palm of her hand.

"That was—uh—original," I say to her. Women are laughing all around me.

Kit ignores me, thriving on the swell of her success. She stretches out in her chair, leaning back as if she's at the beach, so that her legs extend in front of her. She waves away the laughter. "Okay, okay. I'm not in big trouble, if you must know, you bitches."

"So wazzup, bud?" Rhonda asks.

"Did Zullo give you any lockup?" Cody says, without missing a beat.

Kit enjoys putting the women off, and she does. "Not exactly." She's still leaning back in her chair, but now she lets her feet flop apart, and she puts on this teasing half smile.

Dolly says she doesn't need details. Bertie gleefully makes stabs about Kit's encounter with Ron. "He hates to be shown up about anything," Bertie adds, "so I hope you didn't do that."

"Zullo just wanted to clue me in." Kit's on a roll. "They caught the hooch chick. I'm off the hook 'this time,' he tells me. Just like I used to tell Noreen the Bean, innocent until proven guilty."

And then Kit cackles in this eerie way that fills the room, a laugh much louder and longer than anyone else's laugh in Program Room 2 that evening, a wicked-witch laugh right out of *The Wizard of Oz*, and one that I later hear in my dreams, a laugh that forms the foundation of her portrayal of a Puritan woman in our production of Nathaniel Hawthorne's *The Scarlet Letter*. Kit haunts me in that play, grinning toothlessly up at Hester Prynne, waving her script in the air, crying out gleefully, "Show us the mark of your shame! Shame! Shame!"

By now the women are looking around at one another. I'm uncomfortable with Kit's way of dropping tidbits of information. I want to recover order. "Kit, are you in this class or out?" I ask abruptly.

"These bozos are all the same." Kit's still ignoring me, slung back in her seat, comfy, like she's the queen bee. She's blathering. "Give 'em an inch and they take a mile. You know, he leaned over me like a goddam pervert, trying to see down my flannel shirt, fer Chrissakes! Oh, yeah, he knows I don' wanna blow my chances at prerelease with no D. I bet Zullo has it in big-time for you black chicks."

"Kit, that's enough." I'm wondering if she is high.

Bertie and Rhonda give each other looks. Dolly crosses over to Kit and puts a hand on her shoulder. "Jee-sus, Harrigan."

Kit keeps at it. "He just about put his you-know-what in my you-know-where. Give me another chance, my ass!" Dolly edges into the corner. I consider getting a guard. Kit won't shut up. "Maybe I should pee in Zullo's coffee mug, like Strawberry did in Off-i-cer Mar-zetti's. Take my u-rine test the hard way." Then Kit cackles again.

Bertie says she's had enough, and Rhonda tells Kit that she better watch herself with comments about "black chicks." They start to head out the door.

"No one's leaving," I say, firmer than I planned. "Anyone who's in this class will respect my rules. No insults. No one leaves till we're done. Got it?" I say it again, pointedly in Kit's direction. I'm much louder than the first time: "This is a class. *Got it?!*" The women aren't moving. I hand out homework assignments in total silence.

I hope someone will snitch on Kit for something and that she'll get caught, maybe get Iso or do time in Max. I hope that at least I won't see her next week. I think about how I'm looking forward to the drive home, alone, and for a moment, I imagine what it must feel like not to be going home. Sometimes I wonder what the hell I think I'm doing in prison.

. . .

The next week Kit's back in class. And the week after that. And the week after that. In fact Kit writes up a storm all semester. She says she can't get enough of class, and she says it loud and she says it often. As far as I can tell she's straight, but it's hard to know. She's as impenetrable as anyone I've met behind bars. For her final project she can't make up her mind, research or creative writing. I tell her to surprise me.

She comes to class at the end of the semester, almost flinging papers down on the table. "It was Cody's idea," Kit says, breathlessly. "We decided to research why there are no toilet seats in Framingham."

"That's impressive," I say, with a tinge of sarcasm. I feel contentious. Kit looks as if she woke up two minutes ago and dashed out of her cottage to get up to the main institution on the first Upward. Her red turtleneck shirt has stains on the front, and she isn't wearing a belt to hold up her faded jeans. Everything about her sags.

"Cody's in the weight room tonight. We coll-ab-or-at-ed," she says, taking time to pronounce a word that she's obviously trying to impress me with. Bertie muffles a laugh. Mamie, too, makes a kind of grunt in Kit's direction.

"Does Cody know you're presenting this without her?"

"You betcha," Kit replies. "She just got, you know, hung up. She's okay with me sharing the results of our in-quir-ee."

"She needs to be here too, Kit, if you both want credit."

For a moment there's the same silence I'm now used to around Kit. The women all stop what they're doing. Dolly's mid-stitch in her knitting; Bertie looks up from a drawing. Everyone waits to see what will happen next.

Kit runs a finger across her paper, taking in the comment. She tilts her head as if she's getting what I'm saying. I can't imagine that Kit thinks she can pull a fast one with her final. For a moment I consider letting her read the paper out loud. She looks at me, glassy eyed, and then shakes her head and mumbles under her breath, "I shoulda gone to AA."

"Why don't you wait until next week," I say. "There's still time before grades are due."

At first Kit says nothing. Then words tumble out of her mouth. She says, "Don'tcha wanna know why we line our toilet seats with Kotex?" When I give her a blank stare, she says, "I spent a helluva lotta time talking to people." She counts them off on her fingers. "Sergeants, lieutenants, counselors, captains, unit managers, security, maintenance, and even the plumber. The administration thinks we'd bash each other over the heads if we had toilet seats."

The other women aren't talking. I move around in my seat, cross my legs. "Yes, go ahead, Kit. Tell us about your research, but I want you to wait and read the paper next week when Cody's here."

Cody bursts into the room so well timed that it almost looks planned. She's wearing a new blue-and-white Boston Patriots cap. "Hey, sorry I'm late! Had to supervise some girls in the weight room." She still has on leather half-gloves from lifting, a sweatshirt ripped at the neck, and she's been perspiring so much that sweat glistens on her neck and across her brow. "I've got my final. Did Kit tell you that we researched why there are no toilet seats in this godforsaken place?"

"Kit was telling us," Dolly says.

"Zullo says it's for our own protection." Cody's looking around the room from face to face. Kit's nodding away. Cody looks at Kit and then back at me. "Kit did help me write it."

"That's what I said." Kit sticks her chin up into the air and points at the papers on the table like they were awards. "See? We both have copies." She glances around the room and then pushes the papers toward me.

The women give each other looks that say, *Who the hell are you kidding?* Kit watches me and waits until I give her some acknowledgment, a little nod, a semismile, anything she can grab onto. Then the two researchers launch into reading. When it's Kit's turn to read, from the way that the other inmates look down or out the window, it's clear that this is a roomful of women who don't trust her.

The class meets a week later to go over final grades. Kit doesn't show. I hear from Dolly that she's been put in a drug and alcohol rehab program that will control her every move at the prison. I won't see her for at least three months.

. . .

"Carol was a recreation officer, fer Chrissakes, and she's doin' it with an ex-inmate. She deserves to get canned." Kit's outside the classroom all bundled up in her baggy winter coat talking to a dark-haired skittish-looking woman I don't know. It's 1987, a couple of weeks before Christmas, and I've just arrived for our play-reading class. Kit missed only a couple of months of school last year, but she says that with the summer behind her, she's a new woman. "I'm cleaned up and crazy as ever," she said when she returned to classes, and she's been what she calls a "model student" this fall semester. I have to admit that she's completed assignments on time as much as anyone, and she's been involved in class discussion, even if it is with some antagonism. But there's something that still makes me feel squeamish and distrustful around her. I'm wondering why she's waiting for me tonight.

The hall's filled with a few officers and their families, on a "prison tour." They're a group of about fifteen, all dressed up in spanking-new shirts and even some ties and high heels. They're at the end of the hallway, near the Parenting Room, a space filled with old toys and red vinyl couches that's used to teach parenting skills and, I assume, for visits with children. I've been in that area a few times, and its weak attempt at cheerfulness depresses me. An out-of-commission dollhouse is in one corner, its rooms crammed with rolls of paper towels or old rags. An antique trunk holds worn children's books and dolls that have ripped dresses. A coatrack for winter wear is in the entryway, but all hangers have been removed. Windows are propped open with books to let in air because steam heaters on the floor overheat the room.

The recreation officer has explained to me that the tour is a "perk" of being a guard: A couple of times a year families get to see where their relatives work. Now Bernice is leading the way, pointing out something on the wall to the group and simultaneously communicating on her walkie-talkie to the captain's office. The tour passes Kit, who's standing in front of a poster-size drawing of reindeer and a pretty good rendition of Santa Claus. The night sky has stars, and snow-covered mountains fade into the deepest blue. The poster announces that inmates will be singing songs from *Godspell* at next week's service in the chapel.

Kit goes on, still talking to her companion about the recreation officer who was recently fired. "You know what they say, 'Chewin' and screwin' and stealin' money with the best of them.' As soon as Carol got canned, I heard she moved in with the chick. Carol is Framingham's finest."

Now I realize who they're talking about. Carol was Bernice's assistant, a stocky and chipper sort, younger than most of the staff. She talked about her boyfriend's motorcycle and their weekends in Vermont, had a wild laugh that began like a hoot and just got louder. She spent a lot of time with the part-time art teacher watching TV on breaks in the Green Room, so-called because it's avocado green and has couches and a few plants. They brought their dinners in paper bags and ate together while prisoners were at Count in their units.

The other woman snickers and then stops abruptly when she sees me. Kit's still talking. "Last Christmas an inmate was sent to Max when she stuffed pillowcases to try to make a Santa Claus dummy. People go crazy around here without the old mistletoe, if you get my drift."

"Hi, Kit," I say, nearing the classroom. I nod to the stranger.

"What happened to Carol?" I ask.

"She's out. Fired. Gonzo." Kit continues, "That's why Bernice is running around with a chicken whose head is cut off."

"Like a chicken," I say. "With her head cut off." The woman I've never seen before stands next to Kit and smiles tepidly. From the corner of my eye I can see the tour enter the gym.

"This is Rose. She's in my cottage. We're in the program together," says Kit.

"Uh-huh." I try the handle of the door. It's locked. I look around to see if an officer will let me in. I take a few steps toward Bernice and the tour and then change my mind.

"Still no keys?" Kit asks.

"No keys."

"You don't want keys," Rose pipes up suddenly. "Somebody might take them from you. What you have now you can't lose."

"That's true." I study Rose, trying to understand where that comment came from. She looks solemn, serious, in some kind of pain. Maybe it's Christmas, being away from her family. As Dolly told me last year, "Christmas is canceled in prison. Except for the lousy ham and mashed potatoes. The goddam women who spend their mornings upstairs in the Adult Basic Education class can't sing carols in the classroom unless they close the door. No one wants us to be too happy."

Rose has a half-peeled orange in her left hand. I notice that her right hand is withered. The fingers look as if they're stuck together and her thumb is crooked. I'm hoping any friend of Kit's is not interested in joining my class.

Rose begins removing the rest of the peel with her spatulate thumb, using it to peel back the rind. She notices me looking at her. "Want some orange?"

I am about to admit that I can't take anything from an inmate but stop myself. Something about Rose's eyes are even sadder than Kit's. "I just had dinner," I say. "Thanks anyway."

"I'll take some," Kit says. She takes a chunk of pulp and puts it in her mouth, sloshing it around, in order to eat it with her gums. "Hey, Bernice!" Kit yells out toward the gym as Bernice and her group reappear. "Open the door." Bernice waves Kit away. The group troops upstairs toward the chapel and disappears. Finally an officer arrives.

The officer and Kit squabble about something as he unlocks the door. I enter the room, and when Rose follows, I'm surprised. "You know, Rose, you have to register first if you want to take a class, upstairs in Education." She doesn't respond.

The officer says, "You all takin' English?" Kit nods. She pops the rest of the orange in her mouth. He snorts. This one's tall, young, southern, and has a wisp of blond hair that looks dyed across his forehead. It keeps falling in his eyes. "You in this class too, Antonelli?" Rose mumbles that she's making Christmas cards in the Green Room. The officer tells her to get where she's going.

Rose says something to Kit under her breath and then, louder, "Thanks for standing up for me this afternoon. And keep the faith." Rose brushes by Kit and exits with the officer.

I put down my briefcase and take off my coat. "Someone in the cafeteria wouldn't serve Rose this afternoon, and I gave 'em hell," Kit says. "She doesn't wanna be alone tonight, but those are the breaks. Rose has HIV." Kit watches me closely.

"Wouldn't serve her?" I say. Just for a moment it flashes into my head: the orange. I'm imagining Rose with AIDS, a cut, blood on an orange, eating the orange slice. She's not going to bleed on an orange, a rational voice screams back at me.

"Yeah, wouldn't serve her, no way José. Almost broke into a fight. Another broad stepped in, and Rose got her chow. You wouldn't believe how lousy it is here for some of these girls with the virus. One of 'em refuses to come up from her cottage and spends all her time in the crib, singing to herself." Kit plops herself in a chair. "Some of these girls ask for a room change when they hear you have the virus."

"I can't imagine being sick in prison," I say, and begin unzipping my briefcase. I'm still wondering why Kit's early for class. "Kit, how did you get up here before Movement?"

"You know, the usual way. Bribes. Begging. Charm." Kit grins at me and pulls a slip of green paper from her coat pocket and hands it to me. I notice her jacket's ripped at the sleeve. "They know I'm here. I wanted to talk to you." She hesitates. "Could you shut the door?"

I'm a little nervous to be alone in a room with Kit, but I shut the door anyway and come back to the table. Kit's looking at the floor. "I'm gonna be locked for a while, after Christmas. That's what I wanted to tell you. Well, one of the things. No classes for a while." She keeps on, stumbling over words. "My sister's giving away my kid." She looks up at me, a tangle of emotions on her face.

"Giving away your child? What do you mean?"

"My sister Candy's in some detox program again, can you believe it? Granny's got Noreen the Bean, but she can't handle her. Reenie's got some learning problem, and Granny, she can't see to help Jesus. Reenie's only nine, just barely, and Candy, she promised me she wouldn't neglect my kid. Damn." She punches one fist into the other.

"I blew it big time. When I got the letter from Granny that Candy was back on the dope, I flipped. Threw things, broke a lamp. I might do time in Max, who knows? I'll probably miss the class final." Kit starts to get up out of her chair and stops. She plunges her hands into her pockets. " 'She'll be better off with the Department of Social Services.' That's what she wrote."

"I really am sorry, Kit."

"The worst part is that Noreen'll always hate me for this. She won't visit, hasn't been here for three and a half years. Now Candy's jammed me up again. I'll never get to pre-release, never see my kid in that visiting trailer the girls talk about. Never." Again she punches her fist into her hand.

We sit silently together in the classroom. I remember the stinging piece that Kit wrote about her mother, the woman she calls "Granny." When I'd asked the class to write about their grandmothers, I imagined I'd get writing about women in their seventies, with presents for children in lilac-scented dresser drawers. Kit wrote that her real grandmother ran off with some "bum" when she was three, and that her mother "sat all day on the front stoop screaming at her kids to stop fighting, a butt hanging from her lower lip."

Kit sits staring at the floor. I think of how sad it is that most of the women live too far from Framingham to see their kids regularly, and how touched they are when they come to class after a visit with their children. "When I used to work cleanup crew at the front," Kit says, "I'd see the van pull up and kids pile out, other women's kids." With two weeks of lockup, Kit's loneliness will feel even worse.

"Are you allowed to see a therapist when you're locked?" I ask.

Kit cackles, filling the room with her witch laugh. "They gave up on me a long time ago."

Dolly swings into the room, pulling a TV on a stand behind her. "Special delivery."

"Hi, Dolly."

"Hey, Kit." Dolly comes over and touches Kit on the shoulder. "Heard you watched Rose's back in the cafeteria." She coaxes Kit into helping her move the table out of the way and she puts the TV in front of the window.

"Kit, I think it's great you helped Rose out," I say. I erase the white board, try to go over my lesson plans for the evening.

"Hey, Doll, remember what it was like when you first saw a woman in handcuffs es-cor-ted by an officer wearing plastic gloves?" Kit is lining up chairs. "They thought she had leprosy or somethin'."

"We were talking about AIDS," I say to Dolly, heading over to the TV. "God, this thing's dirty."

Dolly plugs the cord into an open socket, noticing the piece of frayed cord in another. "These people in charge, I swear, what's wrong with them?"

"Remember Deanna Louise? Now there was a case," Kit says.

Dolly looks in my direction, explaining. "Deanna Louise managed to get to pre-release. Got thinner and thinner. She moaned in her sleep about going home, until they caught on and took her to the health unit. But Jee-sus, not to her home."

"Lots of girls who have the virus don't want anyone to know, and that's trouble too," Kit continues. "Keeps 'em isolated, that's what Rose says." Other women start to drift in from their cottages, and the noise level in the hall increases.

Almost out of nowhere, a flash of maroon catches my eye. Next to me is Rhonda in a crimson sweatshirt that reads "Harvard University." "Who has HIV?" she asks.

"No one in particular. We're just talking." I hand Dolly my video, and she puts the tape in the VCR.

Rhonda snaps open a metal chair and seats herself. "Hey, Dolly, buddy, let me see that video box." Dolly tosses her *Othello*. Kit mumbles under her breath that at least Deanna Louise got to go to pre-release. A heated conversation between two inmates takes place in the hall. Someone shuts the door.

Rhonda glances at the picture of Othello on the front of the video box. He's standing ominously over his wife, Desdemona, who in this version has blond hair down to her waist. "*Ooo-eee*, who is that hunk? I bet this'll be something." She looks at the description on the front of the box and then says, "Oh, I remember this play. Black man kills white woman. Good for Christmas." Rhonda winks at me. I look over at Kit to see what she's doing. She's standing by the window with a lighted cigarette. She has opened the window a crack so that smoke curls out, and she's humming to herself.

Dolly asks, "What're we watching?"

"*Othello*," I say. Women are gathering around the TV. "I thought we'd watch instead of read, kind of a break."

Rhonda reads out loud, "The story of a man in power consumed by jealousy and the foreboding tale of how he destroys everything, kills his wife, loses his . . ."

"I saw that movie on late-night TV," Kit blurts out suddenly. She puts her cigarette out on the sill. "It was old, old, old. Had another guy who was a sneak. Little. Mean." She pockets the cigarette butt, drags a chair across the floor to the TV, and turns around toward me. "What was his name, that weasel?"

"Iago?"

"Yeah, Yah-go. I always liked him. I remember this thing he said, 'He who steals my purse steals trash,' and then, hey, something like my spotless reputation, now don't mess with that. I relate."

"Right," Rhonda says, shaking her head at Kit.

"Yah-go. Killed a lotta people too. Women. Children," Kit says. "Well, maybe not children." She takes a seat. Someone comments that she's impressed that Kit stayed awake through *Othello*.

Kit grabs the video box away from Rhonda. " 'Running time two hours and thirty minutes.' That's two classes for sure."

"It's good that you know these things Kit," I say. "You're bound to get an A on your final," and I give her a smile, "your take-home final." I think about how ironic it is that Kit is the first inmate I've met in prison who's watched a Shakespearean play on late-night television.

I turn on the TV, and it fills the room with static. Dolly moves in and finds the channel for videos. Kit clasps her fingers behind her head and leans back in her chair. I can see little bits of orange on her upper lip. "Roll 'em," she says into the air.

. . .

It's late February 1988, a few weeks after our first *Merchant* read-through, and I'm on my way into the institution. Kojack is sitting on his stool at the front. He bends over as if he's at a ticket booth, and whispers, "Hey, did you hear about what happened last week?" He slides a clipboard through the wire opening for me to sign in. "Four off-duty officers broke into the side cage, you know the office next to the entrance, looking for God-knows-what. They escaped, even with the whole prison full of guards after them. Somewhere beyond the barbed wire they were arrested for drug and gun possession. I wasn't here, but I heard it was holy hell."

"Yeah, I read about it in the paper."

Kojack takes a bite of his sub. "Because of the break-in, we can't get double shifts so easily. They say someone wasn't paying enough attention at the front."

"Tough job." I slide the clipboard back. "Did you also hear that I had an appointment with Ron Zullo? We're going to put on a play. I mean, the inmates, they want to act—"

"Oh, they act every day, believe me." He chuckles. "They pay for plays now in college?"

"I got a grant."

"Ohhh, a grant. Everybody wants to do something for these women." He smiles and wipes his mouth with the back of his sleeve. It's a relief to find Kojack, even if he sometimes goes on and on about his divorce and playing the horses.

"I just need to check your A & E," Kojack says, referring to the Admission and Entrance form at the front of the prison. Kojack begins rummaging through a pile of papers next to him and almost simultaneously rifling through the index box to his right. Before files are computerized, there is an enormous number of forms at the front of the prison, many forms never in the same place twice. Without someone who knows the entrant, it can take half an hour to locate paperwork and get clearance.

"Inmate Services sent us a special form okaying you," he says, "if I can find it. Here, get started." He hands me the key to lock up my valuables. There are rows of metal lockboxes lining two walls in the cramped visiting room to my left. I always put my car keys and jewelry in the box and keep the locker key in my shoe.

When I come back to the window, Kojack says, "Wish somebody'd get a grant for me." He buzzes me through the first doorway and holds up some photos, mouthing words through the glass: "On the way out, let me show you my vacation pictures. From Malta. They're awesome."

Dolly and Kit are standing against the gym door, waiting for Bernice to unlock it so they can set up for evening activities. I expect Dolly to be up early since she's Bernice's helper, but can't quite figure out if Kit's maneuvered her way into being an assistant. "Hey, Jean!" Kit yells down the hall when she sees me. "Aerobics tonight in the gym. Should I go to sleek instead of speak?" Then she lets out one of her cackles, filling the hallway with that eerie, lonesome sound.

"Who let you up before Movement?" I yell back.

Dolly laughs and answers for Kit, "She's helping us tonight. Leonardo is sick. Hope I won't be sorry." She jabs Kit in the ribs.

Bernice swoops in between the two of them and unlocks the gym. Although I'm planning on an office meeting with Bernice before class, I can't resist the allure of the gym as Bernice puts her key in a lockbox by the door. I enjoy the click as lights go on. This space is bright and hugely welcoming, not at all drab like most of the prison. The windows are so high they have to be opened with a long pole. A proscenium stage, complete with curtain, stands at one end of the room; a removable volleyball net cuts across the center; and a basketball hoop is at the other end. Later the wood floor will buckle from roof leaks, and the space will sit unusable for over two years, but now the gymnasium floor is a perfect place for sports, and the stage for shows. This gym could be plucked out of any high school except for the so-called "dungeon," the secret space behind the stage, where three antique cells are exactly like they were from the late 1800s, when Framingham was a new penitentiary. Bernice took me back behind the stage a few weeks ago, where the cells are stuffed with basketballs and blue exercise mats.

Kit dribbles a basketball down the length of the floor and shoots. "*Hoo-ha!*" she yells out. Dolly and Bernice drag out mats and place them neatly in a stack at the foot of the stage.

"Kit, get out the rest of the basketballs," Bernice says, "and look for the tapes backstage. I think someone left them in the carton of Bibles. I'll be back with the boom box." She almost whizzes by me. "Follow me. We only have a few minutes before the Upward."

I step gingerly around puddles of soap and water that an inmate worker has left in the hallway. I trail Bernice down the hall, and we enter her office, the word "Recreation" on the door. The office is the size of a closet and somehow squeezes in two desks, a large stack of board games, racquets, piles of paper, and assorted boxes. The room smells of old shoes, and the overhead fluorescent lights are too bright, spotlighting dusty floors and shelves. Two boom boxes are on the top shelf above the desk, one with a broken speaker dangling from it. Bernice clears off a chair for me.

"So what's up?" she says, preoccupied with a note on her desk.

"I'd like to rehearse in the gym," I begin. I am hoping to set the play for late June, but with rehearsals only once or twice a week, I need the gym as soon as possible.

"No way can you have the gym, Jean."

"The women need to work onstage, since that's where they'll be performing."

"No way. Not a prayer." Bernice pulls out a chart that lists all the activities in the prison, their nights and times. It's an impressive recreation program. There's movie night, a volleyball league, aerobics, AA, NA, several religious groups, evening academic classes, arts and crafts, and the prison newspaper.

I lean over the desk to see the schedule. "How about Monday? There's nothing on Monday."

She starts to say no, but reconsiders. "Okay, but that's it."

"Could we maybe share the gym on Wednesdays? Half the night to basketball and half to the play?" I ask.

"We'll never get through a whole game. And some of your students are devoted to basketball."

"Gloria and Rhonda both told me those games only take an hour, and the rest of the time the women just hang out. Why not have basketball players come up on the seven-thirty instead of the six-thirty Upward, and my class can head to Program Room 2 for the second half of the evening?"

"You drive a hard bargain." Bernice pencils me in. "But you can't start until the middle of May. We've got another AIDS speakout in April. Oh, and Jean." She smiles. "Take these and answer them." She hands me a small pile of letters. There is a fat rubber band around the middle.

"What are these?" I look at the top envelope and notice it's dated last fall.

"Mail to the 'Drama Department.' I guess that's you."

● ● ●

By the time I get back to Program Room 2, all the women are waiting for me. Kit comes over and whispers in my ear. "Noreen the Bean wrote me a letter, her first."

"That's great, Kit." She's all jittery. "Help me get rid of the table," I say to her.

"She says she'll be moving, wants me to write her at her new address."

The other women pack up chairs while Kit and I push the table to the side of the room. Kit continues, "My old roomie, Nan, writes from a prison in Maine, sends me drawings. I'm gonna send one on to Reenie." She pulls out an envelope with a crumpled-up piece of yellow paper. On it is a picture of a chair that looks like Joseph's coat of many colors. It's rainbow striped.

"Nice," I say. "She'll like it. Send her your writing too."

She smiles at me and winks. "Except for the X-rated stuff." She folds up the picture and pockets the envelope.

I turn to the group. "Let's all make a circle in the center of the floor. First hour we concentrate on acting. Second hour on the script."

"Good we didn't wear our new clothes," Kit says to Dolly. Dolly responds with a thumbs-up. The room erupts in laughter. It looks as if Kit will be cooperative tonight.

"Okay, pay attention. This is a sound-and-movement exercise, otherwise known as give-and-take." I explain that we're going to loosen up, both our voices and our bodies, and at the same time work on spontaneity. "Don't think too much. Just let your body lead you." A few of the women titter, and Bertie elbows Rhonda.

"I'll begin," I say. I pick the same *hoo-ha* sound that Kit was doing earlier in the gym and add a rhythmic clap-clap, and at the end of the phrase I stomp my right foot two times. I'm explaining as I go. "One person takes the sound and movement," and I demonstrate, moving my clapping, foot-stomping, *hoo-ha* into the center of the circle. "When you get into the center you keep doing your sound and movement." I turn in a little circle in the center so that they all can see me.

Some of the women begin to imitate me, and others just stand there, watching. Gloria makes some crack about "crazy college teachers." Someone whistles and another makes no-way noises right through my explanation. I talk above the fray. "Okay. Now the person in the center *gives* that sound and movement to someone else." I stomp over to Kit and face her directly. "Kit, you do exactly what I'm doing."

Kit looks around the room for someone to save her, but everyone's smiling encouragingly. "Aw shit," she says and does a limp stomp and clap, an even weaker *hoo-ha*.

"Keep eye contact. Come on, Kit, let's have some energy." And then the other women join in with their stomps and claps and *hoo-ha*s, and in spite of herself Kit is heading into the center of the circle, trying to avoid eye contact, but her voice keeps getting louder. I'm talking over her. "When you get to the center, you change the sound and movement. You take it and make it into your own."

Everyone watches, still stomping and clapping while Kit manages to slow the sound and movement, like someone who has turned the speed down on a stereo. "Now you *give* that sound and movement to someone else." Kit *hoo-ha*s. Her footwork looks a little as if she's stuck in mud, pulling shoes out one after the other. Her arms are swimming through air. She stands in front of Dolly, and the two of them burst into laughter. The rest of us try to help by doing Kit's sound and movement with her.

We keep the exercise going for a good half hour, adding emotion to the mix, varying the speed and volume, the intensity of our movements. Bertie and Rhonda get into a great moment where Bertie's saying "Uh-huh," nodding her head on the downbeat, a little flick of her right wrist and hip swinging too. When she stands in front of Rhonda, facing her and doing the sound and movement with a sort of sassy sarcasm, Rhonda mimics Bertie. Kit does it too from the side, except that Kit's voice is gravelly and an octave lower, and on Kit the sashay looks anything but sexy. "This is a riot," Rhonda says.

After a while, I suggest they each find a sound and movement to go with their names. By now the women can't wait for their turn, introducing themselves with a gesture and having the rest of the group repeat their creation. Dolly steps into the center with her arms wide, hands forming fists in the air; she announces herself, "Dolly." We say her name and gesture back to her. Bertie is the most creative. She says "Bertie," claps twice, does a flourishy turn, and adds the phrase "is my name."

When it comes to Kit, her face falls, and like a theatrical mask, the corners of her mouth droop down, almost like she can't keep up a good front any longer. She drops into a chair and says, "Enough." She grabs a piece of loose paper on the floor and wipes sweat off her brow. "Who needs aerobics when we've got acting? I guess that's why they call it a warm-up."

I look at Kit curiously but only for a moment, wondering what exactly it is that's caught up with her, and then I whisk everyone into picking up scripts, choosing parts for the night, and readying themselves for our read-through.

"You do Bassanio," Dolly says to Kit. Kit obliges, but without much enthusiasm.

"Let's start with Act Three," I say.

Rhonda and Bertie launch into the dialogue. Kit cracks her knuckles when others are reading. Occasionally Kit comes out with a droll interpretation, but mostly she reads in a monotone, words tumbling out of her mouth, flat. When Bassanio must choose between lead, silver, and gold to win Portia's love, Kit drops her head on the table and says, "Let me choose; / For as I am, I live upon the rack."

"You enjoy this?" I say to her, hopefully.

"Nah. What does he mean, 'rack'?"

"Check out the notes," Rhonda says.

Kit gives her a look that could kill and then squints at the footnotes. "Hey, listen to this," she says. "Rack, instrument of torture, on which the body was pulled with great force, often breaking the joints; used to force confessions, especially in trials for treason." What's wrong with this guy anyway?

"He's in love," Rhonda says and then adds, "Yeah, sounds like love to me, all right." We laugh.

A few lines later Kit says, "Holy shit! Do I have to read all this?" She's referring to a monologue that Bassanio has that's more than two pages long. I tell her to start reading and we'll "translate" together. But Kit takes one look at the pages and says, "Just beam me out the story first."

"Okay," I say. "Bassanio's the good guy. He's the one who discovers that Portia's dead father has willed her to the man who understands the value of love. Her picture is hidden from her suitors' eyes in a lead—not a silver or a gold—box."

"This guy must be nuts. He goes on for two pages before he figures out that all that glitters is not you-know-what."

The women jump in and explain to her that it's dramatic to wait, that Shakespeare knows what he's doing, but she'll have none of it. She repeats some lines and mocks them as she reads aloud, "Ere I ope his letter, / I pray you tell me how my good friend doth." " 'Ope'? Who says ope?"

By the end of the class the women are distracted and annoyed. The reading's been slow, and we've barely gotten through a scene and a half with all the stops and starts. "Translating sucks," Kit says, "but reading these words straight—forget it."

I pull Kit aside. "First you were fine. In a good mood. Then you opted out, didn't do your name, just made fun of everything." The rest of the students are putting away chairs, packing up scripts.

Rhonda's complaining about how it'll take us six months to get through the script at this rate. Someone opens the window for a quick shot of cold air. "What's going on?" I ask Kit quietly.

"Yeah, well. I'm not much of an actress." She pulls out the stub of her cigarette and rolls it around between her thumb and forefinger.

"You've been great at reading, Kit, before tonight."

"I know Dolly wants me to play Bassanio, but he's not my type." Kit's pushing me toward the door. "Seriously, Jean," she whispers, "I won't be able to learn lines. Really. I told you a long time ago, I hate my brain."

I imagine Kit in her cottage, standing with a load of wash, a script in one hand, cigarette and laundry in the other, trying to learn lines. "But we're nowhere near that yet, Kit. We've barely just started with *Merchant*. You'll be great. I know you will."

"I can't memorize anything. Too much scrambled thinking, from the booze and drugs. And anyway, I just—you know—don't want to lose my marbles. I don't want any pressure, or I'm liable to get tanked." Kit lights up the half cigarette and takes a drag, inhaling and exhaling. "Can I go now?"

"How about being our stage manager?"

Kit tilts her head at me. "What's a stage manager?"

"Oh, you know. The person who helps everyone with lines, writes down where everyone stands and sits, general all-around assistant. You could solve some of our technical problems. Maybe tell Noreen about it."

Kit tosses the cigarette butt on the floor and with her sneaker, steps on it. "Can I have a clipboard?"

"A clipboard?" She's looking at me almost shyly. "Sure," I say.

"Okay." Kit turns back to the few remaining students. "Rehearsal's over."

ROSE

[W]e know what we are,
but know not what we may be.

HAMLET, IV.V.43

"I 'm looking to get through my time," Rose says, leaning against the doorframe of Program Room 2. "I thought I'd try acting." There's something uncertain about how she hangs back, waiting to be invited in, hands squeezing each other for assurance. Half hidden in the hallway, she seems almost too defenseless for anyone in a prison setting, but she's got the eyes of a drug addict, glassy irises, that never focus on what's in front of her. They search the room before she enters.

It's mid-January 1988, and word has spread that we're looking for new recruits for a play. Dolly's announced it to her long-termers' group, and Rhonda's advertised it in the cottages. So when Rose appears I'm not surprised.

This particular night, except for Cody, who's expending more energy in the weight room than in class, everyone's here. Kit's piled her *Merchant of Venice* script on top of her books "for effect," she tells me. "I wanna look smart." She's bent over, putting straggly hairs back into a knob on top of her head, so at first she doesn't see Rose. Dolly's

101

busy knitting and throws a lukewarm smile at the figure in the doorway. Bertie doesn't give her a second look; she's all wrapped up in showing off her new turtleneck sweater and talking to Rhonda, who sits at the rectangular table, thumbing through her script. Mamie and Gloria smoke by the window, both of them backslappers tonight, apparently in good moods, topping each other with stories about phone-use hassles in the cottage. They too, at first, pay little attention to our newest class member.

I beckon Rose in like a guest to my home and gesture enthusiastically at the empty chair next to me. But Rose crosses the room, her withered right hand hanging limp by her side, and places herself at the lone desk near the blackboard. She's wearing jeans, a jacket, and a simple button-down blue shirt that make her look tailored, almost preppy. Her black hair is up in barrettes, accentuating the slope of her lightly freckled forehead and its descent into dark Italian eyes. When she pulls out a pad of paper, I notice she can use the hand, but all the fingers crook to one side and her knuckles stick out. There's no trace of a smile on her face.

"Hey, Rose, wazzup?" yells Kit when she sees her. Kit swings her feet up on a chair, still toying with strands of hair that refuse to obey. "Who sprung you from the crib?"

Rose flashes a terse smile at Kit. "Not McNally." Sergeant McNally is the unit manager of Kit and Rose's cottage, Algon, and is rumored to be no friend to the ladies. Kit considers him her personal enemy. She says he won't let inmates come up for evening activities if he doesn't like the way they're dressed, and he insists on random room searches at the drop of a hat. He takes away property "just because he likes to see us squirm."

Rose continues, "I've been cleared by Inmate Services to join the class."

It's as if a bomb dropped on Gloria and Mamie, who've been gossiping about a prisoner and her junkie mother. They give Rose the kind of look I wouldn't want to meet in a dark alley. Something's up but I don't know what. Gloria says to Rose, "You gonna take off that fucking jacket?"

"No," replies Rose, her eyes turning cold. "It's freezing in here."

Immediately Dolly's out of her seat, standing like a sentinel, poised in between the smokers and Rose in her corner. "Ladies, ladies," she says, "this isn't the street."

Gloria and Mamie put out their cigarettes. Otherwise they're not moving. Kit tosses Rose a scarf and says, "Wear this if you're cold." Rose gives Kit a sideways sneer, and suddenly, it seems to me, Kit has no intention of protecting Rose in a roomful of inmates.

"Let's all take deep breaths," I say. "And set up for improvs." There's a long pause, and then Dolly starts moving furniture and the others follow. The sounds of chairs snapping shut and metal scraping across wood distract us momentarily. But there's deadening silence too, and it's not comfortable.

"Hey, that's great, that's great," Kit finally says to Rose, breaking the silence. She keeps mumbling as she pushes the blackboard closer to the wall. "Really. Really, I'm glad you could join our party."

Rose's mouth is set. She's not giving Kit a second chance to get back in her good graces.

"Some of us black folk who've been sick haven't been 'approved' by Mr. Zullo like you white girls." Gloria jabs her words at Rose. "For anything, much less a play." She is stacking chairs along with Mamie, forming a sort of assembly line. I remember how Gloria's been turned down once for her bid to go to pre-release and hasn't been happy about it. She announced that it was Ron Zullo who torpedoed her chances for success.

Mamie groans and shakes her head, and I'm a little annoyed that she's joined in with Gloria. "Let's focus on the work," I say.

Gloria keeps talking. "Maybe if you had the virus," she continues, slapping Mamie on the back, "you'd get better treatment." They laugh, heads close together.

"We all know women who've been ignored here!" Dolly bursts out, raising her voice. "And I don't like it either. Jee-sus, when I was sick one Saturday, I couldn't see a doctor 'cuz there's never any staff on weekends. Happens all the time. But what Zullo lets slip through the cracks is not Rose's fault." Dolly slams the window shut. It's as if she's put a period on the sentence.

Bertie walks over to Rose. "Don't let them bother you."

Rose looks tepidly at Bertie.

"Okay, who wants to go first?" I say, placing myself in the center of the room, striding around as if I'm in control. There's no response from the class.

"They're always mean to newbies," Bertie adds.

"How about a woman meeting a friend at the gym and they find out they're in love with the same guy?" I look around, trying to catch someone's eye.

"Nah, too corny," Gloria says. She's in a chair now, next to Rhonda. They give each other looks as if I just came to work in prison yesterday.

"I'll go up first," Rose offers. She takes off her jacket, drops Kit's scarf on the desk. Heads spin around and eyes stare. A few guffaws.

Gloria puffs up. "How 'bout if we do something real—you know, from life. I'll be a drug dealer." She stands. "How 'bout it, Rosie?"

Rose is out of her seat. She turns toward Gloria, meeting her challenge. "You're on."

Before I know it Gloria's orchestrating the scene, directing Rose to play an addict who's trying to go straight but who finds a wallet on the street. Gloria sets up the problem: What will she do? The rest of us are glued to Rose's reactions, watching to see how she takes Gloria's direction. Rose carefully steals around Gloria toward the half of the room we've turned into the stage, listening intently. Gloria strikes a tough-guy pose, head cocked, feet spread, arms across her large bosom. Rose lands next to her and rolls up the sleeves of her blue cotton shirt. Other students have scattered to unstacked chairs and shush each other as they become audience. I ask the actresses if they're ready, and when they nod, I call out, "Action."

"Hey, wazzup with this wallet?" Gloria bends down to pick up an imaginary billfold. She begins rummaging through it.

Rose stands over Gloria, watching her count bills. "Are there any credit cards?" she asks.

At first Gloria ignores Rose and rises, wobbly and unsteady, as if she's strung out on a street corner. "No identification. Ain't that a bitch." She crosses to the wall and places her buttocks against it. She slides one foot up. We whisper excitedly because Gloria is so believable in this role.

"Gloria. This is a lot of money."

"That's right. And it's ours." She tosses the imaginary billfold into the air and catches it.

"Gloria." Rose tries again, but something stops her. She starts to laugh, a laugh that she stifles with a hand over her mouth. Then she starts to move toward Gloria, but now she can't get a word out without laughing. Gloria looks at her with disgust.

"Stay in character," Kit yells at Rose from the sidelines. When I turn suddenly and tell Kit to be quiet, she looks at me, playing the wounded pup. "I'm trying to be helpful."

"Don't," I say, flipping back to the scene.

"Gloria, I think we have to return this to someone," and at the word "someone," Rose can't contain herself. She begins again to laugh. At first I imagine she can't stop laughing because returning the wallet seems preposterous, but when she keeps at it, I see that Kit's right. It's an acting problem.

Inmates are muttering to each other. Rose is cracking up every other line.

"Don't be tellin' me you want to go straight, when you act like this," Gloria says, suddenly shifting her tone. "Laughing like a hyena, chucklin' for no reason. You's as stoned as I am. We're keeping this cash." We watch with a kind of surprised glee at Gloria's creativity.

Rose keeps breaking up, but now it works. She does seem high. "We have to report this, Gloria," Rose says, in between chortles.

"Wha', you don't need five hundred bucks?"

"Well," Rose looks serious. "When you put it that way. Still, it doesn't seem . . . oh, you know."

"I could use your half, if you be all hesitatin' and such," Gloria says, spotting Rhonda, who's decided to enter the scene. Gloria starts to put the imaginary wallet into her pocket.

Rhonda sashays down the street, her do-wop walk preceding her. The audience roars. She shimmies up to Gloria and puts on her best man's voice, introducing herself as a cop and owner of the loot: She lost this exact wallet a few doors down. With a lot of fast talking, she tells Gloria that she has a witness and that Gloria could be arrested if she doesn't produce the evidence. Gloria secretly passes Rose the wallet. Rose is now enjoying herself, her back turned away from the cop, counting bills. Gloria puts her hand on Officer Rhonda's shoulder, coyly suggesting that if he has all that money, couldn't they go out? Kit whistles from the sidelines.

While Gloria is busy dallying with the policeman, Rose puts the stash in her jeans pocket. Gloria hands the empty wallet to Rhonda. The officer, smitten with Gloria, forgets to check if the cash he lost is still in the billfold. As Gloria starts to steer the officer away with promises of late-night trysts, she looks over her shoulder at Rose and holds out her free hand. With a whoop Rose gives her a high five. The women reel back into the audience, laughing and hollering, so loud that Bernice comes from down the hall with a worried look on her face. We are disturbing the Narcotics Anonymous meeting.

"If you want to go to Hollywood, see that lady," Rose says to Bernice, pointing at me. Her face is flushed with warmth.

. . .

We're in the middle of watching Sir Laurence Olivier's film version of *The Merchant of Venice* when Rhonda taps me on the shoulder. "You always get the best for us," she whispers.

"Thanks," I whisper back.

"Even if we do have to watch this in two parts without popcorn," Kit adds.

I scoot my chair into the row behind Rose, who's sitting at a desk. Everyone else is in metal chairs. I note that Mamie is absent. Cody has sent word that she has a visit, which probably means she won't show up at all.

It's just after Valentine's Day, and Rose is making a card in the classroom while she watches the film. A pink heart filled with glue dollops sits on the desktop in front of her. She pastes the heart onto a black square that she's cut out of construction paper, and then, pulling a glitter pen out of her pocket, she carefully draws silver swirls all over it. She does this with her left hand but manages to use the crippled right one to help her hold the paper in place.

On the screen Olivier is decked out in an elegant suit and tie, meeting his adversaries for dinner to discuss Antonio's plight. He is agreeing to loan money and does it with a bow and a tip of his hat. Kit says, "I like this movie better than that lame first one. That Shylock seemed like a rotten person with a lot of money who would stop at nothing when crossed. This one's got class."

"*Shhh*," Bertie says. "Save it." She's moved her chair in between Dolly and Kit, and sits as close as she can to the screen.

Dolly leans across Bertie to tell Kit that she disagrees. She likes David Suchet's interpretation in the other *Merchant*. "He's a pushy guy with heart, simply headed in the wrong direction. My type of man. This one's too polite."

"You're wrong," Kit says.

"*Shhh!*" Bertie repeats. "I can't hear the Shakespeare." She pinches Dolly playfully on the cheek.

"Oww," Dolly says. "You're dangerous."

Rose looks up from her card and says, "Maybe Shylock can be interpreted in different ways." Gloria makes a sort of deprecating snort, as if she thinks Rose is full of herself.

"Good point," I say. "But Bertie's right. Let's talk about it later."

It's been difficult integrating Rose into the class, since she doesn't make jokes or take things lightly. I don't want to praise her too much or draw attention to her status as a newcomer. Unlike the others who've taken writing, literature, and play-reading classes, Rose has not gone through the college program, and although she's quite bright, she is still not comfortable with the group. In the semidarkness I watch her put the glitter pen back in her pocket and blow on her card. Silver scatters across the paper heart.

Everyone's quiet for a while, watching the film, and then, in the trial scene, after a broken Shylock has been told he must give up his wealth and convert to Christianity, Olivier exits the courtroom. At this moment it seems to all of us that Shylock might not be able to bear his fate. His daughter has abandoned him to a Christian; he's all alone in a Christian world. Then comes Olivier's famous scream, making us imagine he has thrown himself down the stairs or in some way taken his own life. Some of the women are pushed to tears. Bertie covers her ears at the piercing sound.

"I like old movies," Kit says as I turn on the lights. I suggest we just sit and talk for a while.

Bertie curls up next to Dolly. She puts her head on Dolly's shoulder and says she feels sympathy for Olivier's Shylock. "He's the outsider."

Rhonda's the first to head to the window to have a cigarette. She says, "Shylock's driven to revenge, obviously, because his daughter betrayed him." She takes a deep drag on her Newport. "That's why he has to get his pound of flesh. He's been disgraced."

"Maybe," says Dolly, "but he sure as hell doesn't have to try to kill someone for it, does he?"

"Right, Ma," Bertie says softly.

"I'm not sure he doesn't want to die," Dolly continues.

I ask the women to tell me why some of them teared up when Shylock seemed so broken in the last scene.

Dolly says, "It's simple. We believe that everyone deserves a second chance, even Shylock."

"Yeah," Rhonda says to Dolly, "but second chances aside, do you really think most cons in here would care about a Shylock? I mean, really." She takes another weary drag from her cigarette.

"He deserves justice too." Bertie echoes Dolly.

"Maybe, maybe not," Rose says. "But I know his pain."

Dolly crosses to the window and with a friendly nudge, shoves

Rhonda aside to light up. Dolly's been trying to quit ever since Recreation held a weeklong smoke-out a few months ago, but she's back on her Camels tonight. "Remember last week," she says to Rose, "when we came to class late after the Code 99? No one knew what was up. Jean freaked—a buncha guards in yellow jumpsuits marching down the hallway with guns and helmets. We all thought someone had tried to kill herself in Max. I thought it was you, Rose."

"Nahh, she's too stubborn," says Kit. She winks at Rose, who doesn't respond. "But, hey, I don't know," Kit continues. "Coulda been any of us."

"Speak for yourself," Rhonda says, heading across the room. She sprawls out in her chair.

"I wasn't in Max," Rose tells Dolly. "I knew the girl, though. She was in my support group. They say she hung herself."

I look at Rose. I'm imagining belts, clothes tied together, guards on break paying little mind to the possibility of death.

Rose is looking at the floor, her face contorted. It bothers her that someone would think she tried to kill herself. "I've never been in Max or on any sort of Iso, for that matter," she says, and then she twists her hands together, looking around skittishly, "except for, you know, my own." The women are silent except for Kit, who coughs uncomfortably.

Suddenly Rose pulls out a script from under her seat and sits up, waving it at me. "Do you think Rhonda's right? Will anyone in here care about Shylock when we do this play?"

"I think they will," I say.

"But these two-bit bitches ain't gonna see no Laurence Olivier up on that stage," says Gloria. Mamie chuckles.

"Let's try something," I say, brushing Gloria's comments aside. "Ladies, are you game?" I am up, out of my seat.

"You are one wacko," Kit groans. "Nobody in here would expect anything of us after watching that movie."

"Rhonda, you and Gloria are on your way somewhere."

"To a party," Gloria says.

I point at her as though she's won a prize. "Okay, to a party."

Kit perks up a bit at the word "party" and sits up in her seat. I begin pushing the TV into the corner, making more space for an improv. "Bertie, you and Kit will make an entrance, chatting." Kit makes a face, all growl. I ignore her. "You all know each other and aren't interested in people from other neighborhoods coming into your scene. I'll tell you when to enter."

Gloria shoves her chair into another corner and heads to the cleared space. Rhonda pulls Bertie to her feet. Dolly pesters Kit until she's up. By now the energy in the room has shifted.

I direct Rose to the doorway. "Rose, you make an entrance, and as the new kid in town, try to get to know people."

Rhonda and Gloria immediately begin horsing around, cutting up folks they know and others they create on the spot. They hold make-believe glasses of something in their hands, calling out to an imaginary bartender whom they place in the audience. It's clear that on their way to the party they've stopped at a bar.

Rose enters and crosses to where Rhonda and Gloria are toasting. She tells them she's heard that there's a late-night party after the bars close, and she asks where it is. Gloria and Rhonda are acting like they're getting a little tipsy, repeating phrases and slurring their words. They snub Rose. Rose tries again, but as she moves toward them, the two friends make their way around her to another side of the bar.

When I give them the cue, Bertie and Kit come through the door with a "Wazzup?" to Gloria and Rhonda, and the four of them make a minicircle, shutting Rose out. Kit asks the imaginary bartender for refills. From the audience Dolly passes them drink after drink, having decided she's the bartender.

When Rose again asks about the party, they brush her off and drink up. Rose keeps trying to break in, moving behind one or another of the women, even using the tried and true "You dropped your wallet on the ground" routine.

Finally Rose throws up her hands and turns to the rest of us. "I can't do this. I can't. They won't even talk to me." She slumps into a chair by the table, still "onstage." I can feel her sinking. I know I am taking a risk, but I hand her a script and show her where to start reading. She looks at me, her eyes trying to find some reason to trust my direction. I motion the other women who've been in the improvisation to take seats in the audience.

"Go ahead," I say. "Give it a shot."

Rose begins to read, haltingly, "Hath not a Jew eyes? Hath not a Jew hands?" and she pauses. It is Shylock's famous monologue, in which he expresses his sense of being wronged by the Christian merchant and betrayed by his daughter.

Rose is so full of emotion that at first she seems afraid to throw herself into the scene. I ask her to look at her hands, and she does—first one, then the other—and finally, without my asking, she repeats the line, this time with feeling, "Hath not a Jew hands?" She says it louder, letting the word "hands" resonate inside her, letting her sense of injustice build as she goes on, "Organs, dimensions, senses, affections, passions?"

"I get it," she says, turning to me. "Shylock is really talking about how hurt he is, even though he sounds mad. I get it." Tears are in her eyes, but she's unflinching, almost excited. I ask her to finish the monologue.

She pours herself into Shakespeare's words—"fed with the same food, hurt with the same weapons, subject to the same diseases"—and she pauses—"healed by the same means, warmed and cooled by the same winter and summer as a Christian is?"

She stands, clutching her script, walking to the center of the cleared space, and gestures with her free hand, the crippled one, cutting through air. She's forceful now, crying out as though she is accusing us all, "If you prick us, do we not bleed? If you tickle us, do we not laugh? If you poison us, do we not die? And if you wrong us, shall we not revenge?" She walks over to her seat, lowering herself into it, and says softly, "The villany you teach me I will execute, and it shall go hard but I will better the instruction."

Everyone is dumbstruck. Rose places the script on her lap and looks at me. Her eyes are watery, and the struggle gone from her voice. "Does it really hurt like this, for actors, onstage?"

"Some actors pretend," I answer, "but they're not good enough to play Shylock."

Rose nods, somewhat for my sake but more perhaps for her own, drinking in the idea that she can communicate something about herself through this character. She looks at me. "You know, Jean, I want a beard, a long one, white, like those pictures of God. And a scroll. Shylock has to have something to wave around."

• • •

"Rose has a forty-one-page record," Rhonda says under her breath. I'm upstairs in Education, standing outside the school principal's office, where Rhonda works. Since I'm here for a special afternoon class, I thought I'd get more attendance forms. Rhonda, surrounded by untidy piles of memos and official college grade sheets, reaches into a drawer and thrusts some papers in my direction. "She's been a hard-core cocaine addict and a heavy-duty prostitute—as we say, around the block and back."

"How do you know anything about Rose's record?" I am annoyed. It's been almost three months since Rose joined the class, and there's still a pall around her presence.

She leans in, as secretive as she can be. "I happen to have excellent spies."

"I'll take that under advisement." I gather up the bunch of blank attendance sheets and put them in my briefcase. Rhonda goes back to typing.

It's an early afternoon in March, not my usual hour for teaching at the prison. Everything looks different in daylight. There's a thin layer of dust on Rhonda's typewriter, and the lack of color in the room makes even the gray-white walls and black phone look dusty. Besides being drab and barely furnished, this anteroom seems too quiet. Inmates barely talk as they pass by on their way to the computer room, and only restrained conversation comes from the two other classrooms; there's not the uninhibited rowdiness in the hallways that there is at night, or the stream of shuffling footsteps.

"I'll see you downstairs," I say to Rhonda curtly. "Don't be late." As I leave Rhonda's office, I try to brush off her news, with mixed feelings about Rose, in spite of my desire to remain nonjudgmental. After all, maybe Rhonda's just operating on rumor. Since the first improv, in which Rose threw herself into Gloria's challenge, I've watched a hands-off attitude develop around her in the classroom. Except for Kit she talks to no one at length, and even though she's engaged in the play, she keeps to herself. Sometimes when I come into the institution, Rose is still on cafeteria duty, hauling big bags of trash through the hall in her floor-length kitchen apron. Occasionally I see her outside the recreation office, waiting to talk to Bernice. Since

Carol, Bernice's assistant, is gone, Rose wants to be what she calls "Bernice's schlepper." Rose occasionally uses Yiddish words since one of her roommates, the only Jewish woman at Framingham, teaches them to her. "And to think I complained about food service. Try being kosher in prison," Rose has said in passing.

Algon, where Rose bunks, is what the inmates refer to as the "mental health" cottage, and as I head toward Program Room 2, I wonder why she's there. Some of the women have said that anyone with HIV is thrown into Algon. But I imagine that a forty-one-page record probably means plenty of problems.

I reach the bottom of the stairs and turn left. The downstairs hall is quiet too, punctuated with conversation that bubbles up from a line of women waiting for the prison "store" to open. They wait to buy basic foodstuffs to cook in their cottages, like spaghetti and soup in cans or snacks like peanut-butter crackers and Cokes. Here they can purchase stamps and stationery or shampoo, talcum powder, and female hygiene products, all as generic and cheap as possible. A woman says hello to me. I look at her, puzzled.

"Jean, honey, I'm Samantha." I start to apologize for not remembering her name, but she reminds me that I first met her through my trip to Laurel Cottage to take books for Mamie. She says she was hardly herself then, wearing a bathrobe, with tightly wound little pink curlers in black hair. I remember Samantha. She wouldn't stop trying to con me into giving her free books, even though she wasn't enrolled in a college class. I nod at her, expecting some hype.

"Rhonda's told me all about the play and, well, I've been thinking. You know—" Samantha steps out of the line and leans in to me, cupping her hand around her mouth. "I'd be in it, I really would. You know I can act up a storm, but I don't want to be in a class with . . . honey, can I be frank?" I look at her hard. She tilts her head sideways and says, in a voice as hushed as she can manage, "I don't want to be around the virus." And before I can react, before I can remind Samantha that getting HIV from casual contact is just a fear, she's got her back to me and is ordering three cans of beans and franks to be charged to her commissary account.

Samantha is not the only prisoner who stays away from a play because of such prejudices and fears. Three years later an inmate will quit our production of *The Scarlet Letter*. The actress will have no problem with the scenes paralleling the original Hawthorne novel, in which Hester with a scarlet *A* is accused of adultery, nor will the 1850s scenes bother her, in which Hester is forced to be a slave and sexual pawn of a master. But in the 1990s version, in which Hester is in prison with AIDS, the actress will say that she cannot perform. She is afraid one of her peers will think she has HIV.

I pass the poster on the wall, with the caption ANYONE CAN GET AIDS, and reach the classroom.

Ron Zullo has decided to sit in on this special afternoon class since the *Boston Globe* is preparing a story for its Sunday "Learning" section about our Shakespeare play. I've already been interviewed, but today they want interviews and photographs of the women, something that Ron oversees. Publicity, good or bad, always gets the prison's attention, and in this case I am mostly pleased. Even though only a few people from the outside will be allowed to see the production, I feel that a news story gives the project more legitimacy.

When I enter the room I see that the wobbly blackboard's still there, but the table's been replaced by a circle of chairs. A male photographer walks around trying to find the best light, and the reporter, a prim and tweed-jacketed woman, sits next to Ron. The only inmate in the room so far is Gloria, and she smiles at me graciously, as if this is her private interview. After I introduce myself and take a seat in the circle, I watch the reporter make small talk with Ron and imagine what Gloria will say that might cause trouble.

I think about how Zullo's boss, Kerilyn Simms, will react to this interview. Like many in the administration, she fears publicity that will fan the public's perception of Framingham as soft on crime. Sometimes when I'm waiting outside the prison entrance, Simms, an assistant to the superintendent, brushes by me at the end of her day, dangling keys, and always wearing a wide-brimmed hat over coiffed black hair. Early on she tried to sabotage my program by talking to the superintendent about getting rid of what she calls "unearned privileges." Recently, when I called her on the phone to ask if some of my high school students could come to the play, she told me I could be removed for going outside "the chain of command." This is another rule borrowed from the military: don't talk to me; talk to your direct supervisor. Then she hung up.

I watch Ron adjust his tie. Even though it's a bitterly cold day, he's sweating under his collar. I notice that there's a tape recorder on a chair in the center of the circle. The reporter and Ron are agreeing that it's okay to get started even before everyone's here. The reporter, an intense and wiry little woman, waves Gloria on. Gloria, a white cotton headband woven around black curls, sits, chatting up the reporter, demurely crossing her ankles, the picture of propriety in her baby-blue sweatsuit. You'd never know she's hoping to finagle a way to pre-release before our show.

"I come from the inner city, and I didn't learn about Shakespeare or classical music. It's teaching me, and at the same time, it's fun. I'm not being forced, like I *have* to learn this." Turning her head toward the photographer, who is standing near the window, Gloria arches her eyebrows and asks, "Is this for Sunday's paper?" He shakes his head and tells her it won't come out until June. She looks momentarily disgruntled. The reporter is having a field day, scribbling down everything that Gloria says, in spite of the recorder.

I think of how Gloria always plays the coquette. Sometimes she appears outside the classroom, leaning into the door like she's hooking and calls out in a sultry voice, "Hey, baby," sweet-talking male officers doing their rounds. She always jostles Rhonda, a handhold here and there, a playful tug-of-war, trying to entice her out of class. Sometimes they're like sisters. But when it comes to Rose, Gloria is anything but a friend.

Now she tries to work in a question to Ron about her status, but he tells her firmly that this isn't the time for that discussion. Then he turns to the reporter and says, "That's off the record."

Rhonda, Kit, Bertie, and Dolly arrive, rushing into the room, each in her own way acknowledging the tape player. Dolly's pinned up her hair with a banana clip and wears orange lipstick and nail polish. She runs her finger over the recorder, making a scratchy sound with a sharp nail. "It looks like the recorder you have, Bertie, that pink one? Doesn't it?"

Bertie shrugs, smiles at the reporter, and asks not to be in any pictures.

Rhonda checks to make sure that only first names will be used in the article and takes a seat. She crosses her legs with effortless grace, immediately at ease. "A lot of people are afraid of Shakespeare," she says. She's dressed up a little for the occasion, wearing pressed wool pants and a sweater. "But I've always liked the King's English."

While the reporter talks to Rhonda as if the two of them are old friends, Ron looks at his watch and then startles me when he gets up out of his chair and comes across the circle. He asks me if this could possibly be the whole class, and when I say a few are missing, he perches himself behind me, near the door, in that army arms-crossed-legs-spread stance. I know that Mamie is sick; I'm guessing that Cody has bagged the class; I worry that Rose has forgotten the meeting. Ron looks annoyed, and I imagine he plans to have words with any latecomers.

Rhonda uncreases a pants leg and leans in. She seems accustomed to giving interviews. "Theatre is a way of expressing ourselves that gives us a sense of protection; here we are under the umbrella of drama, so pretty much anything goes. In this room we can be free. We can do anything within the guidelines of theatre." Bertie nods her head vigorously. I glance back at Ron. No expression.

"Yeah," Kit chimes in. "That part is good." Kit's less disheveled than usual. She's wearing her ordinary jeans and sneakers, but her shirt's tucked in. "Hey," she says to the photographer, "you can take my photo," and she points to her mouth, "but make sure it's closed."

The reporter smiles in spite of herself. She asks the women to think about what the experience has allowed them that's unusual for prison.

"I think classes in prison open up our eyes to a lot we are capable of doing," Dolly says. "I've written poetry and a play in here." She looks at Ron, who nods approvingly. "You learn something new about yourself every day, even though it's in stagnating surroundings." Gloria whispers something to Bertie, who seems to ignore her. Dolly keeps on talking.

Kit tells the reporter that she's not much of an actress but she likes the "group stuff." She says she likes feeling part of a team and learning that she can do what she didn't think she could. She starts to elaborate about being stage manager when the tape runs out. For a few minutes the photographer snaps some pictures while the reporter changes the cassette. Gloria puts herself in the center of most of the photos. Ron paces.

When the tape recorder's running again, the reporter looks up from

119

her scratch pad and says, "Mr. Zullo, what's your perspective on this project as the coordinator of Inmate Services?"

Ron looks surprised but then recovers, pulling at his tie. "Framingham has always had a history of good treatment models." I notice that Ron's jacket is too tight, bunching up in the shoulders. The flash goes off, catching him off guard. "Don't get me on camera," he says firmly. Ron turns back to the reporter. "I think this project allows them a way to build self-esteem." Gloria tries to interrupt, but Ron keeps on. "This really isn't training for actors but more about offering women a chance to use years of emotion and turmoil to understand Shakespeare." The photographer snaps another picture, only this one's angled at the women.

The reporter thanks Ron and turns to Bertie. "At first I thought, Shakespeare? Shakespeare is too hard," Bertie says shyly. "Too confusing."

"And she still does." Kit is smirking. "Just kidding. Don't write that down," Kit says to the reporter.

"I'm Jamaican," Bertie goes on, "and this play is giving me self-confidence to speak better. I'm learning English, American-style. And Jean will tell you I don't speak well when I get angry." We laugh with her.

Gloria breaks in. "Back there when Ron was talking, I wanted to say something about what he was talking about, self-esteem." The reporter nods her on. "If it wasn't for classes or work, I'd sit all day in my room—it has red walls—and think about my crime. Sometimes I sleep all weekend and do nothing but think, think, think and wait for mail. Pictures of all my kids on the walls and him. I still have his picture." Ron shifts around by the door. "We get awful low in here without something to do."

Just then Rose comes into the room. She looks out of breath, as if she's been running. "Sorry I'm late," she says to Ron. Gloria mutters something about being interrupted. Ron tells her that she's said enough. He gestures to Rose to sit, but she doesn't.

Rose looks at the reporter, who tells her we're about to wrap this up. Rose says, "Sorry, I'm new and I wasn't going to be here, but would you mind saying just one thing from me, anonymously?" Gloria lets out an obviously annoyed sigh.

The reporter flips a page in her notebook and then gives Rose the go-ahead. Rose moves timidly a few feet into the circle, but remains standing behind an empty chair. "You don't have to be on camera if you don't want to," I tell her.

Rose looks relieved and says she'd rather not be photographed. She braces herself, holding on to her arm with her good hand. "It's nice, this class," she begins. "Sometimes I feel different here, like I can be someone else. I've always wanted to make a commitment like this, and I've always wanted to try my hand at acting." She shakes her head, frustrated with herself. "But that's not what I wanted to say. Look—" She grabs the back of the chair. "No one cares out there. No one is interested in my world or why I'm in a play in prison. The truth is nothing will change because of your article."

Ron clears his throat, giving Rose a signal to stop, but the reporter overrides him. "That's interesting," she says, her voice thin but certain. "What exactly do you mean by 'No one cares'?"

Rose backs away from the circle, working one hand into the other. "This prison life isn't important to most people. They're not gonna do anything different when they read about us. But me?" She lets out a little laugh, which is almost painful to hear. Then she shakes her head. It's as though she's having a conversation with herself, trying to sort out what she's feeling. "I get very serious when I set high goals for myself. I have to wake up, look in the mirror, and like who I see.

I have to deal with myself every day in here and face my mistakes. And believe me that's not easy. This class makes me feel I can." Rose pauses and looks at me. "That's the God's truth."

. . .

I find out about the rape, casually, as if the news were revealed in a dream. It's April and the air is moist in Program Room 2, a space much too small for the relaxation exercise I'm teaching. Along with the rest of the women, Rose sits in a metal chair with her eyes closed. Sheets of rain drench the compound. The wind feels as if it will shatter the window any minute, and we're not taking any chances. The small window is shut tight to keep water out, and only the sounds of pounding, the on-and-off-again rumble of thunder occasionally break our concentration.

I'm coaching the students to imagine white light or warm honey or oil swirling around their heads and moving down their bodies, images to soothe them. Most of them came soaking wet into the room, umbrellas not being permitted at Framingham, and only a few women were prepared with ponchos for the storm that came on suddenly. "It's a relaxation exercise," I said to the prisoners when I first asked them to sit, close their eyes, and let go of tension in their bodies. Kit jerked up, her eyes bugging out when she heard the word "oil" come out of my mouth. "Kit, it's okay. It's a way to feel, to let your senses work," I said. "Yeah, sure," she replied, setting off a round of titters in the room, knee-slapping, and general all-around chaos.

Now, after about ten minutes of wiggling around, everyone's settled down enough to pay attention to my directions. "Let the image of white light move into your eye sockets, over the bridge of your nose, and into your cheeks," I say, walking around the room of women sitting in straight-backed chairs. I tell them to focus on their breathing, encouraging each to sink into the chair and let go of tightness in the forehead, the jaw, the back of the neck. Dolly's asleep, her mouth thrown open like an old man's, snoring. Bertie nudges her and she wakes, eyes wide, her breathing loud and heavy.

Rhonda's taken off her sneakers, and her legs bow out, socked feet facing outward. She's having trouble unlocking her jaw and rubs her face with her thumbs, long strokes along her cheekbones. She mumbles something to Kit about me being a "sixties throwback." Kit stifles her laughs and twitches periodically.

Rose asks to keep her eyes open. "Sure," I say, walking over to her where she sits propped up in a chair, palms in her lap, facing the ceiling.

"It's spiritual," she says, responding to my questioning look at her yogalike position. "Something I learned at NA when I first brought up the rape. I imagine I'm outside and the sky is healing me. Through my palms."

"Oh." I'm circling behind her chair. I look around the room and no one else seems shocked by the word "rape." I turn back to Rose. "Try to let go of that wrinkle place between your eyes, and unglue your tongue from the top of your mouth."

She whispers, "I still need to keep my eyes open."

"Of course," I say. "Sure." I touch her shoulder with my hand.

Later I learn that the rape did not occur in prison. It comes up again during a theatre exercise I've given the women. "Go back to your cottage," I tell them the night of the relaxation exercise, "and look for mannerisms in women in your unit, ones that remind you of something about a character in the play. Write them down, in enough detail that you can describe them next week."

Next week things come undone. When I get to the front desk, Kojack says, "There's an order for you to see Ron Zullo before class.

What didja do this time, Trounstine?" He's drinking black coffee from a paper cup.

"I have no idea." My heart's beating way too fast. I try to imagine what Ron could want. "Where am I meeting him?"

"In his orifice." Kojack laughs and puts the cup down.

"You've got to get new material," I say, as he buzzes me through the first door.

"Hey, guess what? They're sending me to Siberia. Seriously, I'm off to the D office. It's a promotion." Kojack's talking through the glass.

I nod, disappointed. Working in the D office will mean day work for Kojack. He'll be the one who'll hear disciplinary actions and make decisions about inmates' lives in prison. "I'm sorry I won't see you."

"You won't miss much. Get it, you won't miss much? Lookit my waist." He laughs and tugs on his belt to show me pants two sizes too large. "Gotta get back in the dating scene, Jean," he says.

When I enter Ron's office, he is sitting behind his desk, holding a red notebook in his hands. "Do you know who this belongs to?" he asks, rhetorically.

I sit, the dutiful teacher, in front of him. "A student?"

"Very funny, Jean." He slams the notebook down on the desk. "This is not a laughing matter."

"Sorry."

"This notebook belongs to Rose. And in it," he thumbs through the pages, showing me scads of writing, "are notes, notes that she calls 'Observations.'"

"Uh-huh," I say, remembering the homework I've given to the women.

"She says that this is part of her schoolwork, Jean, and she calls it . . ." For a moment Ron falters, and then he picks up a stray piece of paper from the side of his desk where stacks of papers are spread out. A stack topples to the floor. "Shit," he says, bending over, banging his head, a knee. Papers reappear from the side of his desk, Ron's face a furious red. He pushes himself back against the window, grasping the sole piece of paper ripped from a notebook, and reads: "An assignment for my acting class. Observation of a woman in my unit." That's what she says. "Is that accurate, Jean?"

"Totally, but I asked them—"

"I know what you asked them," Ron says, waving the scrap of paper in the air, "I have it in writing, for God's sake." Then he puts the paper down and points at the notebook. "The point is, Jean, do you have any idea what trouble this has caused me?"

I shake my head. Ron leans in. "Rose went into her cottage and took notes on another inmate's behavior, and when that inmate asked her to stop, Rose said that the notes were for a class. This went on for several days. That particular inmate has severe psychological problems, and she became so paranoid that she read Rose's journal when Rose wasn't around, to see what Rose was writing down about her. Then she came to see me, hysterical that she was being 'watched behind her back day and night.' You do not ask a woman in prison to observe another woman. Ever. You've been here long enough to know that."

"I'm sorry, I thought—"

"I do not care what you thought. You obviously do not understand the problems you can cause by asking these women to express themselves. If I have one more day like this, the play is canceled. Oh, and when I called in Rose to discuss it—I was planning to send her to Max until I heard that you were responsible—I asked to see the notes she had written." Again he waves the journal around. "Here in this notebook Rose writes about how this particular inmate's eyes—the inmate, Jean, with severe psychological problems—remind her of the woman who raped her, on the street. A woman who raped her with a broom. Now, what does that have to do with acting class?"

I sit, unable to respond to Ron's question. Rose, a prostitute and a junkie, a woman with HIV, raped, raped with a broom, and in prison for forty-one pages of crime. It is too much.

Ron goes on. "Rose happened to mention that some of the women don't make it easy for her in your classroom. Rose has a week of lock-up. She should have known better. You, you're on notice."

I want to ask why Rose is locked, but by now I know better. I let myself out of Ron's office.

That evening we go through the play without Rose. The women want to discuss all the great things they've learned from observations, and we do, but I am only halfway involved. At the end of class Kit hands me a note that Rose has written, telling me she is sorry about what happened and that she never meant for anyone to see her journal but her.

The heartfeltness of that note is not unlike one Rose composes four months later, just before we separate for the summer. She expresses herself on a card that all the women present to me after the production of *Merchant*. On that card Dolly says how much she has changed because of the play and draws a picture of what she calls "our merchant of drama." Bertie writes, "Not on your sole but on my soul is this card being signed," teasing me about her white suede shoes she wore as Gratiano. "Thank you for your encouragement and inspiration," writes Rhonda.

Rose, obviously the last to sign the card, contributes a small paragraph, cramped at the bottom of the page. Her handwriting slants to the right, letters that almost fall over and words that are punctuated with curlicues. She writes about the importance of finding her place in the cast, how her horizons were expanded, and then she says, "You brought out something in me I always wanted . . . to become some-body else . . . even for just 'one night.' " And she signs her inscription "Your friend, Rose (aka Shylock)."

RHONDA

I'll give thee . . .
Adversity's sweet milk, philosophy,
To comfort thee, though thou art banished.
ROMEO AND JULIET, III.III.54

et a load of these pantaloons," Kit says, holding them up for Rhonda's reaction. Rhonda swipes them, drops her jeans, and shimmies into the muslin undergarment as if it were made of silk. She positions a floppy bonnet on her black hair so that a mass of bangs sticks out, and then, without a word, she nabs Bertie to help her step into the unbleached slip and Gloria to hand her the ecru overskirt. Others watch, entranced by the costumes and Rhonda's transformation. She's smiling as if she's onstage, posing in her get-up against the empty chalkboard. Suddenly she lifts her skirts and begins twirling. "You look like you could be Shakespeare's sister," Kit calls out. "You coulda burst outta that play." It's true, I think, watching Rhonda twirl, joining in as inmates clap, enthusiastically encouraging her pirouette. Rhonda carries herself with the confidence of an Elizabethan at a ball. I know she will get out of prison and make a life for herself.

It's mid-March 1988, and I've borrowed Shakespearean costumes from a local specialist in period attire and lugged them past Kojack into the prison. "What next?" he said to Connors when I appeared, loaded down with costumes. "Is this what they do now in college?"

"I want to give my students the feel of the period," I said. "Ron gave me permission. It's a class, remember?"

Kojack muttered, "Maybe a new job wouldn't be so bad after all." Connors, on her stool in the cage, shook her head disbelievingly and mumbled something about "coddling inmates." Then they both complained about having to do the extra work of searching through garments for guns or drugs, and locating the broken-down coatrack to transport the clothing. As Connors took the apparel and me inside the search area, Kojack made a joke from his perch about women "dressed to kill."

By the time I got down the hall, pulling the coatrack on three wheels, the women were waiting for me. Their mouths dropped open when they saw the costumes. I could barely contain them while I scooted through the door, costume rack and all. I got out a few words about Elizabethan history, but before too long Kit reached across me and went for the pantaloons. However, she had no intention of trying them on. It took Rhonda to start the ball rolling. As soon as Rhonda twirled around the room, pretending that she was heir to the throne, others moved toward the costumes and the table I had filled with picture books.

Now Rose is holding up a shirt with removable panels of cloth in armholes. I explain to her that some commoners in the Elizabethan era only had one shirt. Even collars needed replacing. She says, "This is definitely a reason not to get up our hopes about Shakespeare."

"Men and women in Shakespeare's day took baths once a year," I continue. "Without changing those pieces of cloth, watch out!"

Kit almost doubles over at that, and when I add that they also didn't wear underwear or brush their teeth, she cracks, "No use getting my teeth back, then."

I start to clarify how Elizabethans didn't have our knowledge about health issues, but no one is listening. They're focused on the costumes. Bertie finds a child's garment on the rack, a floor-length white dress with delicate work on the sleeves and lace around the neckline. "I'm the only one small enough to wear this," she says to me.

"Go for it," I tell her.

Rhonda helps pull the dress over Bertie's head, her confidence giving Bertie a boost. "You look like a store mannequin," Rhonda says.

"Do I?" Bertie asks coyly.

"Yeah, except for the blue jeans," Kit says. Bertie giggles. She gives us all a sultry look, lips pouty and cheeks sucked in, just like the women whose heads she draws.

Rhonda playfully, as though it were her costume ball, reaches out her hand to Bertie as if she's the queen and Bertie's her princess. Bertie dips into a curtsey and Rhonda smiles graciously, adding, "Welcome to England. My servants will provide for your stay."

"You are too much," I say to Rhonda, enjoying every minute of this.

Kit finds a piece of cardboard on the floor and points with it at the occasional flash of blue denim under Bertie's skirt. "See what I mean?" she says to me. "Blue jeans." Kit folds the cardboard in two and places the scrap inside her college folder.

Bertie ignores her, delighted with herself, and begins swishing the skirt around the table. With her tousled hair piled high on her head, her high cheekbones, and her dark eyes, she is dazzling in her white doll dress.

"Bertie, you are one helluva tease," Rhonda says, returning to herself. "No wonder Hobbs in Laurel always gives you first washing-machine privileges."

"Does not," Bertie quips back.

"My sources tell me that Laurel ladies stand in line waiting for you to finish your laundry," Rhonda goes on. "And you've got some wicked bras, girl." She and Bertie high-five each other, and I can't help laughing, too.

"Something tells me, Bertie, that you give the officers a hard time," I say.

"Shit," Gloria chimes in, "the cops get on us whenever they can. We have to yank their chains. It's survival."

The women continue bantering back and forth while they try on costumes. Dolly starts to put on a pair of brown men's knickers but backs off when I tell her that they are worn with tights. She contents herself with a green velvet jacket, high collar, and cap. Not able to contain her large bosom, the jacket hangs open over her low-cut white blouse. "You look like one of those medieval wenches in a dinner theatre production," I say, helping her place the cap neatly on her head.

Meanwhile Rhonda curtseys around the room to whomever will curtsey back. She's added a velveteen sash to her costume. Whenever she greets one of her "guests," she does a poor imitation of a Brit, using an overdone English accent, jutting her chin into the air and causing us all to tease her mercilessly. By now Kit has found a man's vest. She puts it on and, pleased with herself, throws back her head to let out a huge guffaw.

Gloria, not one to be left out, grabs a cape and ties it around her shoulders. "I just need sunglasses," she says, singing some blues riff to herself and slinking around the room.

"The ladies in the poolroom have to see this," Rhonda announces, and followed by Bertie, Dolly, and Gloria, she is out the door.

"This oughta be good," Kit cackles and bolts to the doorway, where she can get a good look at them parading around the hall. Rose, who's opted out of trying on costumes, joins her. She stands, somewhat dispirited, thumbing through a book about the period while Kit kicks back against the doorframe. "Just waiting for the show, Jean," Kit tells me.

At first I'm not concerned about the costume parade. I watch with pleasure, commenting with others on the interactions in the hallway. Rhonda takes the lead and swings by the recreation officer, urging her to get the prison Polaroid. Bernice does a double-take when Rhonda approaches, her mouth falling open. She stands without moving, clipboard in hand, looking perturbed.

"I've really got it under control, Bernice," I yell down the hall. "They're just having fun, you know, getting the feel of the play. It'll be over in a few minutes." Bernice says something I can't hear and waves Rhonda away.

Meanwhile Bertie and Dolly are posed in front of the beauty parlor, preening. Bertie places her lips up against the glass of the haircutting room, presumably aiming at someone getting her hair cut; and Dolly, tilting the cap a bit over one eye, pulls a Camel out of a crumpled pack, and places it, unlit, in her mouth. Inmates appear in the hall with pool cues, and a few heads turn as the actresses troop toward the gym. Cody exits from the weight room and stands, talking in low tones, her head crooked toward a young Asian woman. They watch as Gloria whisks by, her cape trailing behind her like a rock star's.

"What the hell? *Hold it right there!*" shouts an officer as he comes down the stairs from the chapel. By now the hall is filled with prisoners milling around, whistling, checking out costumes.

I turn to Kit and ask the name of the officer, but Kit shushes me with, "This is just getting good."

The guard wades through the women, shouting, "*Get back to your areas now!*" pushing his way down the hall. The prisoners murmur in response, a few talking back. Two women speak Spanish angrily to each other. The officer writes down their names, still yelling, *"I don't need to tell you twice. Report to your unit. Evening programs are out for you!"* Immediately another guard appears, and prisoners scatter like pinballs.

By now Bernice is rounding up all the actresses and shouting commands left and right for "Trounstine's people" to get back into Program Room 2 or so face disciplinary action. The hall's a swirl of noise and movement.

"I'm sorry, Officer," I say, stepping out into the din. A woman shoots by me and frantically holds up a pass from the chapel. The officer in charge sends her back upstairs, telling her to wait until the disruption is over. Then he moves directly in front of me. He is tall and sandy haired with big shoulders and no smile. He scowls down into my face.

"Captain," he corrects. "Johnson."

I begin again. "It's really my fault. I gave my students permission to walk around with these costumes on."

Johnson looks at me as if I must be kidding. "Costumes? You're letting women in prison wear costumes? Haven't you been trained at all?"

"It's an acting class, for a play. I have permission." Out of the corner of my eye, I can see women's heads peeking out of Program Room 2. Rhonda's hands are waving around. It seems she is telling the others to get out of garb.

"Not to prance around the halls, you don't. Look. Don't cover for them. They know the rules. They sign out for a program. They go to that program. Playtime's over. I want those costumes out of here in five minutes. I'll send an officer to escort you."

"What do you mean, 'out of here'?" I begin to get scared, imagining Ron calling me on the phone and the ultimate ax.

"Five minutes. One of the ladies can help you. The rest, back to their units. Understood?" I nod, penitent. "Consider yourself lucky I'm in a good mood. Or you'd be outta here, too." He turns abruptly and leaves, the sound of keys clanging as he marches back down the hall to the captain's office.

I feel enormous relief, thinking that this incident won't go any further than Captain Johnson, but still, every reprimand in prison is like a punch in the stomach. By the time I'm back in the classroom, the women have hung up their costumes and everyone looks sore. Dolly's complaining, "Jee-sus, Johnson's a prig. I want a cigarette." She crosses to the window and lights up.

"I heard Johnson wanted to make it with a black girl," Gloria offers as consolation.

"Who?" Bertie asks, smoothing out her jeans.

Gloria smiles broadly, "No one in Laurel."

"I bet it was that bitch who pissed in my cup," Kit spurts out. "She's always after the white ones."

"What?" I exclaim, much too loud.

"The broad who peed in my cup. No joke, she likes Cracker cops. Listen, Jean, you don't know what some of these people will do in here." Kit has put her feet up on the table and is leaning back in her chair, holding court. Her ponytail hangs down behind her.

"You need to get up, Kit," I say. "You all do. I know how upsetting this is. I agree, we were only having fun, but let's not take the negativity to heart. You're all bigger than that. Now put out the cigarettes, and pack up. It's just for the night, remember that, but Captain Johnson says you're going back to your units." There's a generalized moan throughout the room. "Rhonda, you can help me carry out the costumes."

"See," Dolly says accusing me. "See. They'll take it away as fast as they give it. I swear to God, Jean, they will." She angrily tosses her cigarette butt on the floor and squashes it with the heel of her shoe.

Rose and Bertie begin to move toward the door. I try to comfort Dolly, but she keeps muttering, "Why should we do this damn play, anyway? I mean, if they don't want it, why should we?" Others stand, disgruntled, shaking their heads in agreement, waiting for an officer to give them an order to head back to their cottages.

"Dolly," I say, walking over to her, trying my best not to give in to my own discouragement. "You know why we should do this play."

"I don't blame Cody for skipping classes," Bertie chimes in, revving up Kit to complain about wasting her time.

"Hold on," Rhonda says. "Dolly, buddies, this isn't a tragedy. Johnson's new here, and yeah, he thinks he's a hardass, and it pisses me off that he sent Martinez and Gonzales back to their units with a D. But, hey, that's not headlines. People get shit for breathing in here. And what officer is not gonna get bent out of shape at me in a party dress? We go back early, kick back, watch TV." Kit says something snide under her breath in Rhonda's direction, but I smile at her gratefully.

"Baby, I need ya," Bertie sings, moving her shoulders and head to some internal Aretha Franklin rhythm. "Baby, I want ya. . . ." She pulls out a cigarette and taps it on top of the pack as if she's playing a percussion instrument.

Rhonda's still talking. "Anyway, I figure Johnson'll last about two years and transfer to the boonies."

Dolly looks at her and says, "Yeah, sure," under her breath.

"Like I said, the cops get on us whenever they can." Gloria's got her notebook up against her chest and is wagging her head back and forth. "I'm not gonna let it get to me."

An officer appears at the door, and all chatter stops. He's another young-colt-type, lanky and pale with freckles, the one who assisted Johnson earlier in the halls. He checks names off a list while students file out. I say good-bye as cheerily as I can, a lump in my throat. It's not the first time I worry, both irrationally and with good reason, that some woman won't be able to take the pressure and I'll never see her again.

Then the lanky officer motions to me and stands by the door while Rhonda and I maneuver the rack, weighed down with costumes, into the hallway. We walk silently down the hall, the prison still filled with sounds from volleyball in the gym, music from the chapel, and doors opening and shutting.

"That can't go through No-Man's Land," the guard says in my direction, pointing with his keys at the rack. "You'll have to make a coupla trips. And you"—he turns and looks at Rhonda with a tinge of disgust in his voice—"you go to the iron door, and that's it."

When we get within two feet of the iron door, I feel defeated and can barely look at Rhonda. I ask the officer if he can help me carry the costumes out. He says, "Not my job."

Rhonda says, "One day soon I'll be able to walk out of here." I nod at her.

The officer unlocks the door, and it swings open, revealing the twelve-foot space between the main institution and the officers' cage. I begin piling up the costumes. The guard leans over Rhonda and says, "This is just a revolving door for you, anyway. You'll be back, like a lot of them." He chuckles.

"Oh, no, I won't." Rhonda is fierce, a nervous smile forming as she fights to restrain herself. She stacks a bundle of costumes in my arms.

"You'll be back."

I turn around and stare at him too, furious. Every bit of me has rebounded. "Not Rhonda. When she gets out, she'll stay out. I know that in my bones."

The officer shrugs and smiles broadly. "We'll see."

Rhonda puts some books in a bag and firmly places the man's cap on my head. "I think I'm gonna have to play that lawyer in *Merchant*, Portia. No one takes advantage of her." She punches me in the arm. "See you next week."

. . .

From my earliest days with Rhonda, it's clear that she's one of the brightest and most articulate prisoners. "Life is going on without my permission," she tells me soon after we meet in 1986. "Sometimes I want the world frozen in suspended animation." Rhonda's not just the Education secretary but, by her own account, a graduate of a prestigious prep school and a former college student, bound to be a mover and shaker when she gets out.

What's not so clear about Rhonda is why she stumbled into crime. I've heard rumors that Rhonda embezzled money at a job and got caught, and that some relative also did time at Framingham. But like most of the women, she is close-mouthed about her record and her personal history, and so it is only pieces of Rhonda's life that appear in our early composition class: "Mama's perfume was the forbidden fruit. It sat on the vanity table in a crystal bottle that seemed to beckon me whenever she left the house." Her work is full of the blues, whether she describes the sweet sadness of going with her mother to get her first pair of shiny black patent leather shoes or she free-writes about a train, asking, "How come they always put railroad tracks by a prison, making you so lonely just to listen, making you just want to get up on that train and ride?"

But Rhonda is not easy to read. She often keeps her feelings under wraps and hides behind her quick wit, specializing in philosophy, clever quips, and comebacks. Then, three months into my first year, we're in a writing class. I've already had a go-round with Connors this evening, who won't let me enter with my dangly earrings. "I'm late," I moaned to her. "There was awful road construction by Mel's Liquors and the Sunshine Dairy."

"Too easy for an inmate to pull off those earrings," Connors muttered, directing me back to the lockers and a twenty-minute delay.

Something's wrong with the class from the start. After Dolly announces that Bernice almost canceled us because I kept them waiting, the energy in the room refuses to pick up. Free-writing is deadly, punctuated by complaints. Someone says that the administration has censored articles about homosexuality and AIDS in the prison newspaper. "We're not presenting the 'right image,' " Rhonda says to the room of women, who are slumped in their chairs. "What do they think this is, a boarding school?"

Mamie responds by shaking her head and clicking her tongue. Women read their writing out loud but without enthusiasm. We comment with the same halfheartedness. The energy in the room drops a notch lower.

So toward the end of class, I'm not in a particularly good mood when Rhonda approaches me. The others are finishing a final assignment. I'm standing by the window, looking at fall leaves scattered around the yard and watching a woman in handcuffs being led away by two burly officers. Rhonda hands me what looks like a Xeroxed copy of a letter. "Thanks, Rhonda. I'll read this when I get home," I say, dismissing her.

"Thought you'd like to see what I wrote to Joe." She leans against the wall. "He's got some cockamamie ideas about prisoners, so I told him about me." Rhonda's referring to her pen pal in what I call our "cross-cultural program," correspondence between prisoners and students at my high school.

I begin to fold up the letter, but Rhonda says, "Wait" and, pointing at a paragraph, "just read this part." We stand together, bent over, reading: "I do not fit the stereotype of a prison inmate. I come from a middle-class black family. My father was a retired navy man and my mother was a hospice worker. Now she's a full-time ordained minister."

I look up at Rhonda. "So that's where you get your preachiness?"

"Read on," she says, punching me in the arm.

I turn back to the letter: "My dad died of heart failure and I went nutty. I don't mean that I ended up in a mental hospital or anything like that; just that I was very depressed and disillusioned with God and society. So I started running with a wild crowd and rebelled. The result was jail."

"I notice you don't tell him what you did," I say.

From somewhere in the room, Kit shushes us. "*I* don't need to hear what she did," Kit says. Mamie makes a guttural noise at Kit.

"Do you tell him about everyone who wants your body?" Mamie asks.

Rhonda says, "I figure Joe didn't need that much information."

I tell her I'm glad that she's writing to Joe and consider asking her more about herself, but Ron's warnings not to get too close and Bernice's appearance at the door stop me. Cody jumps up when she sees Bernice and says "I'm outta here," bombarding Bernice with volleyball questions. Soon after, the others unwind themselves from the hardback chairs and pack up for the evening.

"Keep me posted," I say to Rhonda as she exits, stuffing the letter in her back pocket.

. . .

A month later Rhonda shows me a letter in which she counsels Joe about the girlfriend he almost loses:

> Take Christine out. Make sure you dance your favorite songs together. Let her float around, dance, and talk with whomever she wants, and tell her to give you that same freedom. Don't flirt with other girls, give her compliments all night long, and have a good time. I used to go to clubs with my boyfriend, and we partied together all night. Whenever we danced with other people, we would make a contest to see who could get the most dances, and then we'd talk about our partners when we got home, goofing on them. With all that wild barhopping you do, make sure no one drives who's been drinking. The girl next door to me is doing 9–12 for vehicular homicide.

We talk briefly and humorously about her new status as the Lonely Hearts Club Correspondent, but still, because Rhonda does not volunteer more than what's on the page, I ask nothing about her background.

Then, in May, in our Introduction to Literature class, she turns in what I consider one of her best pieces. We've just finished reading Maya Angelou's autobiographical *I Know Why the Caged Bird Sings* and some of her poetry. Now we're reading Shakespeare's sonnets, and in their journals, the women are writing whatever they feel like writing, responses to the readings or to prison life. We often make poetry from their material, shaping what I call their "stuff" into poems.

This particular night I've asked each student to come prepared to read one of the sonnets aloud. I'm in Program Room 2, and the Upward's late. Dolly, Rhonda, and Gloria are slowly coming into the classroom, all mumbling about Carter Jones, a gang girl who was just caught having sex with another prisoner in a small room upstairs across from Education. Apparently all evening activities have been put on hold while officers string yellow crime-scene tape around the area, pending investigation.

"Be glad we're not upstairs, Dolly says, tossing her books on the table. "You'd be suspected of allowing Carter in a room alone with her girlfriend."

Rhonda stands playing with a frayed string on Gloria's sleeve. "Then they'd call you at work, Jean, buddy, and give you the third degree," Rhonda goes on. "I listen to those calls, you know."

"It was a mess," Mamie says, limping in. She drags her leg behind her, an old injury that seems to ache more these days. "We were locked right from dinner. I barely finished eating when the sirens went off. I'm surprised they let you in." She sits, breathing heavily, and pulls out her red folder, fanning herself.

Other women stream in, including Kit, who's commenting about what she calls the "sex of the century" incident.

"Maybe you should cancel class," Gloria says. "There's a big ol' volleyball game tonight. I need my best player." Gloria's not enrolled in college classes yet, but she hangs out with Rhonda and tries constantly to tempt her to forget everything for volleyball.

"She means you should cancel class," Rhonda says.

"Does that mean you don't have your homework?" I am pointing my question at Rhonda.

"I always have my homework." She tugs at Gloria's headband. "You go, girl. I got business here." Gloria wheels around and exits. Rhonda sits next to me and hands me a piece of paper. She's got on some kind of musky perfume that reminds me of the sixties. "It's just a journal entry, first draft," she says, "but I like it."

Bertie and Dolly ask me simultaneously if they can have a few minutes to read over the sonnet assignments. I agree. They bury their heads in their books, mouthing words. Other women settle in or talk quietly among themselves. Meanwhile I read Rhonda's piece:

> Often I sit in my room, especially late at night, and look wistfully out my window. I should say, peer through my screen and scrutinize the scenery. It's usually misty, faint, and sometimes eerie. Sometimes there are bright, clear stars spangled across the dusky night. Each look brings a forlorness, an isolated, lonely, wish-I-were-somewhere-else-feeling. I always, always, always think about lost loves. My father's death, my first boyfriend, my *last* boyfriend. Friends that I wish I could write or visit, stay on my mind. A very special friend who left before I could really tell her good-bye, or wait—even she flashes momentarily in my mind's theatre. She is an ongoing, long-playing Broadway show that will not shut down. She doesn't get the critics' reviews because they don't know where to find her act. The public isn't aware that she's onstage. Only she and I were there when the man built her dressing room. I'm her understudy; and I don't know how she can say her lines without me. No wonder I haven't heard from her; the show must go on.

"What a great piece of writing," I whisper to Rhonda, adding how I love the theatre metaphor and the word "spangled." "I can really hear your voice," I say. "There's definitely something there. Let's work on it."

"I'm glad you like it," Rhonda says. She pulls out a stick of gum from her pocket and unwraps it.

"Do you want to read it out loud?" I ask.

Rhonda shakes her head no. "Not interested in sad tonight."

"Stylin' Jean," Bertie says from across the room. "That's Rhonda. Cool as what is it—a piece of cucumber?"

Rhonda shrugs and says, "I do what I do to keep myself together."

"Who's the woman in the piece," I ask. "Do I know her?"

"Not likely," Rhonda replies. She pops the gum in her mouth. I wait for more but Rhonda adds nothing. I look again at the piece, searching for other clues, but there's just a page filled with Rhonda's handwriting, letters as crisply formed as her demeanor.

"Did you know Carter Jones?" Bertie asks looking up from her book at Rhonda. "On the street?"

"Nah, but I know her type. Like me, rebel from the moment go."

"I know what you mean," someone says.

"Carter's eighteen, and a half-assed dealer who got slammed for a gang murder and went loco, but basically she got hooked up with the wrong crowd." Rhonda's looking away from me while she speaks.

"I knew it," Bertie tells Dolly. "I bet Carter will get a whole month in Max," Bertie says. Dolly nods emphatically.

"At least," Rhonda calls across the room, "you'd think there were guns or drugs involved, and not just sex."

"Maybe if we had conjugal visits, like the men do in California, we'd be better off," Dolly says. Bertie agrees.

Rhonda continues, caught up in her own thoughts. "Like I told Joe, after my dad died, all hell broke loose. Bank robberies, stealing cars, passing bad checks, you name it. My cousin was here once, so it didn't really faze me." Rhonda turns toward me. "And I was a kid, a bad crook and a kid."

I hand Rhonda back her writing. I say, "I know you as the writer of pieces like this."

"Are we gonna read these poems anytime soon, before I qualify for social security?" Kit asks.

Soon we're plunged into poetry, and the women are taking turns at rendering sonnets aloud. Kit's taken center stage, reciting lines of verse but stumbling over words and doing her deadpan monotone in Dolly's direction: "Shall I compare thee to a summer's day? / Thou art more lovely and more temperate."

Dolly says, "I don't think so." She laughs.

"What does 'temperate' mean?" Bertie asks.

"Mild mannered," I say.

"Like Superman," Rhonda says to her. "Or in this case Super-woman."

" 'Temperate,' my ass. How many chickies you know who are temperate?" Kit says.

Mamie shakes her head at Kit. "There's no teaching you anything. Lordy, you have to finish the poem in order to understand it." Kit immediately gets defensive, crosses her arms, and tells Mamie to stay out of her sonnet.

Other women insist that they stop arguing. "Let's get this over with," Dolly says. "I picked Sonnet forty because I identify with some of it." She reads: "Take all my loves, my love, yea, take them all; / What hast thou then more than thou hadst before?"

"Good, Ma," Bertie tells her.

"Listen to this," Dolly continues, fortified:

I do forgive thy robbery, gentle thief,
Although thou steal thee all my poverty;
And yet, love knows, it is a greater grief
To bear love's wrong than hate's known injury.

"Reminds me of my life, particularly the 'love's wrong' part." Dolly sits back in her chair. She's done her bit.

The sonnet readings creep along until we get to Rhonda, who announces to the room, "Now don't get all nutty on me, but I read these in prep school and I actually understand them."

"Well, *la-dee-dah*," says Kit, who's still moping.

"Maybe you can show us how to read them, girl," Bertie says, animated, hands waving like flags, "because for my Jamaican self, I could use it."

"That's a good idea, Bertie," I say. "Read the sonnet, Rhonda, and try to make the meaning behind the words clear to us. My suggestion is to really focus on the language."

Rhonda sits up straighter in her chair and holds her book away from her. "Okay, pay attention." She begins, her voice louder and fuller than usual, enunciating clearly, stretching out her *o*'s in a way that makes me feel I'm in church: "When in disgrace with Fortune and men's eyes, / I all alone beweep my outcast state."

I'm thinking she's going to move us, tap into meaning, but she takes a breath, and like a teacher, turns to the class, "See, you have to read to the place where there's a natural pause." The women stare at her.

"Do it again," Bertie says.

Rhonda rereads the first two lines and goes on, her voice sweeping gracefully, "And trouble deaf heaven with my bootless cries / And look upon myself and curse my fate."

Then Rhonda abruptly interrupts herself and says, "I like how Shakespeare calls heaven 'deaf.' When you're down, that's how it is. No one listens."

She goes back to the poem, reading and analyzing, almost spurning the emotion in the words: "Yet in these thoughts myself almost despising, / Haply I think on thee."

"See, Shakespeare knows what's up. Just when he feels the worst, he's thinking of her." She continues, ". . . and then my state / Like to the lark at break of day arising / From sullen earth, sings hymns at heaven's gate."

She stops again, explaining to everyone how Shakespeare's soaring high now. "He's dropped his mood, and it's all because of a lady, although some critics say that the muse was a man." Kit's staring at the floor. Dolly's busy looking at her sonnet. By the time she gets to the end lines, Rhonda's lost most of those who were listening.

Seemingly unscathed by the lack of interest, she looks at me, triumphant. "Boarding school was a real boost to me. I can take almost anything apart."

For the next few months Rhonda continues to show me pieces of writing that are full of feeling, but in class discussions she often plays the detached one, clever and analytical, not invested in emotion. She's much deeper than she wants anyone to see. When we read texts such as Jean Giraudoux's *The Madwoman of Chaillot* in the fall play-reading class, she tells us coolly about the power structure in the play and calls the women "do-gooders"; with *Othello* she's critical of a black man's involvement with a white woman and calls Desdemona "Des-de-moaner."

Then, somewhere around our early rehearsals for *Merchant*, all hell breaks loose for Rhonda. She falls in love.

. . .

I hear about Lynn from Bertie one midwinter evening in 1988. It's a few weeks after the infamous costume parade, and I've reassured the women that I haven't heard anything about it from Ron and that no news is good news in prison. We've been discussing the trial scene, and I've suggested we perform that scene, setting it in New York's 1920 gangster era, with Antonio as a Mafia boss and Gratiano and Bassanio as his "associates." Bertie has said she wants to play Gratiano because "he gets to say mean things." Rose has claimed Shylock and Dolly, Antonio. We're all pointing Rhonda toward Portia.

Rhonda has just come out with "So why does Portia have to get dressed up like a man to be believed in the courtroom?" Someone says that undisguised, Portia would never have been taken seriously "in those days." Rhonda is staring down at her book as though she's studying the words, but every few minutes she glances over at the open doorway. I'm about to bounce the question back at her and ask her what she thinks, when Bertie, who is brushing her hair, blurts out, "Rhonda, your new girlfriend has to be at least six feet tall."

"Bertie," I say quickly.

"Who has a girlfriend?" Kit asks. She's organizing notes, ripping pages out of her notebook and attaching them to her newly acquired clipboard, the one I promised her as our stage manager.

"Where have you been?" Dolly asks, looking up from knitting a pale green child's blanket—the only color yarn she could get from the Property Office. "Rhonda, I do believe you're blushing."

Rhonda's trying not to smile, rifling through papers as though she's lost something. "It's okay." Rhonda says to me. "I do. Have a girlfriend." Then she shrugs it off. "It's a jail thing."

Kit leans in toward her and says, "Better not let Bernice see you. I heard she rats out to the cops."

Rhonda levels Kit. "I'm not Carter, if that's what you mean. And this is my business, buddy." She looks over at the doorway again.

Dolly returns us to the play. "I think Portia should just walk right in there and give those guys what for. Be herself." She is pointing one of her knitting needles in the air. "Rhonda, you have to play her."

"I will, I will," and she turns to me, "undisguised."

"Undisguised?" I say.

"Yeah," Rhonda answers, "the only woman in the courtroom. She's a real underdog advocate, and I'll play her, but straight, in a way I wasn't able to in real life. Before I came to Framingham I was a prelaw student."

All heads turn. "Yeah, yeah, I know," Rhonda says. "I woulda been a great lawyer. Sounds like that old refrain. You never know what you got till you throw it all away."

"What's that lawyer show? You know, *L.A. Law*?" Kit asks. "Those are some fancy women lawyers. They say what they think."

"But Portia doesn't try to be fancy. She's on a mission most of the play," Rose cuts in. She has brought hand cream up from the cottage and is opening the tube. It smells like lavender. She rubs it on her wrists and the backs of her hands. "A mission that has something to do with love."

"Could be," I say, "that Portia disguises herself because she knows what she's up against."

"She knows that taking a pound of flesh from someone is barbaric," Rhonda says. "Sounds like a woman to me. The only woman in a man's world."

Suddenly a very tall and very ebony-skinned prisoner appears in the doorway. She has her arms full of gym equipment—volleyballs, a boom box, what looks like a piece of netting. Gloria comes from behind, yelling over her shoulder, "Sorry, Jean, a big tournament to-night. I have to be there. You're lucky I let you have Rhonda."

The first inmate hands Gloria the equipment and tells her she'll catch up in a sec, flashing a smile that is meant only for Rhonda. Under her breath Dolly says, "Jee-sus," but the rest of the women say nothing.

Rhonda looks at me. "Just give me a minute, Jean." I nod, wondering, as I watch her cross to the door, if I have a choice.

"That's Lynn," Bertie whispers at me from across the room.

Rhonda leans against the frame, her foot sweeping the floor shyly like a moon-eyed teenager's. Lynn, a big, hulking woman who could easily have been a trucker on the street, seems out of place next to Rhonda's fine-boned body and chiseled silhouette. Lynn's in a dark green T-shirt that hangs halfway down her baggy jeans, and she wears wide-laced hightops that bunch around her ankles. Her cheeks are pudgy, and when she looks down at Rhonda, her face is almost cherubic. She says something we can't hear, but something that catches Rhonda for a second and keeps her smiling. I try not to look, but I can't help it. Their two bodies, as close as possible without touching, compel me. The whole exchange lasts only a moment, but when Lynn places a hand on Rhonda's shoulder, it is as tender as anything I've seen between two people.

Rhonda comes back to her seat, noticeably changed, softened. An officer comes in to do Count, and again there's a quick transformation in Rhonda's demeanor, fear flashing across her face. When the officer leaves, there's relief.

The women pick up scripts to resume our discussion, but I say, "Let's try an improvisation on the text tonight. Rhonda, you read the 'quality of mercy' speech and let's see what happens when the rest of you respond." I look at the other women. "Forget the script. Just pretend you're all in court. You can pick any kind of character you want. Except you, Rose. You play Shylock, a modern Shylock."

Immediately the women take up poses all around the room with a kind of comedic energy that is catching. Kit yells, "Hey, bozo, get my name on the docket," to Dolly, who's walking around, laughing at Kit and pretending to be in charge of something. Dolly grabs Kit's clipboard and begins writing notes. Rose harangues Judge Bertie, who'll have no part of her. Bertie's using her hairbrush, pounding it like a gavel.

There's no real scene, no real focus. All four corners of the room are filled with individual courtroom shenanigans, and Rhonda's sitting by herself at the rectangular table. I cross over to her. "It's your turn to get them to believe in what's true. Quiet the whole lot of them. And don't interrupt yourself."

Rhonda nods and, without missing a beat, moves behind a chair. It is her podium. The noise in the room keeps erupting from corner to corner, but Rhonda brandishes her book in the air as if it's a Bible. "Shhhhh," she says to the four corners, "Court's in session." She looks from face to face, not stopped by those who are still talking. She says, "Mercy, we're talking here about mercy." Then, as a hush begins to fall over the room, she begins reading: "The quality of mercy is not strained; / It droppeth as the gentle rain from heaven."

She takes off with Portia's monologue, modulating her voice and dramatically drawing out words.

But the hush is momentary. As soon as Rhonda is a few lines into the speech, the room gets noisy again. "Mercy is above this sceptred sway," Rhonda says to Kit, who mutters something unintelligible back to her. She turns to Rose and adds, "It is enthroned in the hearts of kings."

Rose waves her away, saying, "We're not listening to you," and she and Bertie keep their patter going. "I want justice," Rose says to Bertie, trying to grab her hairbrush. Bertie keeps her at arm's length.

Kit breaks out of character and says to Rose, "This is no Chelsea court, believe me. Any judge there woulda creamed you."

Rhonda is not deterred. She steps out from behind the chair, one hand on her hip and the other holding her script high. Through the glass, snow covers the barren expanse of yard, and even in the darkness, casts a kind of sheen into the room. Rhonda is still when she speaks. "Mercy is above the law," she says at first to Kit, and then, as though she's on a mission to persuade, she begins moving around the room, improvising on Shakespeare's lines.

"We do pray for mercy," she says to Rose, who as Shylock tries to shrug her off. But Rhonda is passionate now, looking into the eyes of all of us, her courtroom. Words seem to come easily, tumbling out of her mouth: "And that same prayer doth teach us all to render the deeds of mercy." She wends her way from woman to woman, the preacher's daughter ministering to her congregation.

Kit begins clapping, and then Dolly follows, caught up in the momentum.

"Mercy is enthroned in the hearts of kings," Rhonda continues.

"I want justice," Rose says again, insistent. "Justice and the law."

"I am saying all this—" Rhonda is now next to Rose, "—to convince you," and as Shylock brushes her off, she says it still louder: "—to convince you." The clapping builds.

"The law!" Shylock cries out, waving Portia away. "I want the penalty of the law!"

And now Rhonda repeats the line yet again, drawing it out still more: "I am saying all this to *convince* you." Her voice rises above the clapping, and then she lowers it dramatically as she almost hisses at

Shylock: "I have said all this so you understand," and she leans in still farther, "that mercy is an attribute to God himself. Mercy seasons justice."

Someone from outside the classroom yells, "Tell it like it is!" as they are passing by, and that breaks us all up. The women dissolve into chaos. But Rhonda is not laughing. She stands in the center of the room, waiting to see the effect she's had on her audience.

"You were terrific," I say. "Who says Portia can't preach?"

"I always wanted to be a lawyer," Rhonda says. "One of the good ones."

"You are better than any lawyer I had," Dolly says, slapping Rhonda on the back.

When the class ends Lynn is outside the door. She's pretending to be waiting for Bernice to call the Downward, leaning against the wall, a cigarette in her hand that she will smoke on her two-minute walk to the unit. She and Rhonda stand together, talking quietly, acting nonchalant. They are almost like any two women I might find in the hallway except for the fact that Rhonda can't stop smiling. Her hands are in her pockets, her hair's a mass of tangles, and she's got her script under her arm. On my way out of the classroom, I overhear Rhonda say to Lynn, "This play is controlling me better than all the tricks the Department of Corrections has ever had up its sleeve."

MAMIE

They'll give him death by inches.
CORIOLANUS, V.IV.43

When I get to know Mamie, it never occurs to me that she will die in prison. A big woman, seemingly sturdy, Mamie works hours in the greenhouse, a glass-domed building near the main entrance, where she weeds and waters, transplanting rootbound plants into larger pots. When she's not in the greenhouse, she spends her days landscaping prison grounds, growing flowers inside the compound, and taking clippings to the cottages. But Mamie's energy and passion do not preclude her from a deeper fragility. Even before she gets sick, she keeps on her coat in class, along with a frayed wool scarf and an attitude of humility. It's hard to conceive of Mamie setting a woman on fire. Sometimes she seems washed out, more like a down-and-out homeless woman than a dangerous convict.

She arrives one evening that first November, long after the leaves have turned, with what she calls "a chapter" of a book she plans to write. *The Other Side of Dignity*, she tells us, is about a woman who enters the state prison on a jewelry bust.

153

"It's based on a woman here," she says, with a nod to Rhonda. Mamie is wheezing. That, and something about the way she knits her brow when she shifts in her chair, makes me think that she is physically uncomfortable. She goes on, "Remember, the one who got snagged with hooch in her cottage and sent to Max?" From the knowing looks women exchange, it's clear that they all remember this inmate's infraction.

Rhonda jumps in. "The narcs here say—they *say* Strawberry made hooch out of Kool-Aid and leftover something from dinner, pineapples, I think. She works in the kitchen and has access to anything she wants. Strawberry's story is that she just put the stuff in this enormous ol' glass jar in her room and lo and behold, it fermented. Who knows if she's telling the truth?"

"Last month they tried to lock us in our rooms for that, which I feel was very wrong," Dolly says sharply. "Strawberry didn't even get a hearing. She went straight to Max."

"I never liked that girl," Rhonda's brought photos to class and is thumbing through them.

"It's not supposed to be guilty until proven innocent," Dolly adds, pointedly at Rhonda.

"My novel's like that, too," Mamie says. Compared to the others, she is amazingly soft-spoken. "Paula gets caught with a hot engagement ring from her fiancé, swearing she didn't know he had stolen it. Judge gives her two years."

"Happy Veterans Day," Kit says. "Welcome to 'You Survived the War, and Now You're Gonna Pay.' " The women groan.

"Why don't you read it, Mamie?" I say. "I'm impressed." I nod at the twenty or so pages she places on the table alongside her notebook.

"Nah, it's too long."

Bertie echoes, "Read it. I need to listen to a good story tonight."

Mamie turns to Bertie. "Girl, how do you know it's good?"

"I know," Bertie says. "All those poems you write. I know."

I think about the poem Mamie brought to class a month ago. She prefaced her reading by announcing it was just "some little verse" she wrote late at night when she couldn't get to sleep.

> From a small box at the foot of my bed,
> I rescue dried petals, still deep purple and soft white
> from an envelope long since buried.
> I retrieve the remains of old mint plants,
> scent long gone, just a shapely bunch of flat leaves.
> Glasses low on my nose, and papers in my hands,
> I snip and I cut. I paste and I glue.
> There is silence all around.
> I can hear my blood flow.

The class had loved her poem, but I wanted to take out that last line. It felt dangerous to me, evocative of Mamie's crime. I didn't want to picture Mamie setting someone on fire, and with that line I saw her revving up to kill. I liked the image the poem gave of her without it, the prison gardener who sent cards made of flowers to her family in Georgia. When I suggested she take out the line, Mamie firmly told me that the poem needed those words, a "peaceful image" of her deep involvement in the moment. She knew what she wanted to say.

Now, as she thumbs through her novel chapter, Mamie has her specs low on her nose. She's shaking her head at the pages in front of her. "Pick a section if you want," I say, "but I think we'd all rather hear the whole chapter."

Most of the women agree, except for Kit who's in a belligerent mood. Mamie holds papers out in front of her, and we settle in as she reads. No one says a word as her protagonist, Paula, comes to Framingham a fearful young woman, struggling with prison life, and becomes hardened by assaults from both inmates and guards. As Mamie describes how Paula eventually ends up in Max, where officers push food through a slit in the door and ignore her when she cries out for help, Bertie crosses and uncrosses her legs. "Is this true?" Bertie finally asks.

Mamie is squinting, her eyes caught in the glare of the overhead track lighting. Rhonda's arm hangs loosely over the back of Mamie's chair. "It all happened here to someone, so it's true," Mamie says. "But it's really my story, in a way."

"Not that you look like a skinny twenty-something broad," Kit says. "Or that you spent months in Max."

Mamie studies Kit. She snaps the papers back inside her three-hole binder as though with women like Kit around, she'd rather not say anything, much less read aloud.

"Don't pay attention to the negative," I say. I push Mamie to keep reading.

"You," Mamie says, pointing a finger at Kit. "Not another word." Kit gives Mamie an elaborate shrug as though she couldn't care less. Mamie picks up her notebook and holds it in the air. "Sorry, I need new glasses," she says to me, and then, still squinting, she goes through the final pages, ending with Paula in Max where she does push-ups to relieve fear and has trouble sleeping. Finally, Mamie tells us, an officer appears, kind at first, stepping into Paula's cell, urging her to sign papers, the D report. Mamie reads:

"Why am I here? I didn't do anything wrong. I tried to tell them that before they beat me up," Paula sputtered.

"Come over here. Sit down," coached the officer.

Paula allowed herself to be led like a small child, hanging on to the officer a bit longer than was necessary.

"The report states that you were found with hooch in your room, and during your search, you attacked Officer Dixon in the presence of four other officers."

"I did not! I did not! You've got to believe me. They jumped on me when I snatched my arm away from that black officer. I tried to tell them that it was Kool-Aid. I bought it at the store." Pleading and crying, Paula reached for the officer.

The officer jumped back, keeping herself out of Paula's reach. She began talking. This time there was harshness in her voice. "Two officers are out of work because you hurt their backs."

Paula sensed the difference in the officer but continued to protest. "I did not touch them. I did not hit or hurt anyone." Hands trembling, Paula exposed her thighs. "Look at me," she demanded. "Look at these bruises."

The officer examined the bluish-green flesh but made no comment.

"Nobody seems to care what they did to me. I didn't touch them. They beat me up. Look! Look!" she accused.

The officer put the pink sheet at the foot of her cot and left the room.

Paula buried her face in her pillow and felt herself slipping. All the anger, the bitterness, and the disappointments since that snowy day in December came crashing down on her. There was but one thought in her mind before she surrendered to the world of nothingness.

This is the other side of dignity where there are no human beings.

The women all begin talking at once when Mamie finishes her story. "Great last line, and man, oh, man is it true." "Who's the real officer?" "You got it right, girl." "Those bastards, those bastards." "I hate to see women as victims, but hey, there it is, your word against theirs." "Judge shoulda known better. First offense, no way two years." "Paula's a lot like me." "Nah, she's white." They go on for a good five minutes.

Mamie holds up her hand to quiet everyone, as if she's in church. "It's only my first chapter." She smiles, obviously pleased that she's generated so much noise. "I've got work to do."

"Does Paula die?" I ask her. Heads turn toward me. "The ending, the way she sinks into 'nothingness,' I thought maybe she might be contemplating suicide."

Again the women erupt as one. "Hell, no." "Don't you realize that's how it makes Paula feel, being called a liar, like nothing that's what." "She has to sign those damn papers, so it might as well be death." "She'll probably get time added to her sentence." "You've been in the free world too long, Jean." Mamie chuckles and shakes her head.

"So will we learn more about Paula's past in the next chapter?" I say.

"Yeah," says Kit, "like why she'd front for some scumbag?"

Mamie starts to say something, but she's having trouble again with her breathing, little throat sounds coming out on each exhale. Kit sits back in her chair, cocking her head at Dolly as if they share some private joke. Dolly doesn't respond. Instead she crosses over to Mamie. "Are you all right?" Dolly asks.

"I am," Mamie says, "I am. Haven't had this much attention in ages." The women hoot at that, and for a few minutes they make jokes and tease Mamie about how sexy she sounds when her voice gets all raspy. As Dolly sits, pulling a chair near Mamie, the room becomes quiet and I think about the deeper issues in Mamie's story, the despair that must come with isolation.

Mamie turns to me. "You know the girl this story's based on doesn't talk much about her past. But I heard . . . ," and Mamie hesitates, "that she was raped by a neighbor. He sliced her throat open, dragged her to the garbage, and left her for dead." She pauses, again, to catch her breath and take in the somber faces around her. "It was a miracle she made her way home. But, Lordy, there's always a price for surviving." Mamie takes off on a prolonged round of coughing. "I guess that's chapter two."

"Just keep writing," I say. Others echo my sentiment and continue the discussion, and then they veer off into prison gossip. I give them a break, and before we launch into another women's writing, I walk around the room, picking up scraps of paper from the floor, cleaning up absentmindedly. I move behind Mamie, leaning over her shoulder to give her another bit of praise.

On the back of her notebook Mamie has scrawled, "Oh where did our innocence go?"

. . .

"Does anyone know exactly what's wrong with Mamie?" I ask. I know this is against policy, but trying to get information from the Education Department has been like trying to squeeze water from a stone.

"It's this damn medical neglect," Dolly says. She sighs and reaches into her shirt pocket for a Camel, talking as she lights up. "Mamie's been very sick, something with her brain, I think. And these damn people, they try to make her work when she can't even walk, can't even remember, for God's sake, how to put on her shoes."

It is December that first year, heading toward the holidays, and Mamie's begun to miss classes. The rest of the women are gathered around the rectangular table, notebooks, papers, and pens spread out in front of them. They've been reading journal entries, daily assignments from the past week. They nod and mutter, agreeing with Dolly.

Dolly heads over to the window, and when she opens it a shot of cold air hits us. "Jee-sus," Dolly says. "What I do for a cigarette."

"Mamie's not my business," Kit says, turning away from Dolly. She's unwrapping something that looks like a burrito, but when she gets it open, I see that it's a napkin full of cookies she smuggled up from the cottage. "My business," she says, pleased as punch to the other women who eye the sweets longingly.

"Mamie still works in the greenhouse," Bertie says hopefully.

"But she did have a nasty fall on the way to get her meds," Rhonda adds. "I heard she was only wearing slippers." Rhonda's working on something that looks like a volleyball schedule.

"All I know," Dolly says, "is that Mamie needs a doctor. Hell, a real hospital. The infirmary here can't handle anything serious. And bein' sick at the Shattuck? Forget Shattuck Hospital. Nobody should ever be sick there." She squashes her cigarette. "I hate these things."

"So, she can't see a doctor here?" I ask.

The women give me the once-over. Kit laughs outright. "Would you want to see a doctor who works in a prison?" she says. "Sick or sore. They make you work, sick or sore." Kit pops a piece of a cookie into her mouth.

Dolly crosses back to the table. "When Mamie complained about going to get her meds, they threw it back in her face. 'You could stay at the hospital unit,' they told her. Sure, with six or more women to a room who are sick. Hell, they come in here with crabs, strep, hepatitis, you name it. Padding along in her slippers, fer Chrissakes."

"Why don't you write about this, Dolly?" I say.

"Yeah, maybe send a letter of complaint to the super," Kit says. She snaps her knuckles. "She'll listen."

"I know it's not the only answer, Kit. But maybe Dolly should send a letter of complaint. Take action." Dolly looks up at me. "At least put down what you feel. I'll write with you."

Dolly scoops up a bunch of writing paper from the table. Others do the same, but some are distracted. Bertie stares at the paper, not writing a word. Cody scrunches up a few tries, tossing wads of paper like basketballs into the trash can. I watch them, disturbed that there is such poor health care in a place where it seems pretty likely that people will get sick. I begin to write my frustrations, and finally, by the time we hear noise in the hallway and Bernice on her walkie-talkie directing the seven-thirty Upward, we have all moved into free-writing.

Rhonda is on her feet when she sees the door open. "Mamie, you made it!" Rhonda opens her arms wide, about to give Mamie a hug, but freezes when she sees the pained look on Mamie's face.

"I'm okay, girl, I'm okay." Mamie thrusts a thick arm into the air, brushing past Rhonda, and shuffles into the room. As usual she doesn't take off her winter wear, and when she sits at the table, heavy in her chair, her parka puffs up around her and makes her look even bulkier than she is. The women immediately begin to quiz her about her medical issues, but she says, "Lordy, that's no way to greet a friend."

The women erupt into noise, and the blue mood lifts.

Kit pulls out the list of complaints she's been scribbling and says, "Listen. Listen. This'll tickle your fancies." She scrambles to sit up straight in her chair.

"Fancy," Rhonda corrects.

Kit blows a mock kiss in Rhonda's direction and turns to Mamie, reciting a list of what she calls "the gruesome chow" she had for dinner.

When she finishes, she looks at Mamie, the proud child waiting for approval.

"Hey, girl, no joke, I wrote about food, too, a few days ago." Mamie licks her thumb like a postal clerk and leafs through her journal. "Here it is," she says, adjusting her specs. Kit's a little bent out of shape and sinks down in her chair. Mamie reads:

> The menu is—pork chops, mashed potatoes, carrots and gravy. In reality, the pork chops are just short of being raw, and if you are unlucky enough to be the first there, the fat stares back at you. If you've stood in line for twenty minutes, then they taste like shoe leather. The mashed potatoes are of the instant variety and watery. Carrots—even Bugs Bunny wouldn't eat these. Instead of orange, they're rust colored and salty. Now the gravy—no mother would claim it. The meat is clothed in it like a winter coat.

"I remember that meal," Rhonda says. "Brutal." She high-fives Mamie.

"I bet the men wouldn't stand for that," Dolly adds. "Frank says they're gonna get a real Christmas dinner this year, and lengthy visits."

"The truth is that all institutional food is the same," Rhonda says. "When I was in college, we complained about it, too. And hey, buddies, what do you expect in a prison?"

The women bat their complaints around and read more journal entries out loud. But it's clear that Mamie's arrival has been a gift. They're full of smiles, the kind of jokes that families make at Christmas. At the end of class Mamie announces, "I might not be here next week, but if not I'll send up my work. Don't go worrying about me or I'll wring your throats. For my final I'm writing a play."

. . .

Mamie rallies and makes it through the end of the semester, and for her final grade, I arrange to have her one-acter read aloud. Unlike in regular school, classes still can be held in prison during the holidays. As Kojack says when I arrive one blustery evening just before New Year's, "I guess no one's going home for the bubbly."

"Bernice is off for the week," Darlene, another recreation officer, reports as soon as I pass through metal detectors and make my way through No-Man's Land. Darlene is at least seven months pregnant, and she moves slowly toward me down the hallway. I've had one woman in and out of my classes who's been pregnant, but Darlene is the first officer I've seen this far along.

I meet her in front of the open iron door in the barren hallway. "No one mentioned to me that there was an evening program tonight," she says. She moves in front of me, blocking my entrance.

Immediately I feel my pulse racing. "I arranged to meet my class through the college program coordinator."

"Well, no one told me." She eyes me up and down.

"Ron Zullo knows about it too. It's all been approved."

"We'll see about that." She turns abruptly, and now I am following her, back down the hall, toward the recreation office.

"Could you please call the cottages and tell the women I'm here? There's a final tonight." She makes a sort of snorting sound. Random thoughts hit me: let there be a note from Bernice; think of a compliment, or ask Darlene when she's due; drop the name of some politician who supports my program.

Darlene unlocks the door to the recreation office, and as she enters, the steam heat hisses from the overhead pipes. I stand outside mumbling about how much I appreciate her doing this. She thumbs

163

through papers on Bernice's desk, trying in vain to find some directive. "No papers here," she says.

"We probably only need an hour and a half." I rifle through my briefcase and pull out my class list. "There aren't a lot of women. Maybe you could call the captain's office?"

"No one told me." Darlene takes the paper, says she needs me to step outside and abruptly shuts the door. I wait, leaning against the wall. It's deadly quiet in the halls, and there's not an officer to be seen. I wonder if Darlene gets overtime for working Christmas week. Across from me Ron Zullo's office has a fake wreath on the door, plastic pine needles and a few crimson berries. Otherwise there's no sign of Christmas.

When Darlene reappears, she looks annoyed. "The captain says you can have the women for an hour. I have to take you all upstairs to Education and lock the door while you're in class."

I'm so relieved we're able to meet tonight that I don't ask any questions. I just follow Darlene upstairs to Education. Even the entryway is a big room, twice the size of my regular classroom, with a high ceiling and wooden floor. There are no tables or chairs. "I'll be back," she says and exits.

I walk around the area, peering through a glass wall into a classroom where desks are in neat rows. A huge bound dictionary lies open on a table, and the blackboard is filled with the cursive alphabet—I figure an Adult Basic Education classroom. Searching for chairs, I try doors to the computer classroom and to the office, but everything's locked.

By the time the women get up from their cottages, they are angry and look as if they've been roused from sleep. There are complaints: no one reminded them that they had school until five minutes ago, and why do they have to have a damn class anyway this week; no one let them have time off from their jobs today, so naturally they haven't had time to do their laundry, make phone calls, or write letters; Darlene, they say, should be home and setting up for her baby—at least she can give birth in a place that's clean and doesn't have roaches; and although they don't say it directly, when Kit blurts out, "Christmas sucks in prison," I know that for most there have been no visits from family.

Maybe it was bad planning on my part, I tell them. "Now you think of it," someone says.

Winter jackets are strewn, hats and gloves in piles. The women are all disheveled, in sweaters or heavy shirts. "I guess we'll have to sit on the floor," I say.

Mamie says she has to have a chair. Cody bangs on the door to the outside, trying to get someone's attention, but Darlene could be anywhere in the institution, and there's no response. Cody bolts past me, doesn't listen when I tell her that all doors are locked. Scouting for chairs, she jiggles doorknob after doorknob, cursing.

Rhonda tells Mamie she can sit on her butt, and that breaks up the tension. The women grudgingly sprawl out on the floor, except for Mamie who stands, her face in a knot, scanning a copy of the one-act play she calls *Misgivings*. Mamie hands a script to Rhonda—she's made Xeroxes—and says, "I'm Jackee. You play my sister, Christine."

"What's she like?" Rhonda asks, thumbing through the pages.

"A crazy bitch, whaddaya think?" Mamie smiles. At the words "crazy bitch," I catch my breath. Suddenly it's her sister I imagine as the woman in flames. No one else seems concerned.

"I don't know why she couldn't have just turned her work in like the rest of us," Kit says. Last class, she and Cody submitted their research, the "collaboration" on toilet seats. Kit's flopped down on the floor, her chin propped up on her elbows. "Then I'd still be in bed."

"Plays sound better when you read them out loud," I say.

165

"Yeah," Dolly echoes, shifting around, trying to find a comfortable way of sitting. She discovers the wall and leans back, stretching her blue-jeaned legs out in front of her. "I'll read a part," she says to Mamie.

"You be the beautician in the scene where Jackee gets her hair done." Mamie turns to Cody. "You play Alonzo, my husband."

Cody halfheartedly takes a script and places it on her lap. She flips through it to find Alonzo's lines. She reads them to herself, practicing aloud the Spanish phrases Mamie's given her character.

There's the sound of a key in the door, and Darlene reappears. "Bertie's down for the evening." I nod at Darlene. This is during the time that Bertie's particularly distraught about her crime and too distracted to finish her final. It doesn't surprise me that she refuses to come up for this class.

"Hey!" Cody calls out. "Darlene, we need chairs."

"She's right," I say. "Some of the women are having difficulty sitting on the floor."

Darlene shakes her head. "Sorry. I don't have authorization to go into any classrooms tonight." She exits quickly, locking the door behind her.

Watching Mamie struggle to sit on the floor is painful. She has to place one hand against the wall and squat slowly, the other hand braced on her knee. "Ohhh, this is work. Mercy," she says, "my back's not what it used to be." Someone makes sure there's something for her to sit on, a coat, a hat, something softer than wood. "Thank you, girls," she murmurs. The women protectively edge in, sitting in a sort of semicircle around her. "I don't know what I'd do without you girls."

"You should give her an A just for being here," Kit says in a spurt of kindness.

"I give you all a lot of credit for being here—considering all the hassles you have to overcome on a daily basis. I'd probably have blown it and spouted off to someone, been in Max for weeks by now." At my comment they all burst into laughter and begin talking about times they almost went to Max or when they were locked for days or how some women scam the D officer and avoid lockup.

"Let's begin the play," I say to Mamie. Everyone rustles through her script. By the time we get through the first scene, in which we learn that Christine tried to steal Jackee's husband when they were first married, their energy is back. They cheer Mamie on at the end of the opening monologue, when she holds up her pass from the cottage, treating it as though it were an old photo of the sisters. She talks to it: "Hah! When I finish with her, Alonzo and everyone else will see the envy and jealousy all over her face."

"Scene Two," Kit announces: "The Beauty Parlor."

Mamie is animated, eyes wide, hands in the air. Her voice has vibrancy as she reads, talking to Dolly, "Hello, Bertha. A slight change this week." Her fingers fly up to fuss with her hair. "I want my hair up, something . . . something regal. I'm having a very important dinner party tomorrow night."

"Act it out," I whisper to Dolly.

Dolly gets up and crosses behind Mamie. She runs her hands through Mamie's locks, looking studiously at Mamie's mass of black hair as though she is deciding what to do with it. Kit snickers. "Good, good," I say to Dolly.

Mamie sucks in her cheeks and acts as if she's looking in a mirror in front of her. Dolly takes her lead and stares into the imaginary mirror, too, discussing hairstyles with her client. Suddenly Mamie turns toward Rhonda, as though she's just walked into the salon. She says, "Why, hello, Christine, nice to see you. Where's Paul? Doesn't he usually do your hair?" "I heard he's off on one of his trips."

Rhonda plays Christine by adopting a sort of rich-southern-belle posture, a dame getting a mud pack treatment in the salon. She closes her eyes and throws her head back. Mamie's Jackee tells her, "I guess all those hot lights during your modeling sessions and all that makeup are very damaging to your skin, huh?" Rhonda smiles sweetly.

"I'm enjoying the hell out of this," Kit says.

"*Shhh*," Dolly says to her and tilts Mamie's head back into the pretend sink to begin applying shampoo, rubbing her head this way and that. Mamie blinks as though she has soap in her eyes, which wins a huge laugh from Kit. Then she sits up, improvising to Bertha that she has to wipe her eyes. She's adjusting her specs, holding her script toward the light as she reads: "I saw your picture in *Vogue* magazine last week, Christine. You still look beautiful in your clothes, as usual."

"Wouldn't Christine say something?" Rhonda says, recoiling.

"Nope," Mamie says. "She just smirks at Jackee. I get the last word in this scene."

They breeze through the next scene at Jackee's home, where she and her husband discuss their lives and ready themselves for the party. Pretending to shimmy into a party dress, Mamie talks to Alonzo, played by Cody, who can't stop fidgeting with her baseball cap. After Jackee sends Alonzo from the room to deal with guests, she says to her mirror, "Move over, Christine, this will not be your *night*."

Now I'm thinking about the next scene, wondering if it is revenge that Mamie has in store for her characters. But for a few pages we're at a typical dinner party filled with repartee. When Christine arrives in the same dress as Jackee, looking twice as beautiful, Jackee has a TV moment, fleeing to the kitchen and breaking down. But with Mamie and Rhonda, it seems anything but ordinary, and we're all listening closely as Christine follows her sister into the kitchen and reveals how much she envies her.

The two begin talking about their sisterly competition. "I never paid much attention to directions and tried to do things my own way, which usually got me into trouble," Rhonda reads, "but you, even when we were at camp, you were able to pitch a tent in record time and groom a horse as well as ride one."

"Oh, yeah, and even then, Alonzo was always watching you," Jackee counters.

"Alonzo knew I couldn't swim and was afraid I'd drown. That's all, Jackee, honey. Things are not always the way they seem."

It's a saccharine-sweet ending, the kitchen reconciliation, with Christine asking Jackee to be her matron of honor at her wedding. But perhaps because of Mamie's crime, I have been hanging on every word and sit dumbfounded, soaking up clichés like "No more tears" and "You're still my best friend." I'm hoping that this play is a way for her to resolve some of her feelings about the arson.

Before the women can clap for Mamie's play, Darlene's back, unlocking the door. "Okay, ladies, that's it for tonight. Captain says 'Heave ho.' "

"Great job," I say as they all grab coats and bundle up. Rhonda helps Mamie to her feet. "Why do you call it *Misgivings*?" I ask Mamie as we all pour out into the hall.

"Something told me to," Mamie says. "It's hard to explain, but Christine is not as evil as Jackee thinks."

"So they are Jackee's misgivings? She's the one who misjudges?"

Mamie nods. "Maybe we all misjudge. I've been thinking a lot lately about this patient I used to have at the nursing home." Mamie's holding onto the rail as we walk down the stairs to the first floor. "I always wondered if I hurt her in some way when I rolled her over to change her bedding. Even though I paid special attention to the temperature of the water when I washed her clean, and even though I tried to soothe her, I

know she felt such indignity. How long, I wonder, how long before in-
dignities turn into a hardened shell? Those are my misgivings."

A few months later Mamie's out of class more than she's in, but
she sends up a note about the book we've been reading in our literature
class, Elie Wiesel's *Night*, his Nobel Peace Prize–winning memoir
about surviving concentration camps as a young man during the Ho-
locaust. She tells me that she read the whole book in one sitting and
wants me to invite Wiesel to our class. She writes, "I need to find out
how he got back his faith in God."

. . .

Mamie gets through summer and fall, but by March 1988 she's been
hospitalized at Shattuck. I hear about it from Dolly and Bertie, who
swear that she'll be back any day now. When she returns, they say,
she'll need her schoolwork, and so I bring books to her cottage.

We are having tea at a table in the day room, the main living area
of the cottage, and the TV is blaring behind us. Dolly pops the question, "Do you think you could go visit Mamie?" From the corner of
my eye, I'm watching the unit officer, framed by glass, nodding at
women who hustle inside and flash their IDs.

"Visit Mamie?"

"I've written a card for her," Dolly continues. A few ladies in bath-
robes pass by with food on plates. "Maybe you could deliver it?"

"What about mail?" I ask. "Can't she get mail in the hospital?"

"Teacher Jean, stamps cost money," Bertie reminds me. She empties a packet of sugar into her tea.

"Oh, of course," I say, feeling stupid. "Sure I'll take the card. And
maybe I'll just take her books too." I'm wondering how I'll ever get
permission to enter a prison hospital.

"Good, good," Dolly says, and darts into Mamie's room to rescue the books from Mamie's cot. A woman in curlers and a fuzzy yellow bathrobe, glass in her hand and toothbrush in her mouth, plunks herself at our table. She takes the toothbrush out, drops it into the glass, wipes her hand on her robe, and sticks out her dry hand for me to shake.

"I'm Samantha, honey, Rhonda's friend." I smile at her with reserve. "Heard about your classes." I notice her looking around the room as she speaks, as though she wants to see how everyone responds to her. When Dolly returns Samantha browses hungrily through Mamie's books.

The officer in the glass at the front waves at me. He has reddish-blond hair and a moustache that reminds me of my kid brother's.

"Hobbs, now there's a hot ticket," Samantha quips. "He winks at anyone in a skirt." She thrusts a paperback in my direction. "Any chance I might have this dictionary? I'm a terrible speller."

"These are Mamie's books," Bertie says, guarding the rest of the pile. "She'll be needing them, and girl, you know she'll be back." Samantha tosses me the dictionary and, with a sigh of disgust, drifts away into a conversation with an inmate waiting to do laundry. Hobbs waves at me again.

I gather up books and papers as Dolly tucks her card into the copy of *The Merchant of Venice*. "Give Mamie a hug for us," she says. Bertie places her hand in mine and squeezes as I awkwardly say my good-byes. I want to give them all hugs, but I sense that staff are not to touch inmates. It's an unwritten rule, and Hobbs is watching. I walk past him, and this time I see a man sitting in a glass booth; I imagine him watching day and night.

• • •

The next day I call Shattuck Hospital to see if I can visit Mamie. Shattuck has, at the time, several wards for patients who cannot afford medical care, some dying of AIDS, others diagnosed with mental illness. Convicts from all over the state are hospitalized at Shattuck, and most outpatient procedures for prisoners occur there as well. After several phone calls, because I am Mamie's teacher, my visit is okayed.

The first thing I notice is the smell. It's cold, antiseptic, but mostly the hospital smells of emptiness. There's barely any furniture in the large lobby, and as I walk toward the back corner, a man in pale gray striped pajamas wanders past me to the lone couch. He is sipping a soda from a straw and gazes off into space. A few flyers, advertising special programs, are taped on posts, and an occasional chair is tucked into a corner, but this large space, populated with so few people, seems markedly forlorn. I follow a sign pointing visitors to the prison ward. A prison officer at a desk tells me to wait while he checks me out.

I flash back to the few hours of training I received when I first came to the prison and the video with simulated scenes of inmates portrayed as tricksters and sneaks. Now, time under my belt, I know that conning is only part of the truth of what goes on inside. I'm betting the women are right: it took so long to get Mamie to Shattuck because no one in charge took her seriously.

"Trounstine?" I turn to see a female officer with a clipboard. I nod. "I'll escort you now." We head upstairs in an elevator, secure my jewelry, and go through the standard pat-search, only a few feet away from the locked unit, where a guard sits in a chair next to a control panel that opens two sets of doors. The patient area is hospital-clean but run down, with the same sparse feeling as the lobby, and with more prison guards than nurses. As I enter Mamie's room, an officer stations himself outside the doorway. There she is, in a pale green hospital gown, her brown arms on clean white sheets. We smile at each other, and I take in the cool, light, and airy space that surrounds her.

"I have some kind of tumor," she tells me almost immediately, and then, without a trace of self-pity, "cancer." She shows me a stack of letters and cards that have come from friends and from her family. I notice a crayoned picture of Easter eggs she's pasted on the wall behind her bed, along with some photos, and she has a few books piled neatly on her bedside tray.

"I don't know when I'll be back at the prison," she says. "Sometime after my treatment." I nod, pulling a chair near. "But I'd like to stay here," Mamie sighs. "It's almost like being free." She points out that she has a room to herself, and that her window has no bars and a good view of pine trees. "I can look out on a patch of green."

"Dolly sent you a card." I hand it to her and watch Mamie carefully open the envelope as though she might keep that too. She silently reads the card and then lets it rest on top of her covers.

"I'm afraid of the cancer, Jean. I've seen too many patients suffer when I worked with the terminally ill. I've seen them, Jean, organs rotting away, one day depleted bags of bones and the next gross bloated bodies. I want to go home." She grimaces as she pulls herself up a bit in the bed. "You know I applied for a pardon." Mamie points to a copy of the forms she filled out and the letter she's written to try for a compassionate release. I don't feel hopeful.

"What can I do?" I ask.

"Tell me about everyone." She plumps up her pillow. While I unwrap a straw for her apple juice, Mamie hangs on every word about the prison. She wants to know who is back and who got out. She is unable to read right now, she tells me, but is delighted when I show her the books I brought. "They make it cozy in here," she says, and asks me to put them on her bedstand.

"We're going to put on the play in late June, you know, costumes, props, the works," I begin. "Do you think there will be enough interest in *Merchant?*" Mamie always has her pulse on the prison, even from Shattuck.

"Absolutely," she looks thoughtful, pulling her tray table closer so she can reach the saltines left over from lunch. "The girls love trials. They can't get enough of them, I guess."

A doctor slips in on his rounds, and Mamie reaches out her hand for him. "Doctor, this is my English—no—my drama teacher." We both laugh, and then Mamie catches his eye. "She's helping me."

The doctor introduces himself to me and talks kindly to Mamie. "He's one of the good ones," she teases, enjoying all the attention. As she breathes in and out for him, his stethoscope on her chest, she looks up at his glasses. "You know some of these doctors don't give a damn about me or anyone on this floor. That boy across the hall has AIDS, and he moans all night."

"Just breathe, Mamie," he is counseling. Then he feels her pulse and checks what looks to me like charts. He sits on the edge of her bed.

"Doctor, why can't I see well?"

"I'm afraid I don't have any more news for you, Mamie."

"Does reduced vision have something to do with cancer?" Mamie stretches out her hand, squeezing and releasing her fingers as though they hurt. "It's all right, Doctor, you can tell me. You know I was a nurse once."

"We will do follow-up tests, Mamie. That's really all I know now." He stands up, gently brushing a few crumbs off the top cover, and leaves the room as quietly as he's come.

Mamie's face grows more solemn after his visit, and she asks me to pull the curtains. Then she settles into herself.

"I think you'd better go," she tells me, eyelids heavy, chin touching chest. She pulls a crumpled sheet up almost to her lower lip, an arm thrown over the top of the covers to one side. "I'm sleepy."

"I'll be back. Next week. I promise."

In the hallway I hear her call after me: "Don't forget, I want a full report. And when I'm back, a part in that play."

. . .

Mamie is moved to New England Medical Center at the end of May. Her condition has worsened, and I am no longer allowed to visit. Rhonda says how sad it is to see Mamie's handwriting, all scribbles, with words running off the page as though she's spilled water on ink. Still, Rhonda and the others write often. Mamie's children desperately try to get her released so that she can be with them when she dies, but they are unsuccessful. One night, when I come into the prison ready for class, I hear the news.

Dolly says softly, "I wanted to call you, I really did. I knew they wouldn't tell you." She reaches out her hand, and I take it.

"It was beautiful," murmurs Bertie, "the memorial service. Even her older sister came."

"Beautiful but still a funeral in prison," says Rose. She is playing cat's cradle with a piece of string.

Outside the window I can see officers accompanying a woman across the yard to the medical building. The wind is blowing green leaves around them, and steam rises from the grate in the cement below. Even in May the heat's not turned off in the prison. I want to ask if Mamie was alone when she died, but I don't, trying instead to imagine how they feel about losing one of their own. We hold on to each other with our breathing.

"Reverend Ryland led the service upstairs in the chapel, and everyone who wanted to spoke about Mamie. Then we sang songs," Bertie says. She moves her chair in closer, resting her head on Rhonda's shoulder.

We sit around the table, mostly quiet, remembering Mamie. It is a spring night, the kind of rare evening that comes and goes quickly in New England, the smell of lilacs in the air. "Heartbreakingly beautiful," Rhonda says about the service, the first to break the silence. Dolly offers the address of Mamie's mother, who doesn't know much about her daughter, suggesting that she might appreciate hearing how Mamie has written a play, started a book, and planned to perform onstage. We decide to send her all Mamie's written work, and a card with pressed flowers that Mamie made. Bertie volunteers stamps.

"I don't feel like doing improvs tonight, but maybe we could get on our feet, do something," I say. I suggest we warm up with a group vocal exercise. The women nod, all except Kit. She's been waiting for a phone call from her lawyer and has gotten into a fight with her unit manager. She says she is in "no mood for jumping around." She helps us push chairs back but just wants to sit. The rest of us move into a circle.

We stand, arms loosely around each other, eyes closed. I begin by humming. Each woman adds her own sound, some sharp and punctuated, some open throated and soulful. There are low and high notes, even some harmony, sounds that seem gospel, some that sound like prayer. Without words, the music moves from its initial lament to a cacophony of sound. Someone starts stomping. Another claps, and one by one, we are open eyed, waving arms and shaking bodies to the sounds of our own voices.

I swing into the center and begin initiating a repeatable movement and sound, taking it to Bertie who, facing me, copies it. Then she brings it to the middle of the circle and transforms it into her own. The energy swells. Bertie and Rose face each other, *ooh-ahh*ing, with a jump and a punch to the right; the other women do the same. Rose lets the sound flow and adds more shoulders. Soon we are all blues, and shortly drift into a kind of bebop, with Kit on the sidelines occasionally yelling "Go girl!" to whoever has the lead in the center.

Not interrupted by recreation or officers, we stay on our feet for a good half hour, letting sound and movement shelter our pain.

At the end of class, Dolly picks up her books from the table as others move slowly into the hallway. "Remember the night Mamie brought her play to class? That awful Christmas week?" I nod. Dolly is looking at the play script, a small, thin paperback. "She told me on the way back to the cottage that she had been sick and thinking a lot about God and the right-to-die movement. She asked me if I believed people had a right to decide when to die."

"What did you say?"

"I said I wasn't sure it was what God wanted."

I remember what Mamie said in the hospital about her fears of death; she didn't want to end up suffering like some of the patients she'd seen. I think of the title of the book Mamie wanted to write, *The Other Side of Dignity*. "Do you think Mamie held God responsible for her death?"

"Not really," Dolly says. "But I know Mamie was like a tiger about God. She once said, 'I believe in God but not in the blind sense that most people do. I have experience with him.'" I laugh, the kind of laugh that happens at funerals, and then I find myself wiping away tears.

Dolly puts her hand on my shoulder. "Mamie argued a lot with me, but I know she must have been ready to go. 'Only when the light has gone out of our eyes and we can't tell you or God how we feel. Then we have a right.' That's what she said."

"That's what dignity must have meant to Mamie."

Dolly comes closer and I turn toward her. We hug goodnight.

. . .

One evening a few weeks later, toward the end of class, Bernice knocks on our door. She says, "I've got a letter that came here for you." She produces a tattered envelope with my name, barely readable, scrawled on the front.

A few women head to the corner of the room after Bernice leaves, and in spite of the fact that smoking has recently been banned in the main institution, they light up cigarettes. But tonight I'm not playing enforcer.

I study the letter. "It's from Mamie's mother," I say. We all look at each other, and it's almost as though Mamie's in the room, tiny dried flowers between her thumb and forefinger. Her glasses are low on her nose, and she's shaking her head, chuckling in wonder that her mother actually took the time to write us. I look at the few small paragraphs. The mother's handwriting is wobbly and tight and looks as if it is not often practiced. She thanks us immediately for the package we sent and says, "I didn't know my daughter ever wrote anything." She doesn't talk about the children who were once estranged from Mamie and are now in her care, or about Mamie's crime, but she encloses pictures and tells us she is sorry that her daughter went wrong. The letter ends with a prayer for all of us. I turn the page over, wishing there were more about Mamie.

Dolly shakes her head and puts her cigarette out on the windowsill. She is smoking in spite of herself, and her fingers are yellowed.

"Mamie would have given her right arm to see those kids before she passed. I don't know why they couldn't have sent her home." We share the pictures, silent. Her son sits on a fence, waving at the camera, and in the corner of the photo, two girls scooped up by a young Mamie are squealing under a hose. In another shot Mamie stands smiling next to a woman who's bent over a vegetable garden, weeding.

Dolly is the first to leave the room, and most of the women file out quietly. Rhonda remains. "I know it's against the rules, but I'd like those photos. You know, to remember." Every bit of me says no as I hand them to her.

As Rhonda exits I remember what Mamie said to me on my last visit to Shattuck Hospital before they moved her to New England Medical Center, where she eventually died. She'd become too weak to write letters, her stomach bloated, her eyes swollen, but she talked about the greenhouse and her work at the prison. "I dream about pine trees and a place clean as fresh sheets," she told me.

That night I think about Mamie all the way home.

THE PLAY

Nothing of him . . . doth fade
But doth suffer a sea change
Into something rich and strange.
THE TEMPEST, I.II.399

D on't get me wrong, Jean, I like the King's English." Rhonda's
following me down the hall after class, tossing from hand to
hand two apples that she's snagged from other inmates in exchange
for God-knows-what. I'm semi-ignoring her. "But if we're going to
do Shakespeare in here, we have to do it so that everyone gets it, even
the Spanish women who don't speak English."

It's May 1988, six weeks before the production of *Merchant*, and
although by now we're meeting twice weekly, we're still not allowed
to rehearse in the gym. I'm on my way to complain to Bernice, figuring
that volleyball or no volleyball, by next week we've got to be onstage.
We pass a display of photos from a recent family day, women and
their kids posed up against barbed wire.

"Latinas," I correct. I try the door to Bernice's office.

Rhonda leans against the wall. She's not giving up. "That means,
Jean, we have to translate the script."

I stop in my tracks. Change Shakespeare's words in performance?

180

Use modern American speech? I look sideways at Rhonda. She's always fooling around in and out of class. Maybe too many improvisations have led her to this.

"Sure, we can play around in rehearsal," I say, "but not in production."

I knock on the door, just to be sure Bernice is not hidden away doing paperwork. "Damn. She must be making rounds." I pull out a piece of paper from my briefcase and scribble a note. I slip the scrap of paper under her door.

"Jean, buddy, I mean it. I know Shakespeare's the Bard and all. But believe me, I know my audience." Rhonda turns on her heels and heads down the hall, calling out behind her, "I'll take care of it." Then I hear, "Hey, Lynn, wazzup?"

Before I can scramble to speak, Rhonda and Lynn have rounded Four Corners, the crossroads in the institution, where two paths intersect. At the far end of the hall, Bernice is skirting around, busy with doors. Inmates pour past her, undoubtedly on their way to have a last cigarette before heading to their units. I hurry outside to find Rhonda.

Walking down stone steps into the expanse of the yard, I am struck by the warmth of the spring evening. Stars, bright as comets, shine overhead. In the distance I see a line of women waiting in the moonlight for meds. I look around for Rhonda and see her standing by a tree with Lynn, their conversation sotto voce.

"I'll think about what you said," I call out. And before anyone can tell me I'm "out of place," I turn quickly back into the institution and head toward No-Man's Land.

The next week we are once again in Program Room 2. The women are frustrated but I explain that working twice a week, we still can be ready by late June. I casually mention Rhonda's idea of "translation" but couch it as an aside, emphasizing that I've been taught that Shakespeare's texts are sacred, and that a good director is faithful to the author's language. "I'm sure the English director Peter Brook didn't change one word in production and his *A Midsummer Night's Dream* was famous, almost gymnastic. I mean there were acrobatics, wooing of lovers on swings."

"We don't want to do this play in England," Dolly says. The others nod vigorously.

I then bring up how weeks ago we decided to set the trial scene in New York's 1920 gangster era with Antonio as a Mafia boss and Gratiano and Bassanio as his associates. Portia's to be undisguised, I remind them, the only woman in a man's world, and our Shylock, a recent Jewish immigrant to the United States, will be the ultimate outsider. We've already cut out Nerissa, Portia's lady-in-waiting, and we've left in the magistrate, turning him into a more modern judge. We've decided to copy Laurence Olivier's idea of putting Shylock's famous "Hath not a Jew eyes" speech just before the trial scene, in order to link the trial, in which Shylock seeks revenge, to his daughter's betrayal. "Isn't that enough adaptation?" I ask.

Heads wag no.

"Okay, okay, I'll give it a shot." They smile at each other like kids who've gotten their way. "But I'm not promising it'll work. We'll try Rhonda's suggestion. For each line of Shakespeare's, let's figure out what exact words we need to make his meaning our own. Kit, you copy down the changes." Kit pulls out her clipboard filled with lined paper and hunkers down to take notes. Bertie gives Rhonda a thumbs-up.

We spend the rest of the evening going over the script, line by line, not only simplifying some of the "thous" and "thees" but, more important, searching for metaphors that the women feel will affect their audience, reach their community. At the place where Shylock tells Bassanio that he distrusts Antonio—"What, woulds't thou have a serpent sting thee twice?"—Rose comes up with the phrasing "Oh, I suppose you'd have a pit bull attack you twice?" When Shakespeare's Shylock says he'd rather his daughter go to the biblical thief Barrabas than be married to Bassanio or Gratiano, Rose points to Antonio and his cohorts, saying, "I would rather my daughter be married to a vile murderer than one of them."

Bertie, playing Gratiano, comes up with a few ideas of her own for the trial scene. She decides that because she is so much younger than Dolly, she should play Gratiano as Antonio's nephew. In the scene when Bassanio tells Antonio he would sacrifice everything to save his friend from having to pay back the bond, Bertie considers Gratiano's original lines: "I have a wife who I protest I love. / I would she were in heaven, so she could / Entreat some power to change this currish Jew."

The lines Bertie paraphrases become: "If I were married, I would love my wife, but if it would help, I would rather that she were in heaven and whispering in God's ear so that he'd change this doggish Jew."

But, discussing the script this way, the group process takes so long that by the end of the class we've only reworked part of the scene. On their way out, some of the women complain. I overhear Bertie tell Rhonda, "This is deep."

By early June we're still blocked from rehearsing in the gym, and just as I'm trying to imagine how we'll ever get to stage this play, Rhonda appears at the door, a typed manuscript in hand, with copies for all. "I couldn't take too much more of this group collaboration," she says, brushing off the task she's accomplished. "I knew we'd be adapting this thing for the next six months if I didn't take over. I took Kit's copy to my room and worked on it. Here's my favorite part."

And with that, she crosses over to the window and opens it, reading from the script, as though she's talking to Shylock, turning the original line, "Do you confess the bond?", into a more lawyerly, "Did you sign the contract willingly and in full knowledge of the consequences?"

Kit swings into the room and sees the pile of typed scripts on the table. "I saw you working on this in the office, Miss Education Secretary."

"Well, there is that," Rhonda says, a huge smile on her face.

As women enter they each take up a copy of the "adaptation," which Rhonda says is mostly filled with Shakespeare's words. "I've just updated some of the language." Things, she says, we've discussed in class, or discovered through improvisation. Impressive, I think, and I tell the class to look over the script. At Bertie's suggestion I promise them colorful folders.

With that the women are off on a tear, laughing and cutting up, and soon they're into the text, pronouncing lines aloud, enjoying their words. By now all parts have been claimed much less competitively than in my drama groups in the free world. Cody is our on-and-off-again Bassanio, and although I've been a little concerned about it ever since Kit vetoed the part, I'm holding my breath. Gloria is standing in as the judge magistrate, "until you get a real one," and although she continues to say she has "no intention of sticking around this joint," she shows up for class.

After the women have a chance to read what we are now lovingly calling "our translation," I ask them to respond. Dolly's head is buried in the script. "I like the way you kept in all that mercy talk," she says to Rhonda.

"I knew Jean would have killed me if I changed anything in that speech."

"Why don't we try a read-through of this new and improved script,"

I say. "Then we'll get on our feet. There might be more changes when you're actually moving around."

The women are game, and they breeze through the text, but tonight no one wants to try it standing up. "We need the gym," Rose says, the only one who even attempts getting on her feet. She's so into her part that every time Portia makes what Shylock considers a fair ruling in the courtroom, Rose jumps up, waves her fists in the air, and, using Shakespeare's words, cries out in thanks: "A Daniel come to judgment."

At the end of the evening Bernice knocks on the door of our classroom. Immediately the women besiege her, asking her to promise that the gym is ours next class. To my relief, she agrees.

. . .

" 'I might as well play a part; I've got nothing better to do.' That's what Gloria said two days ago, I swear to God, just two days ago." Dolly is standing outside the door to the gym, waiting for my arrival. "Now Gloria's gone to pre-release and I've scoured the cottages and all I can find is Claire. Jee-sus."

"Don't panic," I say as I approach the locked doors. Transition is not something the prison spends much energy on. Beds in halfway houses or lower security facilities are always at a premium, and consequently, most women get final word of their transfer one day and disappear soon after. As concerned as I feel, I shouldn't be surprised. Most likely I'll never see Gloria again. "Where's Bernice?" I ask.

Dolly's preoccupied. "Claire. You remember her from our early improv night last fall?" she asks.

I look down the hall, but no Bernice. "I think so," I say carefully.

I think back to the evening that Rhonda invited Gloria and two other women when we were first looking for recruits. Claire, a tall slim young woman who professed she'd finished three years of college and starred in several plays, hung around, bragging that she couldn't stop her family from frequent prison visits. "We're all so close, like sardines," she said. Dolly and Bertie looked at each other while I gritted my teeth, all of us trying to keep from saying something horrible to Claire. But Claire didn't notice anyone's disdain that evening. She talked nonstop until someone suggested she think long and hard about volunteering. Kit complained under her breath, "All we need is another druggie in this crew," and she later wrote me a note and slipped it in my briefcase: "Get rid of her. I'll play two parts."

Dolly looks around frantically. "I told her to come up from her cottage. We have to have a judge, Jean."

"You did the right thing, Dolly."

Within minutes Bernice has arrived. "It's not my fault. Ron said he had to have the gym later tonight for some sort of special program. It was last-minute." She's heading across the hall. Dolly and I follow anxiously. I'm trying to keep Dolly from swearing. Now she worries that it's not just Claire that's the problem, but the possibility of never getting the gym. Bernice is talking constantly on her walkie-talkie. "Program Room 2 is taken," she says. "I'm putting you in the Green Room."

"Jee-sus," Dolly says while Bernice unlocks the door to a large dusty space, where couches line walls and a TV on a stand is shoved into a corner near a lamp. Dolly shouts, "Bernice, this place is fulla cobwebs!"

"You can't be picky in prison," Bernice says as she exits.

I walk around, setting up for rehearsal, trying to relax. The Green Room is actually avocado green, and it seems to have character. It is filled with racks of old magazines, art supplies, broken pieces of pottery, and articles cut from newspapers in stacks by the window, but the main attractions are the fake leather couches and an overstuffed chair, split down the center.

"Watch out when you unfold those metal chairs," Dolly says angrily, nodding at the pile in a corner. "Spiders, creepy-crawlies, God-knows-what." The hall fills up with women's voices.

Claire is the next to enter. She says hello warmly and places herself in the cushiony leather seat. She crosses her legs, and an expensive sandal dangles from one foot. She's wearing leggings and a big shirt, her black hair up in a banana clip. She's says that she's already gone over the script Dolly gave her and has just a few questions about her part. I sit on the arm of the chair, and together we look at the script.

"Comfy?" Kit says as she arrives, moving past us and plopping herself on the couch. I glare at her. Doesn't she realize we are desperate for a judge? Others troop in, placing themselves around the room, in various states of annoyance when they see Claire.

I try to be the diplomat, but it is tough. Rhonda, who knows Claire the best and is often the mediator, is cold. Bertie and Kit are downright hostile. When we read through Portia's entrance, the part of the play in which the judge welcomes Portia into the courtroom, Rhonda deliberately ignores Claire. "You have to pay attention to her," I say severely to Rhonda. "She's the judge." By the end of the evening, Cody says we might as well throw in the towel. The others protest, but not with much conviction.

The next class we are finally in the gym. Claire comes to rehearsal early. I have already been setting up for half an hour, carting a few orange plastic chairs across the room for our defendant and his cohorts, putting them all in a row, stage left. Bernice has made sure there's a table, and although it's scratched up, it's sturdy. I've moved it center stage for Shylock. Now I'm enjoying the silence, writing blocking notes in my script, and I hardly notice as Claire moves across the barren wooden floor and props herself up on the stage rim, sitting next to me. The faded lime green curtains frame us like a photo.

"I'm feeling out of it, Jean," Claire says, her dangling sandal hitting the STAGE OFF LIMITS sign. I notice that her toenails are fiery red. "I don't really understand what it means to be a judge in those days. I'm not ready to block the play." She goes on, fussing that it doesn't make sense, Shakespeare's duke of Venice. "I don't get what you said, 'akin to a governor.' What does that mean?"

"I see the duke as part of an old-boy network," I say. "He's—"

"I want to quit."

"Claire, you just started a week ago."

"I know."

"Don't you think you might try to find out about your part before you give up?"

She gnaws on her lower lip. "It's not just that. . . . How can I figure out where to sit or stand when no one wants me near them?"

"You can't expect to be accepted immediately. These women have been working together for months."

"But there's this drugged-out thinking of mine. I'll never be part of this group, and I'm afraid—I mean, I don't have anything to offer. Bertie doesn't like me, and Dolly and Kit, well, let's be honest—they think I'm a flake." She slumps down, pulling her knees up toward her chest. "I feel so uncool telling you this."

I try to be reassuring, but I'm not all that sympathetic. Something about Claire is so fake. She's someone who seems to have a supportive family and a decent education. For some reason I feel annoyed that she blew it in college, experimenting with drugs and crime, ending up in prison. What irony, I think: Claire, of all people, playing Shakespeare's judge. But we need her. "You know, Claire, sometimes I want to quit too. Maybe you're blowing this out of proportion."

"I've never finished anything. Sometimes I'm scared I can't do it."

"Stick it out."

"I don't know."

"I know you'll enjoy it when you perform the play."

"Maybe," she says, carefully, pulling at a toenail. "Let's forget I said anything, and I'll be the judge—tonight. But if I get any more flak, give the role to someone else. Okay?"

I start to disagree, but then the others bound noisily into the gym. Rose lets out a boisterous laugh when she sees the stage and then, climbing up on it, winces and glares as Shylock. Rhonda, Cody, and Kit begin playing basketball, while Bertie stands in the gym doorway arguing with a female officer. Dolly shakes her head at the dirt on the stage, finds a broom, and grumbles, all the while moving chairs and sweeping under them. It takes fifteen minutes plus a relaxation exercise to get everyone settled down. I explain that tonight we're concentrating on putting the play on the stage. I encourage them to both make movements natural and keep refining our adapted script, allowing for changes. "Let's try the opening," I say, "and see what movements you come up with."

Claire has found a podium backstage and is pushing it stage left. She says I have to get her a gavel. "Sure, sure," Kit replies, shaking her head and sighing. "The super's just dying to let us knock each other over the heads with gavels." Kit hops on the stage, handing Rose a cardboard knife she made for the scene in arts and crafts. "Use it wisely," she says and elbows her in the ribs. Then she places herself in a chair next to me, facing the stage.

"I'll make you a gavel," I say loudly to Claire. "Tonight use Bertie's

Jean Trounstine

hairbrush." Bertie reluctantly gives Claire her brush. "Rhonda, you know where you enter from. Bertie, you and Cody take your places off left with Dolly." As they move into place, I see Cody show her cohorts a wad of fake dollar bills she must have discovered in a box backstage. She stuffs them in her pocket.

As the scene begins Rhonda makes her entrance, stage right, complete with my briefcase. She's Portia, coming to solve this famous case, even though, as a woman, she obviously is a surprise to Judge Claire, who looks at her surreptitiously. Claire hams it up, following Portia with her eyes, standing stiffly at the podium, fiddling with her glasses and clearing her throat for effect. She tackles the adapted lines, "You heard what Bellario has written. I take it you're the famous lawyer? Times certainly have changed, women in the courtroom." And, looking Portia's body up and down, she adds in a half whisper, "Are you any good, honey?"

The cast lets out a roar. Claire continues to ogle Portia, and although Rhonda has to act calm and collected—to keep her job as a lawyer, Portia cannot respond to the judge's almost blatant sexual harassment—all of us can see that Claire has found a way to make Rhonda squirm.

"I am the lawyer sent by Bellario," Rhonda insists, trying to be dignified. Claire presses on, grilling her on her credentials, embarrassing Portia over her lack of knowledge about the case, so that when Rhonda finally says, "Which one is the merchant and which one is the Jew?" we all see not only a lawyer being hassled by a judge but also a woman trying to keep her poise in a court of law.

After the scene is over, Rose tells Claire that she has defined the part through her improvised lines. Even Rhonda, who hates to be one-upped, is pleased that she actually felt embarrassed onstage. "Some men always try to psych you out," she says to Claire, "and you

190

really made me feel queasy. I despise that, having to flirt to get a job."
I agree, and Ron Zullo's overeager smile pops into my head.

Kit, who's written down the additions to the scene, then organizes
the women into a circle on the floor of the gym. They sit at her feet,
copying down the changes. Thus our script evolves as the women's
lives find their way into the text in subtle but definite ways. Claire
leaves that night chatting it up with the others. For a few rehearsals
I breathe easy.

. . .

Two and a half weeks before the play, Rhonda and Lynn meet me on
my way into the gym.

"Cody's officially dropped out," Rhonda says. "Couldn't take the
pressure."

"Yup," Lynn adds, and before I can react, she takes a breath, her
chest puffing up like a wrestler's. "I'll do this for you, Jean." She's
cocking her head at me as I watch, dumbfounded, gawking at her easy
stroll past me into the gym, the oversize arms swinging by her side as
if she's headed for a fight. Lynn's wearing a Walkman, and her chin
goes up and down to the music.

"It was my idea," Rhonda says, following. "Lynn can be Bassanio."
I stare at her. One by one the women enter. No one else seems surprised to see Lynn.

"I guess news travels fast in prison," I say, and Lynn shoots me a grin.

The inmates go about our new routine, creating our "set"—setting
up the stage with table and chairs—and then, pulling out blue mats
from the dungeon for our relaxation exercise. I'm still adjusting to the
idea of Lynn playing Bassanio while women lie down on mats, spreading out arms and legs. When I ask them to close their eyes, suddenly
Lynn announces, "No, suh." Rose tells her to pipe down and do the

exercise eyes open. But Lynn guffaws all the way through my "Take deep breaths and sink into the mat," muttering to herself lines like, "God knows who's gonna come in this room and do what."

"*Shhh,*" I say, but she won't let up.

I can tell it's going to be equally difficult getting her to understand the play even with a quick summary, which is all Lynn can tolerate. "Just give me the basics, Jean," she says, on her feet as soon as the exercise is over, "but don't go off on me."

Seeing that she has no intention of reading *Merchant*, I corral the group into a circle on the floor of the gym to do a talk-through of the scene. We try to translate the character for her in terms she can grasp.

"Bassanio has a thing going with Portia, you know what I mean? But he is also Antonio's best friend," says Rhonda. "He's in court to try to help his friend get justice."

"Portia has to do her job," I add, "which, in this case, means she can't show favoritism toward Antonio or Shylock. She has to represent the law fairly."

Bertie says, "Bassanio is . . . what do you call it in English? . . . Antonio's protector."

Lynn seems to liven up with that explanation, and says she wants to get onstage. But after a read-through, I can see she still doesn't understand Bassanio's motivation.

I hear my voice, shrill and tight, order women around. Bertie stops and stares at me. Dolly glowers. "Look, Lynn," I say harshly, and then force myself to soften. "Imagine you want to use your relationship with Rhonda to get help for a friend. No, make it a friend in trouble with the law, someone who needs you," I add. "What would you do? How would you move? Remember, no one up there can know about your relationship with Rhonda or else they'd declare the trial unfair." It is a dare, and Lynn jumps onstage.

Rhonda, as Portia, stands in front of the old table that we dragged stage center. Claire stands at her podium, and Rose as Shylock sits at the table, head in hands. All the women have scripts, but I've given them permission to continue to add words when they feel they need them.

"Curtain," Kit says.

Rhonda looks at Dolly. Antonio and his cronies are all seated in chairs to Shylock's left. Rhonda crosses, approaching Lynn and reads, "Isn't he able to pay the money?"

Lynn stands up, placing one hand on Dolly's shoulder, and as if she is vouching for her friend, declares, "Of course he can pay the money! I brought twice the original loan. If that's not enough, I will pay ten times that, or sacrifice my own flesh and blood."

At this point Lynn literally grabs Rhonda's wrist and pulls her downstage, improvising, "Come on, twist the law a little. Let's break this Jew's will."

"I cannot do that," Rhonda says firmly, intimately, and close into Lynn's face, meaning that Portia cannot break the law, even if she agrees with Bassanio.

It is a surprising moment, and Kit and I are glued to the action as though the two actors are frozen in time. Rhonda is dealing not only with the original text, in which Portia, disguised as a man, struggles with her personal values and feelings toward her secret lover, Bassanio, but also with her own allegiance to her girlfriend, Lynn. We watch the resolution as Portia pushes Bassanio away and moves back upstage into the legal problem she must solve. Kit and I look at each other. Because of Rhonda and Lynn's relationship offstage, the texture of the scene deepens onstage.

That night we make Lynn promise to stay out of trouble on the compound, not fight in her unit, and memorize all her lines.

. . .

We are rehearsing the play's final few moments. Portia has stopped Shylock from taking his pound of flesh, proving that it is against the law. She's also uncovered Antonio's legal right to get revenge. Antonio, bloodlessly, has ordered Shylock to convert and give his inheritance to his renegade daughter and Christian son-in-law. Rose, as Shylock, sits motionless onstage, rumpled, her hands in her lap. Judge Claire has managed to cough and wipe her glasses, and as if those distractions aren't enough to pull all the attention away from Shylock, now she drags a chair across the stage, wood scraping against wood.

"Claire," I say abruptly, "for God's sake, don't sit down when Shylock is falling apart like that. You're stealing his thunder."

Almost like a chain reaction, Bertie throws down the scroll we've been using as Antonio's "bond," the contract, and curses at Claire under her breath. Claire turns and yells back, daring Bertie to say whatever she has to say aloud. Bertie eagerly steps into Claire's space, thrusting the word "cunt" at her. They edge toward each other, screaming obscenities, a chicken fight, each one continually upping the ante while the rest of us watch, speechless. Before I know it I have placed myself between the two of them, saying, "Knock it off, both of you." Suddenly Claire bolts, crying, quitting, out the gym door. I run behind, trying to stop her, both of us with arms flailing, as we head down the hall. A guard intercepts Claire and orders me to go back to the gym.

The women are in an uproar. Bertie storms back and forth across the stage, swearing, "That bitch is going to ruin everything for us." I say something about solving this problem with reason, that we can work it out, but Bertie tosses her head at me, continues her pacing, and blocks her ears.

Dolly blurts at Bertie, "Cool your jets. No way am I going to get a D for Claire's personality problem."

Then everyone quiets down for a while, although tension still seems to pour out of the walls. Rhonda and Lynn walk away from the group and sit on the stage rim, their feet hanging over the STAGE OFF LIMITS sign, cracking jokes. Rose too isolates herself and sits at Shylock's table, thumbing through a script, occasionally mumbling obscenities. I walk in a circle on the gym floor and try to figure out what to do.

The officer who intercepted Claire appears at the door.

"Oh, shit," Kit says under her breath. "It's Marzetti."

"The captain wants to see you right away," Marzetti announces in my direction. I can feel my heart racing. It is as if I'm being sent to the principal's office.

"Did you hear me?" he says again. He's a stocky little guy with a punched-in-looking face and thick black eyebrows, someone I dislike immediately. This time I answer yes, in a voice that sounds unfamiliar and small. I fear the worst. Kicked out for mishandling the women.

Bernice comes into the gym, her walkie-talkie blaring. "I'll stay here until you get back, or whatever," and then the gym door slams shut as Marzetti and I walk down a hall noisy with jarring voices and the scuttle of feet. I turn right. Claire is sullenly leaning against the wall at the end of the hallway and stares out a window, refusing to look at me. The captain's office is directly in front of her, and Marzetti parks himself alongside Claire.

The captain on duty that evening comes up to the half door when he sees me. It is Johnson, the captain who caught the women in costumes parading around the hall. He looks exhausted, his face almost ashen, and he smells of aftershave.

"Jean, is it?" I nod. I am almost holding my breath. I catch a glimpse of a few other officers behind him. They are eating dinner, pizza and chips. "Officer Marzetti tells me there's been some disruption in your area. Is that true?" I nod again. "This isn't the first time, is it?"

"No, sir."

"Whenever there's a problem in the institution, you must get an officer at once. Didn't you learn that at training?"

"I guess I thought I could handle it myself."

"Don't make this mistake again. Civilians have no business solving these kinds of conflicts. Get an officer immediately. Third time's the charm, Jean." As the captain pulls out a folder and pen, I think, he's right. I shouldn't have put myself in between two women screaming at each other in prison. But my instincts told me we could all work this out together if given a chance.

The captain is writing as he talks. "We're isolating Claire, sending her back to her cottage until further action can be taken."

"Does that mean she'll miss the play? It's in two weeks."

He looks up and catches me straight on, his mouth curling at me as though I am ridiculous. "I advise you to tell Bertie to calm down or she'll be sent down as well."

"But the play's in two weeks. What about rehearsals?"

"This is a prison, not a drama school." From the side Marzetti muffles a laugh.

I stand looking at Johnson, knowing that I can't say anything to change his mind, but sure that if Claire doesn't come back, she'll lose face with the women, and what's more, we'll have no play.

Johnson doesn't look up. "That's it, Trounstine. The case is closed."

. . .

"Jean, if I didn't think what you were doing was good for the women, you never would have lasted this long." Ron is standing behind his desk, newspapers spread out in front of him. He gapes at me like an open wound. I sit submissively in a straight-backed chair, listening. It's late afternoon, two days after the "Claire incident," and I've come to see Ron on my own.

"Have I not been a constant supporter?" He turns and pulls down the window shade behind him and then, turns back to face me.

"Yes, Ron."

"Have I not given you chance after chance?"

"Yes, you have."

"The business with Rose, the costume fiasco. Those were minor infractions." His face is as flushed as I've seen it. "This time you've really taken the cake."

"Ron, you're right, I—"

"*Quiet!*" he yells. Then, as if to calm himself, he places both hands firmly on the desk and balances himself, lowering his voice, "Look. You have to cooperate with us. You can't pull stunts like this—placing yourself in between two women in a fight. I gave you the *Globe* article, Jean, and you know how much I despise, *I despise* media. Take the breakfast program. We decide to do up posters, trying to get the girls to eat healthy. Next thing you know they're creaming us for coddling inmates with breakfast buffets. But in spite of that, I let the girls be interviewed, didn't I, Jean?"

"Yes, Ron, you did. And it'll make the prison look good, I know it will. And it means a lot to the class."

"You can't try to get close to these women. I told you that!" The window shade snaps spontaneously and spins back up into a tight little roll. "Damn shade!" Ron pivots around and forces it down, fiddling with the tension. I look at scuff marks on the floor and think about a colleague of mine, recently ousted for interviewing her students and publishing information about them. Sometimes it seems like a crap-shoot, which misstep causes the final blow. I remember what Bernice said early on, "When push comes to shove, art isn't welcome in prison."

I look up at Ron. He is busy with the shade, having managed to get it to stay down but not able to get it to go up without winding it by hand.

I clear my throat. "Ron . . ." He ignores me. "Is there any possibility of getting Claire back for rehearsals?"

Ron pivots around and looks at me, eyes riveted on mine. "You just don't get it, do you? Security always takes precedence over program-ming. Claire will be back when Security says she'll be back. And if she has to miss the play, you'll find someone else." He sits now, his eyes narrowing into a warning. "And if Claire is back, Jean, I do not want you to try anything funny. No encounter-group crap. No jour-nals. Just class. You get my drift?"

I nod. "Ron, why don't you come to a rehearsal, just to see what we're doing?"

"Jean, I hear about you from the officers. I hear about you from Bernice. I don't need any more headaches." By now Ron sounds weary and is rummaging through papers on his desk. "Here, look at this." He thrusts a newspaper article into my hand. "I admit it's not just you." There in bold black letters is a headline about a social service agency contracted for programs at Framingham, followed by a huge spread with recently released damning facts about health care at the prison. "The agency did not clear this article with anyone, and as of two P.M. yesterday they're not allowed back. As I said, you're doing good work here, but ultimately I have the last word. Don't disappoint me again."

. . .

I stand staring at the empty stage, alone in the gym. We've just had our dress rehearsal and it's what Kit calls, "the witching hour" in prison, the time when everyone's locked for the night and thoughts of home fly through the air. I'm still a little charged up from the rehearsal. After the chaos of the past few weeks—a week without Claire and rehearsals influenced by visits, court worries, and family issues—tonight was a blessing. The women were all here.

The door to the gym pops open, and an embarrassed voice says, "Excuse me. I'm looking for Bernice." I direct the two women who are new AA volunteers down the hall to Bernice's office. As the gym door closes, I hear one say to the other, "That's the play lady."

I move a few chairs back into place, pleased that Bernice managed to find more than 150 seats, including the blue mats on the floor in front, and I drift back into the events of the evening.

"We've got a show. I'm sure of it," I announced to the cast. I did worry during the early part of the evening, when they all broke character and rehearsal almost fell apart. "For God's sake, pull yourselves together!" I yelled. Dolly still doesn't know her lines and is using cue cards in the middle of the scene. Bertie has a habit of laughing out loud whenever she forgets something, and tonight she forgot half of her blocking. Although Claire hasn't offended anyone since her blowup, she keeps whining and seems on edge. But still, I think, walking toward the empty stage, they're ready. "Get a good night's sleep for tomorrow. It'll be a long day," I told them as they all left on the Downward, giddy as kids on Christmas Eve.

It is a sweltering June night, and there are still sounds of steam from overhead pipes. I am dripping with sweat and worried that the

199

weather will be worse tomorrow. I take in the freshly painted back wall of the stage. Two inmates, who heard about *Merchant* from Rhonda, volunteered to paint our backdrop. These prisoners, part of an art group set up by a local mission society, have turned the backstage brick wall into a courtroom, with New York's skyline peering through a window. In one corner is a painted sign, complete with a scales of justice and the words: THE LAW . . . READ THE FINE PRINT. Bernice is thrilled because the new wall spruces up the gym.

I pick up a pen someone left behind, wondering if this belongs with the props, ones that are now stored in the beauty parlor, things I couldn't bring into the prison—a tinfoil knife for Shylock, a cardboard gavel for Claire, and scales for Rhonda to weigh the flesh.

I think how weeks ago we spent an hour deciding what everyone would wear. "We have to look good," Dolly asserted, "otherwise the audience won't pay attention." I tossed and turned over what to do, realizing after the hall parade that costumes could literally stop the show. But since we'd set the play in the 1920s, the magic of disguise seemed necessary. Permission came to rent costumes. Bertie took measurements, putting them on three-by-five cards, and I made several trips downtown to the Boston Costume Company. "What do you mean, they're putting on a play in prison?" the young man behind the counter said. "Don't they just stay in their cells?" With each trip I told him more about Framingham, apologizing profusely when the suit for Bassanio had to be altered after Lynn took over the part.

Rhonda wanted a subdued flapper outfit with dark pumps and a cloche hat. Dolly, Bertie, and eventually Lynn jumped at the prospect of "pimp" suits. Bertie suggested a man's hat for each, with a colorful hatband matching pocket hankies in bright red, blue, or yellow. For Shylock I borrowed a prayer shawl and black yarmulke from a local synagogue. In Claire's absence we were relieved that the judge's robe was big enough and small enough to fit just about anybody.

The costumes are now neatly stored in plastic on a rack, behind closed doors, with the props. Although no one searched the costumes particularly thoroughly tonight—in later years the process could take up to two hours—I've heeded Ron's wishes. "Keep a chart so nothing is 'lost,' if you know what I mean."

Bernice pokes her head into the room. "I'm locking up, Jean. You ready for tomorrow?" I walk across the room as she slips a key in the switch by the door. A *clank* sounds as the key turns off lights.

"I don't know. I never know. Thanks for storing the costumes, and for everything else." Bernice has sent notes, asking that the captain on duty avoid announcements over the PA system in the middle of the show. She's arranged for earlier meds for the cast, and coordinated show time with the Upward. She has finagled first dining privileges so the actresses can have extra time to get into makeup and costume, and received approval for us to remain late in the institution and clean up after the show.

"Glad I'm not working tomorrow. Too much trouble," Bernice says, as we walk down the hall. "Darlene will take pictures for you."

"That's great."

"A lot of problems putting on a play behind bars. I don't know why you do it." She opens the iron door.

I shrug my shoulders, hesitant to explain. Bernice seldom has the luxury at work to focus on inmates' talent. " 'Night." I walk through the glass doors and metal detector, three buzzers separating the prison's interior from the world. Kojack and Connors are playing cards. I wave at them and wonder what they would think of prisoners performing a trial scene. There is always tension when Shylock wields his knife in that scene, but the tension takes on new meaning when one criminal is about to exact a pound of flesh from another.

. . .

On the evening of the production, the inmates gather onstage to help one another put on makeup and get into costumes. With the heat so high and tempers so short, I've borrowed two huge fans to circulate the air. Dolly fans herself with her script. Claire asks Bertie to pin up her hair, acting as though their fight never happened, and Bertie says sure, in a minute. Now Bertie paces the stage, repeating parts of the play aloud. Rose has made a special scroll for her contract and tied a blue ribbon around it. It sits next to her makeup mirror, the plastic kind—no glass in prison—and she's staring into the mirror, reveling in her transformation with wig, beard, and Jewish prayer shawl. "I look like one of those guys from Brooklyn, what do you call them?"

"Hasidim." I stand on tiptoes adjusting Lynn's pimp hat.

Rose pulls her shawl around her shoulders and then strokes her long gray beard. "I wish my kid could see this."

Lynn pushes away the blush I aim at her cheeks. "It's too much of a girl thing."

Rhonda, her hair in curlers, sits peering into a mirror, dressed in a robe she brought up from the cottage. "Pass me the cold cream," she says to Rose.

"You use that after the show," Rose replies.

"Can you help me with my tie?" Dolly says, turning to Bertie. Dolly sits at the long table littered with makeup. Her mirror has a yellow border and is propped up on a Kleenex box. Bertie comes over to her.

"I like your moustache." Bertie tucks the white tie neatly under Dolly's collar. Dolly wiggles her nose. The moustache, a fake black one attached with spirit gum, scrunches up with her face.

"You look like Jackie Gleason," Kit says, clipboard in hand. Heads turn to see.

"Oh, my God," Claire says. "You do."

"Watch out," Dolly says jokingly, "or I'll give you eyebrows." She waves her black pencil in the air and then carefully pencils dark brows over her own. She places the cue cards in her pants pocket. "We might not look nervous, Jean, but we are."

After the women are ready, we clear the stage. While the cast does a prolonged relaxation exercise, Kit runs around setting up props and I help her with the stage. We leave the table in the center, place the podium down right, and arrange three chairs for Antonio and his cohorts stage left. Kit closes the curtain. I tell Dolly, Bertie, and Lynn to go into the beauty parlor and wait for Kit to give them a warning. They will enter the gym after the audience is seated in our "court-room." Rose also takes her place outside the gym to come in through the crowd, and Rhonda and Claire hide in the wings, ready to enter from backstage. I wait to greet the audience in a room full of empty chairs.

That night the security is especially heavy. Three officers patrol the auditorium. One stations himself at the doorway; another, at the side entrance, with Darlene and her walkie-talkie; a third stands at the rear of the room. Ron sends word he'll arrive at the last minute, escorting the invited guests, including representatives of the college and the Foundation for the Humanities. "Upward for the play is now in prog-ress," reverberates over the loudspeaker. It has never sounded so loud.

As women pile noisily into the gym, I start to worry. I watch in-mates run to sit up front. What on earth was I thinking, inviting ten guests from the outside to join 150 inmates from the prison to watch this play? We are stacking the deck against Shylock throughout, en-couraging the audience to oppose him, and then hoping for the turnaround that Shakespeare's script promises. What if the audience disappoints us? What if a fight breaks out?

The officers are roaming around the gym, forbidding prisoners to go past the front row of mats, instructing them to sit down, telling them not to rearrange chairs. More and more women keep pouring into the space, and noise mounts as fans whir and women call to one another across the room. Ron files in with the guests, placing them close to the front, and then, taking his place in the back of the room, arms crossed, he leans against the wall. When he motions to me, I send Kit to tell the actresses that we are about to begin.

Turning off lights in a gym full of prisoners is not permitted, so in order to signal that the play is beginning, I walk up the small staircase we've placed at the front of the stage. "Good evening," I say loudly, and the audience, as if they are at an AA meeting, yells back, "Good evening!" Looking out into the room, I can see faces upturned, hopeful, smiling from the floor seats, and women way in the back crowded onto a ladder perched against the rear wall. The officers have opened the side door for air, and four or five women sit in the doorway, arms around knees.

"This is the start of a new drama program at Framingham Women's Prison, and the women you will see tonight have worked on this project for six months." The audience claps and yells. We might be at a ball game or a high school graduation. I can hear the actresses onstage behind me whispering excitedly, and I raise my hand to quiet the cheering audience. Then I introduce the play the way Shakespeare might have, by telling the story, and I take my place in the audience.

Women go wild, whistling and stomping their feet, when Dolly, Bertie, and Lynn enter in their gangster suits, complete with white ties and dark shirts, hats tilted on heads. Dolly as Antonio swaggers, followed by his defenders, greeting the audience as friends, and improvising hellos as though he owns the prison. The three sit in the "courtroom" amid whoops, howling. As Shylock enters for his monologue, I hold on to my script like a lifeline: "They knew, none so well as they . . . they knew of my daughter's flight. . . . Running off with a Christian . . . My own flesh and blood to rebel!" Heads turn to see Shylock slinking in from the door to the gym, lamenting the loss of his daughter. Rose points her scroll into the air and then at the audience. Good, I think, watching her hunched form slither down the center aisle, accusing onlookers with her eyes. A woman coughs; others shift in their seats, perhaps not used to this character, so rigid, so foreign. Rose is not deterred. "And I have made another bad match, loaning money to Antonio, / a bankrupt prodigal who treats me like a beggar in the marketplace."

A few snicker, perhaps at the prayer shawl and earlocks, obviously preferring the rowdiness of Antonio and his friends to the strangeness of an immigrant Jew. For a moment I feel unsafe. It is possible that the audience might walk out with more prejudice against Shylock's ethnicity.

But Rose stands tall in the center of the gymnasium, walking up and down the aisle of seats, her eyes digging into the onlookers. "Revenge," she hisses, and whirls around, leaning over an audience member. "The villainy you teach me, I will execute, and it shall go hard." Rose bites out her words, filling the room with anger. "But I will better the instruction." She turns and exits, a crouched figure sweeping through the stage side door, her crippled hand clinging to the prayer shawl. I sit on the edge of my seat, watching the play unfold anew, sensing the danger of art.

Now Antonio and his pals strut to the stage for the next scene, and they've got the audience in their grip, tipping their hats and acting as if they've bought drinks for everyone. The audience erupts into laughter, and for a few moments the tension subsides. Onstage Judge Claire, clothed in her black robe, moves quickly to console the trio about Antonio's plight: he must pay Shylock with a pound of his flesh for forfeiting his bond. She seats the defendants. "I am sorry for you, because you have to answer to a hard enemy, an inhuman wretch, incapable of pity or the least drop of mercy!"

There's a hush as the judge calls "the Jew" into the courtroom and Shylock storms in from the wings, ready to get his justice, ignoring the fact that Bassanio offers money to settle the case. Bertie almost laughs as she calls Shylock names like "despicable dog." But disguised as Gratiano in her suit and hat, she manages to come off as cruel, and stands, pointing angrily at Shylock, her words clipped and harsh, "Can no prayers pierce you?" Antonio tells his friends not to worry, and at this point Dolly takes her hat in her hand and pulls Bertie and Lynn close: "I am like a sheep ready for slaughter. You couldn't have a better job than to live and tell my story."

Judge Claire paces, saying she will dismiss this case unless a solution can be found. As Portia enters there's another round of applause from the audience, and a few whistles. They love Rhonda's confidence as she takes over, grabbing attention and throwing verbal retorts at Judge Claire's obvious sexual innuendos.

But then, as Portia turns her attention to the case and as Shylock continues to demand his penalty, there's a shift of mood in the room. All are silent as Shylock sits, hoisting his bond into the air, staking his claim for what the law allows. Portia leans over him, arguing for Antonio's life, trying to stop the inevitable. She pleads, her voice full of emotion: "The quality of mercy is not strained. . . . / It blesseth him that gives and him that receives. . . ."

Rhonda is amazing, preaching not only to Shylock but to the audience, who nod and *yes* her, caught up in the outpouring of her plea for mercy. She circles the stage, her voice rising and falling, and she ends by grabbing on to the back of a chair, close to Shylock: "I have said all this to try and persuade you to drop this case. . . . You are asking for this man's life!"

But, in spite of Portia's impassioned speech, Shylock waves her away with his fist. Antonio's and his friends' outcries are futile. They cannot convince Shylock to change his mind. Even the judge has no effect.

Shylock is immovable: "My religion will take care of my sins. Here I demand justice, the penalty for forfeiting the contract." Rose begins sharpening her knife. She brandishes the blade, casting it above her head like a wand, and then improvises a slitting of the throat. There are titters from the courtroom.

Unable to persuade Shylock to take the money and tear up his contract, Portia moves to the podium to render her decision. She picks up Claire's gavel. "A pound of this merchant's flesh is yours. The court awards it and the law allows it." Rhonda pounds the gavel. I marvel at her steady rhythm: pounding, words, pounding. It is the heartbeat of the courtroom, the judgment the inmates fear. Rhonda wields it like a hammer.

Heads turn to see Shylock slowly rise from his chair: "Most righteous lawyer." Still pounding, Rhonda pronounces, "Then you must cut this flesh from off his chest. The court awards it and the law allows it."

The gavel is insistent, like a drum. "Most learned judge." Rose takes her knife and slowly walks toward Antonio, who by this time is flanked by his friends, hat in his hand, jacket over a chair. He holds his other hand close to his chest, just over his heart. Rose stands only a foot away, one arm in the air, pulled back. She's a rubber band about to spring.

"Come, prepare," Shylock says ominously and lunges at Dolly, dagger high above their heads.

Rhonda grabs Rose's wrist, yelling, "Wait a minute!" and the audience gasps and sputters as Portia dramatically stops the moment. She quickly picks up the lawbook, pointing at a page, thrusting it in front of Shylock. She has found the loophole in the law, and Shylock's knife descends, as does his hope of taking Antonio's life. The audience now has every reason to feel triumphant for Antonio and his cronies, to hate Shylock even more than before, and to curse him for distortion of justice.

But here is where the story changes. Not only does Shylock not get his bond, as Portia tells him, pacing the stage with her book of law, but he, an alien, must be punished for trying to take Antonio's life. "I will pardon your life before you even ask," says Judge Claire in her most noble voice. And then she adds, "As for your wealth, it is Antonio's and the state's." She hovers over Shylock in her robe.

"What mercy can you render to him, Antonio?" asks Portia.

Antonio, buttoning up his shirt, now swivels full force to face a beleaguered Shylock. Dolly, without using her cue cards, orders Shylock to turn over half his estate to her and to give half his money to his Christian son-in-law. Pointing her finger toward heaven, she threatens and bargains for his life: "For this reprieve, you must convert your religion to Christianity." Gratiano leaps forward and spits on Shylock just as Claire steps in and takes away Shylock's skullcap, the yarmulke, symbol of his religion.

"That's cold," cries out one woman in the audience.

"You can't take away a man's faith," calls out another.

"Ain't nothing wrong with being a Jew if that's what you are," proclaims a third. And I sink into my chair, a sigh of relief, grateful they have understood: There are some things you cannot do even in the name of justice.

Before the play ends Shylock, alone and embattled, retrieves his skullcap from the floor and, looking up, from his chair, wonders aloud if he can be excused. Rose plays this moment for all it is worth, her long walk across the stage, a counterpoint to the backslaps and antics in the courtroom of celebrants. I watch her take one last look at the merriment onstage before she exits, broken. As Kit pulls the curtain closed, all the audience hears is Shylock's lonesome howl.

It is the end, and the audience rises in a wave from mats and chairs. There are screams and yells, whistles and clapping. The cast members bow and bow, trying to stay in a straight line on the stage in front of the curtain. Dolly calls me up too, and presents me with a plant and a card, and the actors clap—for me, for the play, for themselves. "We did it!" Dolly yells.

The actresses break from the line and hug one another. Audience members wander up and hug their friends in the cast. Someone weeps on Rose's shoulder. The guests shake hands with the performers and chat with each other. Even Ron and the officers congratulate the actors. But what strikes me most, standing onstage surrounded by the cast, is the swarm of women cheering for fellow prisoners, a generosity I hadn't anticipated. It is as if the onlookers too have imbibed Shakespeare with the cast, and they all are drinking up the success. They shine because their friends shine.

As I look around the room, I realize the performers were right. They knew their community. In prison every line in a script must be clear to an audience in which many speak Spanish as a primary language, many believe that Shakespeare is "white man's theatre," and many have never seen a play. While Kit gathers up the props, Dolly and Bertie are animatedly bragging to Bernice. I am proud of them all. They have impressed their friends, surprised the officers, and pleased Ron. But, more important, they have found that classic texts belong to everyone, and that what they consider most difficult can be within reach.

...

After the gym empties out, we hold our "cast party." We all sit around on the stage, amid props and set, eating potato chips and drinking Cokes. Suddenly Rose says, "Do you think a judge in the real world would have taken off Shylock's yarmulke?" A heated discussion follows, in which Rose and Claire argue about the correctness of the choice. Rose is sure judges "back then" wouldn't touch a plaintiff, but Claire disagrees, reminding her that many stranger things probably went on in courtrooms.

By now Dolly's wiped off most of her eyebrows and is busy pruning leaves off the plant she has engineered into the prison for me. "You know, Jean, I thought about Mamie tonight."

"Did you?"

"It was when Rose was coming at me with the knife. I felt like Mamie was watching, almost looking out for us, helping us really. It was a trip." She hands me the moustache and looks solemnly at me.

Bertie, who's kept on all of her makeup, claiming it makes her feel like she's someone special, moves indecisively from potato to corn chip. "In my country you know we believe in spirits."

Rose says, "I have to. Mandatory sentencing." In her crippled hand she holds the yarmulke. She gives it to me. "Wish I didn't have to give back the beard." She's snapped the thin black string that held the whiskers to her face and now the beard sits on the table next to her, a gray lump. She passes it to me, too.

Rhonda has gathered up at least twenty programs to send home, and is taking a swig of Coke. She says, "Old souls. That's what we are. I think Claire was right about that moment with the yarmulke. Some judges think they can take away anything, even religion."

"Can you believe this?" Rose smiles. "A real party in prison. Is this what it's like out there after a play?"

"Probably not drug-free," Kit says. And I laugh, head back and heartily. Rose is right. Here we are, sitting together as I would with any cast from any play in any context. When a lone figure in blue appears at the door to the gym, our theatre, it takes me by surprise.

"Last Movement down," he calls out, stopping me in midgulp of my Diet Coke. We all look at one another.

"I think we get to stay until nine," I say, trying not to overreact. I had imagined that on this day we were free of rules, that we could, like kids, stay out till all hours.

"Nope, wrap it up. The ladies have got to get a move on." He stands there, at the door, waiting for us. I look around the room, doing my best to keep from sinking. It would only be fifteen more minutes, but right now that seems like hours. Rhonda rises first, picking up her programs, and says something about cops and good timing. Kit's up next, but she's trying not to grumble, which spurs the rest of us to our feet.

We hurriedly tidy up the stage, throwing out our cans and empty bags of chips, moving chairs and tables. The women help carry costumes, bags of makeup, and props to the big iron door near the gateway. The officer unlocks the door, and for a moment no one moves.

"This is where we say good-bye," I say.

Rose puts down the suitcase filled with shoes, her beard, and Claire's wig. I look at her, wanting to say something wonderful, something important that might protect her the way Mamie had protected Dolly. But she beats me to it:

"We were stars."

EXITS

As many farewells as be stars in heaven . . .
TROILUS AND CRESSIDA, IV.iv.44

Mamie

On Graduation Day, late June 1988, Mamie's presence is again among us. I'm in the gym, along with at least one hundred inmates and most of the Education staff, straining to hear voices that crackle from an ancient sound system, straining to look past heads in front of me, past rows and rows of women, to ten officials sitting in the front of the room, at the foot of the stage.

With the play over, I'm pleased to be a spectator. Although we're crammed into the gym on a warm afternoon, we're all here to recognize those who've earned their GED or taken college classes, and those who have completed skill-based courses such as manicuring or gardening. In later years both Dolly and Bertie will be awarded associate's degrees at ceremonies just like this, but without the college caps and gowns. Bertie will wave to her friends sitting in the audience as if she's a movie star. Dolly will get choked up on her valedictory

212

speech. Women will rush up to get cake after the ceremony, edging each other out in line and gulping down ginger ale as if there's no tomorrow. Still later a new principal will make the mistake of putting decorative green balloons on the gym wall. They'll get taken down by Security because inmates can put drugs inside and slip them into their vaginas.

Now the prisoners are complaining to one another about how long this ceremony is taking. Hushed whispers and outright nasty cracks cause officers to patrol the room. They occasionally lean over an inmate with a warning or usher someone out. Already we've had a senator rush in for her requisite five minutes and rush out to a legislative meeting, and we've sat through the superintendent, the deputy, and the principal—all polite speeches about what Framingham is doing for prisoners. The women who've heard it all before are shifting in their seats, impatient, hot, ready for cake. Some are there to collect certificates, wanting their names in calligraphy to post over their cots; others come to cheer for their friends or land a white carnation from one of the graduates; but most are restless for the event to be over.

One of the teachers gets up from the first two rows, where most full-time staff sit, and announces, "The class of 1988." There's music, Elgar's "Pomp and Circumstance" march, a scratchy rendition that barely fills the gym played on Bernice's boom box, and this year's high school graduates march in, huge smiles on their faces, all in white robes. They teeter in high heels; some are wearing nylons. The administrators in straight-backed chairs clap politely at each name while the inmate audience hoots and hollers. The students are praised by their teachers, and they stand at attention while voices drone on with award after award, recognition for the five or ten or fifteen students who completed each class.

When the gardening teacher gets up to speak, a noticeable change comes over the room. Those who look as if they've been falling asleep sit up. Others lean forward. Some heads tilt to the side, curious, ready. Everyone knows that Mamie was the gardener who most devoted herself to her work. Everyone's thinking of Mamie.

The teacher explains what it means to recognize someone after their death, how their good deeds, the work they've done, and the mark they've left live on "posthumously." The teacher is petite, a mass of curly hair framing her face, and she's in khaki pants and a white shirt with the sleeves rolled up. She takes off her glasses and wipes them, visibly moved as she talks. She asks for a moment of reverence for Mamie. I can see Dolly and Kit at the side of the room, heads bowed. Bertie's head appears a few rows up, poking out from behind a tall woman. She turns around and winks at me. I smile back as the teacher goes on, holding up the certificate that honors Mamie, blessing her name.

At the end of the event, most women swarm to the food table, but Dolly comes up to me. She holds up a card she's just received from her student pen pal, Debra. "She asked me to write her a college recommendation," Dolly says.

"That's a real vote of confidence."

Dolly beams. "Wellesley." Then her face drops, all her age returning, eyes somber. "It's really lonely to go through stuff like this in prison. I've gotta go back to my cottage." I nod, patting her on the shoulder. "I gotta have a cigarette," she adds.

"I thought you stopped smoking."

"I did. Months ago. You know how that goes." Dolly pulls a Camel from her pack of cigarettes and palms it. "Listen, Jean, after what we went through this year, Mamie's death and all, next year we need a comedy."

Before I can do more than say, "Yes, absolutely, a comedy," an officer appears. "Pronto, Ms. H," he says to Dolly. I leave before the women empty the gym.

Rose

Rose is noticeably absent the summer of 1988. Although Education closes down after graduation, Ron's given me permission to hold a special afterplay meeting. So, in a sweltering July, I'm once again in Program Room 2, setting up the VCR. The room feels like it's ninety degrees. I drop to my knees in front of the TV, concentrating on rewinding the videotape of *Merchant* filmed during dress rehearsal and prescreened by Ron to make sure there's no one on camera except for the cast. Women troop into the room in shorts and T-shirts, fanning themselves with rolled-up pieces of paper, brimming with after-production good cheer.

They especially brighten when they see the plastic pink roses I've brought for them to take to their cottages, gifts that weren't authorized the night of the show. "We tried to get these flowers through Control," Bertie says, "but Johnson was on a rampage." She plants her feet on the floor and crosses her arms, mimicking the captain's obstinate stance: "No permission slips." Her voice is an octave lower than usual. "I'll be damned if I'll take the rap for letting you ladies have flowers in your units, even if they are plastic." Turning her head sideways and throwing us a sarcastic "Uh-huh," Bertie drops into a chair. Then she takes one of the pink roses stamped APPROVED, places it, like a bookmark, in her script, and scoots her metal chair toward the TV.

As others settle in to watch themselves on camera, Dolly's telling Kit, "We were a hit. I heard it all week on the compound. I couldn't believe how much they loved it. You shoulda been in it."

"Next one," Kit says, kicking back in a stray orange plastic chair.

"I'll be in the next one. But let's face it, I ran the show." She cups her hands behind her head, elbows spreading out to her sides.

"You're a piece of work," says Lynn. "Hey, Jean, why did'nja bring snacks?"

I'm trying to get the sound turned up on the TV, which is not easy since the knob is broken and I have to fiddle with what looks like a twisted paper clip someone has stuck in the knob hole. "I'm ignoring you, Lynn."

"By the way," Dolly says to me, "Did you hear about the trouble Johnson gave me when I tried to go to dinner with my moustache on? He said no 'disguises' are allowed in Framingham. Did he really think I'd try to escape in drag?"

"At least not on the night of the production," Rhonda says.

The women continue to joke with Dolly and reminisce about moments from the past few weeks. I wonder if Rose is in the infirmary with pneumonia or, worse, sent to Shattuck for her HIV, but with everyone in a good mood, I'm hesitant to bring up Rose's whereabouts. Instead I focus the women on filling out evaluation forms from the Humanities Foundation, promising them the video as a "reward." They groan a little at the chore but come around. Even Claire, with pen poised in hand, is cooperative. She teases, "Should I mention the fights or just stick with the good parts?"

"I'm ignoring you, too," I say, smiling.

When the video begins, they *ooh* and *aah* at the title and the music I've added, but as soon as Shylock enters, there's silence. Suddenly Antonio and his cohorts are on screen, and the women scream much the way the audience did during the performance. They point at the TV as each new character appears. Bertie moves her chair closer. Dolly keeps shaking her head in disbelief, mentioning times when she didn't use cue cards. Rhonda can't take her eyes off the video. "Damn, we're good," she says, and I can tell by the wry smile spreading over her face that she is as surprised as she is pleased. They all get caught up in the story, making me realize, once again, why Shakespeare's tales have lasted through time.

As names roll up on screen to music at the end of the show, the women read them aloud. Lynn insists we replay the ending credits so she can see her name again.

"Where is Rose?" I finally ask the room, a shot of fear in my voice.

"It's good news," Bertie responds quickly, grabbing my arm. "She wrapped up her sentence."

Rose's card arrives a month after that class, addressed to "The Merchant of Drama": "My daughter is a hell of a baseball player but she can't act her way out of a paper bag. She brags about me. I'm looking to enroll in an acting class. Say hello to everyone and tell them I'm well. I almost miss prison."

I write her back and send her an evaluation form, and after that exchange, we lose touch. Five years later, I hear that Rose lived in a halfway house for several years and helped others with HIV until she came down with full-blown AIDS. In my imagination she spent her last days in hospice care, loved and nurtured by health care workers and, unlike Mamie, died with her family around her. It is not her prostitution charges, the cocaine addiction, or hooking that I remember but the image of her in a gray beard silencing the audience with the slow, deliberate turn of her head.

Rhonda

By the fall of 1988, when I return to Framingham for a new semester, Rhonda's been transferred to a federal prison to complete her time. With Lynn gone to pre-release, I can't get news of Rhonda.

"She's got to be writing some of the girls," Bertie says one afternoon when I bring up Rhonda at the end of a late fall literature class. There's a new principal at the prison, and she's instituted afternoon college classes so I'm teaching upstairs now, in a room just past the entrance to Education. I'm near the flag-making room, an old sweatshop, better known as "Industries," the only part of the prison that makes money, complete with a half dozen creaky sewing machines and white walls tinged with soot. Dolly and Kit, the other old-timers, have already left on the Downward. I sit atop a real teacher's desk, my legs hanging over the side.

Bertie thumbs through her copy of the novel I've handed out today, *Black Like Me*, by John Howard Griffin. "I think Rhonda's the type to keep to herself. She won't stay in touch with anyone here for long."

"I'd like to write to her, Bertie, so if you get an address, let me know."

A few weeks later, I discover that letters are prohibited unless instructors have official business with students. "You're a teacher or a friend, but not both," the new principal says when I ask about writing Rhonda. And so, for a few years, we have no contact.

In the mid-1990s, a colleague tells me that she ran into Rhonda while teaching in a New Hampshire prison a year or so before. Rhonda was serving more time out of state, and I hope not on a new charge. When my friend learns that Rhonda was incarcerated at Framingham, she asks her if she ever took a class I taught. "Are you kidding?" Rhonda says. "I was Portia."

The next year I'm in my office at the college, where I've been teaching full-time since 1989, and the phone rings. "Portia here," a voice says. Rhonda talks nonstop, witty as ever. She says she's been out for a while and finally found me through the "prison grapevine."

"I hear you've been sending tapes of more recent plays to the ladies' families, so, hey, where's my *Merchant*?" She tells me that she's landed a job at a local health care office in Boston where she's the "head honcho" of some sort, dealing with paperwork and questions, and guess what, she wants to finish her degree. "Can you help me?" Sure, I say.

For the next few months, Rhonda and I keep in touch while she writes a paper about her adventures with *Merchant*. That paper gives her the experiential credit she needs to complete her course load, and within months of her first call, Rhonda earns her associate's degree. In her final paper she writes:

> For this group, working together, taking risks was harder than robbing a bank. To court ridicule and apply themselves to reading and writing was ten times more difficult than jumping out of a john's car going forty miles an hour. Assimilating the thought pattern of a playwright from the past was a miracle.
>
> How I fit into this scheme of social misfits is interesting at best and sad at worst. But my involvement in this play was a pivotal point for me as well. I was able to go back to my academic roots, enter the comfortable world of make-believe and shine. . . . Playing Portia, I *was* Portia. I could create the female lawyer, underdog advocate that I was forbidden to become in life because of my record and circumstances.

"I'm sending you a photo of me, Jean," she says, the last time I speak with her. "And, yes, I'm staying out." I hope so, I say to myself, and we talk of how Gloria came back on a violation from Lancaster and had to do more time behind the walls, how Samantha had to go to a drug rehab after she got out—the second time—and how the deck is stacked against those who don't get an education. Rhonda says, "I have a son now. I won't be back."

It sits on my desk, this picture: Rhonda at home in her own apartment, clothed in an elegant dashiki, smiling, radiant, full of hope, holding her son in her arms.

Kit

Kit tries her hand at acting before she goes to pre-release in 1991. But like everything else for Kit, in spite of her hey-no-problem attitude, it's not an easy venture.

First there's *Lysistrata*. In 1989 she decides to be both the stage manager and the understudy for our adapted version of Aristophanes' Greek classic. "We need backup, Jean," Kit says early on in rehearsals. "You never know who'll hit the deck." I agree. That spring, she's a pistol, contributing ideas for the production, right and left. She's the one who spurs on our conception of the show, insisting, "We're not doin' this play in togas. After all, we don't want to look like *Animal House*." She likes the idea of setting the play in 1918, a year when suffragettes struggled to get the vote, America's Great War paralleling Aristophanes' Greek crisis. And she's gung-ho on Aristophanes' premise that women can attain world peace by withholding sex from the soldiers. She tells me that she has no intention of learning anyone's lines, and bristles when Bernice says that inmates' handling of clipboards is now forbidden. However, she cooperates in other ways, moving props for rehearsals into the yard, and suggesting production details that make each of the characters come alive. For Dolly's Lysistrata, Kit comes up with two ideas: draping her with a banner proclaiming NO SEX and giving her a huge megaphone and a white billowy dress to symbolize her role as a suffragette, "the one who disbands armies." For Bertie's Kalonike, "the one who primps," Kit suggests that she use a nail file on stage. Her best idea is for our Myrhinne to be pregnant in the first scene and then, in the second scene, to come out with a baby on her back. For a few months things go well, and she stays behind the scenes.

When I come onto the compound one evening, four days before the show, the cast is waiting for me in the yard, our performance space for this production. Concerned looks spread from face to face. "Tell her," Bertie says to Kit, pacing from tree to cement steps. Dolly sits on the stone steps that lead up to the gym door, her head in her hands.

"I've figured it out, Jean." Kit is talking in a soothing manner, as if she is comforting a child. Sweat forms around her hairline and across her upper lip.

"Tell her," Bertie says again, this time louder and more insistently. Dolly stares at the ground, and Bertie braces herself against a tree, eyes aloft.

"What's wrong?" I search Kit's face for clues.

"I can learn all the lines," she continues.

"Damn." Bertie swings around.

"What are you talking about?" Looking at the women, I count five. Someone's missing. "Where's Myrhinne? *Where's our Myrhinne?*"

"She's in Max," Kit says flatly.

"Max?" I echo, hardly believing what I am hearing.

"She got into a fight with someone in her unit and was put in Max," Dolly says. "She'll be in for at least ten days, and then, after a hearing before the D Board, she might get more time in lockup, or she might be returned to population."

"I can play the part," Kit keeps on. She smiles, all gums. She directs her words at Dolly. "I'll get the baby backpack from the Parenting Room. No one will miss it."

"Couldn't I talk to Kojack? He works with the D Board now, doesn't he?" I say.

"No power," Bertie says, swatting a fly with her script.

"She's right. Working in the D office means dealing with disciplinary reports and such. That's it." Dolly says.

"The costume's a problem. I'm not a lot smaller, but enough. You know, in the hips." Kit has her script open and is marking lines with a contraband yellow highlighter.

"I can't get the costume adjusted four days before the show," I say.

"Maybe you could talk to Ron?" Dolly tries. "He'll help with the bigwigs."

"Doubtful."

"I think there's a doll that fits in the backpack. Used to be, when I took Parenting." Kit pauses and then whisks her yellow pen over a phrase. "Cute little black baby."

"Will you shut up?" Dolly says.

"Ma—"

"Ladies," I say quickly. "The last thing we need now is an argument. We'll make do with Kit." And, turning to her, "Learn the part."

The night of the production she shows up late and gives us all a scare. But by the time the play begins, the veterans have calmed her down. Kit can't keep a straight face when she makes her first entrance, laughing after every few sentences. The audience doesn't help, clapping and whistling, enjoying a pregnant Myrhinne. She tries keeping her head down, mumbling words, but then she's hardly audible. She does look the part—blush and lipstick bring out her color; her hair's up under a wide-brimmed hat, and she's wearing dowdy stockings rolled down below her knees and white pumps, not exactly elegant but in character. In the second scene, when she comes out with the baby in her backpack, as though she's had a child in spite of Lysistrata's prohibition against sex, the audience applauds her.

Later she follows Bertie, who sweeps through the audience in her taffeta dress and suffragette bonnet, and the audience points and hoots, enjoying the warm July night's entertainment. Behind the actresses, banners posted on the institution's brick wall proclaim war efforts. Some members of the audience whisper, staring at the "stage" from seats set up on the basketball court; others rest comfortably on the grass or lean against trees. No one seems bothered by the fact that Kit is carrying a script. Even Ron is caught up, clapping as the actresses sing for their finale, "There'll Be a Hot Time in the Old Town Tonight." The cast gives Kit a special round of applause at the end of the show for filling in at the last minute. Kit barely sticks around to receive any congratulations and shrugs off what most women agree is a special experience, making the video and talking to their family on camera. But at least she pulls through.

She says she wants to be in the next play, *Waiting for Lefty,* Clifford Odets's drama about a taxicab strike during the Great Depression. At first she comes to class, saying that studying the 1930s gives her a chance to talk about her grandmother, who stood in lines for relief, ate mostly potatoes, and stashed whatever money she did have in socks. Like Bertie who keeps repeating, "I can't believe this is really American history," she seems to enjoy the opportunity to learn. She wants to play the factory worker who becomes a cab driver after her boss tries to blackmail her, and decides to model her character on her grandmother. But she never shows up for rehearsals, and eventually we replace her. As a Puritan woman in our adaptation of *The Scarlet Letter,* she promises me she'll be better with attendance, and she is, but she is also vicious to the woman playing Hester Prynne, a prisoner serving time for sexual abuse. Kit relishes crying out lines like, "Whore! Tramp! You're polluting the town!" When I tell her those words aren't in the script, she says, "I'm improvising." She talks constantly about going to pre-release but watches inmate after inmate get placed before her. She stays through the production, spewing hate at the figure on the scaffold.

The last time I see Kit is at Lancaster, the pre-release she longed for. I'm there with a college class I teach in prison literature, getting a tour of the facility and listening to prisoners talk about their lives. Kit appears in the cafeteria where my students and I stop for a visit. She sits by herself at a table, surrounded by chatter and the noise of silverware clinking against plates. When she sees me, she smiles and waves me over. A plainclothes officer is engaging my students in the history of this particular building, so surreptitiously I edge toward her.

"Hi, Kit," I say. "Good to see you here. How are you?"

"I've got my teeth back." She opens her mouth and turns her head so I can get a look.

"Great. That's great. How's school?"

"Nah, I'm not doing that." A woman walks by her and says hello. "A lotta the girls are here, so that's good." She digs into her mashed potatoes and what looks like creamed corn and chicken. "But no Reenie."

"I'm sorry to hear that."

She spreads the corn around her plate. "Yeah, I was counting on that trailer program. I was sure I'd get an overnight with Reenie, but no such luck."

From across the room, the students start to move toward the door and I apologize to Kit for leaving so abruptly. "I wish you the world, Kit," I say. "For you and for your daughter." She looks up at me, a smile masking the tears in her eyes.

Years later I hear from Dolly that she's out, living in Chelsea, and that she and her kids are getting by as best they can.

Bertie

Bertie performs in four more plays before she leaves Framingham. When I tease her that she's going to lose her Jamaican accent if she keeps going this way, she says it would be better for getting a job in the free world.

She's both gorgeous and funny as Kalonike in *Lysistrata*, talking nonstop, shimmering onstage in her blue taffeta dress and flouncy hat. She steals the show when she throws open the doors of the gym and comes down the stone steps, sashaying across the grass from tree to tree. Twirling her blue parasol, she sings *Won't You Come Home, Bill Bailey*, to a cheering audience. She and a southern belle dressed in crimson who also misses her man, Bill, sing the song together, dueling with parasols.

Back in the gym the next year, at the dress rehearsal of *Waiting for Lefty*, Bertie dons a simple flowered cotton dress that hits her midcalf, and a hat with a veil that covers her eyes. "It's not a look I like, Jean," she says to me. But as soon as she takes her place onstage for the opening moment, she's in character. When Bertie comes downstage for a scene, she sits on a bench, head slightly turned, staring wistfully over her shoulder. While others carry on, Bertie just sits, absolutely still. We can read Bertie's face—the longing, the despair—and without a word, she makes us see that her character is not able to marry the man of her dreams. "Bertie," I say, "you are a natural."

Bertie is not much more than twenty-four when she stuns her peers, playing Pearl in our arena-style production of *The Scarlet Letter*. She slides gracefully through the audience in a bright red satin dress, a

Pearl grown up, transplanted out West in the 1850s, looking for the mother who abandoned her. Her skirt touching the floor, she enters as if she's made for the role, speaking clearly with a slight lilt to her voice. "I'm looking for my mother," Bertie says to those who sit in the circle surrounding Hester Prynne's scaffold, stage center—to those who include the real daughter of the woman playing Hester. Seating herself on the edge of the scaffold, Bertie takes a silver hairbrush from her traveling suitcase and brushes her hair. She unravels the story of Hester, found guilty of adultery, and reveals Pearl's feelings of loss. I wonder if Bertie thinks about her own mother as she speaks the lines:

> My mother was the perfect woman. Always working, always helping others, never taking anything for herself. Once the life had been drummed out of her, they began to think better of her. They came from miles around, almost as if what she made with her sinful hands was specially valuable and desirable . . . it was the fashion. . . . I never saw my mother fight back. I never heard her complain.

Bertie stays at Framingham another year. She is one of a handful of women, at the time, who earn their associate's degree, and by the time she graduates she has excelled in subjects she never thought she could handle, such as history and psychology. I see her through her college graduation and through *Rapshrew*.

In that play she not only swishes across the stage as Bianca, winning approval every time she teases her beaux, but she also comes up with ideas for our set. For a backdrop that gives us a feel of graffiti on an LA street, we roll out huge pieces of silver paper, and Bertie suggests the women paint their rapper names all over the drop, adding glitter and plastic ornaments. Bertie then makes black handprints on the silver, and all the women follow. "It takes two to make a thing go right," Bertie sings in the finale of that show, swaying with lover Lorenzo, her teal blue dress shining against the silver backdrop.

I never get to say good-bye to Bertie. Rumor has it that after she's out, she goes to New York, but no one is sure, and no one can tell me why. Eventually I hear from Rhonda that Bertie was deported to Jamaica. Before she went, she had another child. "It has to be healing," Rhonda says in the mid-1990s, talking to me on her office phone.

It has to be, I say to myself, in silence and out loud, still praying for Bertie.

Dolly

When Dolly plays the lead in *Lysistrata*, she is again a star on the compound. And when Dolly becomes the second woman in the history of Framingham to earn her associate's degree, she seems at her peak—there is nothing she cannot achieve. Dolly, who once wrote, "My biggest dream was to be a hairdresser," plans to complete her bachelor's at Lancaster Pre-Release, where she is sent to serve the remainder of her sentence. At least that is how it seems in 1989.

I go to visit Dolly six months into her stay. From the moment she walks down the rickety staircase at the women's housing unit, I can see through the natty tweed jacket and trim jeans that she's lost weight and feels good about herself. Lancaster Pre-Release, resembling a sprawling college campus, is without barbed wire, chain-link fences, locks, or uniformed officers, and surrounds prisoners with space and country air. The stretch of land looks more like farming fields than a minimum-security prison. Except for the run-down brick buildings, similar to the ones at Framingham, and the fact that guards know where prisoners are every second, it seems like a new world for Dolly.

"I can have money here," Dolly says as she ushers me into the visiting room, a smoky couch-filled space with soft-drink and candy machines. We both get sodas, and she seats herself on a checkered couch; I sit in an overstuffed chair near a wooden table with a game board, puzzle pieces strewn on top. She tells me how she doesn't have a prison job yet but is hoping to be in the outreach program, in which she'll travel to high schools and talk to teenagers about crime and punishment. "I hear it opens up kids' eyes to what really goes on here," she says, sinking back into the couch. "But you know, sometimes that's discouraging too, all those stereotypes kids have of criminals."

"I know," I say. "Maybe you should do something related to counseling? You'd be good at that."

"The world doesn't want people like me talking to kids." Dolly is running her fingers through her newly cropped hair. "And Jee-sus, I'm not a fighter anymore, Jean. I just don't have the juice. But my kids—lookit this." And she pulls out photo after photo from the last visit, bragging about her family and a recent overnight she had in the trailer.

That is the first of my visits to Lancaster during which Dolly and I pore over school brochures together. She's heard about a college program in Florida, a correspondence course she'd like to take. Maybe she'll enroll in paralegal. Eventually she tells me that in spite of support from her family, she can't get motivated. "Heart problems," she says. "I'm just waiting for the other shoe to drop."

Dolly comes to my college in the early 1990s as part of the outreach program, along with members of the Framingham Eight, women who killed their batterers, many whose sentences were commuted. There in the cafeteria, she steps up to the podium before a crowd of two hundred to retell her story of domestic violence. She explains how she was beaten by one man and verbally abused by others, including Frank, her codefendant. She isn't a murderer, she tells the students, but her sentence is for life. After the talk Dolly and I sit together and eat pizza.

In 1994 I run into Dolly in the hallway at Framingham. "What are you doing here?" I exclaim to the worry etched on her face. I am shocked by her frail body, skin sagging in pockets under her eyes, the blotchy cheeks.

"They brought us back, anyone on a murder charge. The state says we have to finish our sentence here. 'Truth in sentencing,' they call it. Jee-sus."

She shakes her head and tells me about new policies, whereby offenders on a murder charge, having spent years in pre-release, are being yanked back to more secure facilities, often in the middle of the night. The majority of prisoners, she says, face frequent lockdowns, cell searches at midnight, and fewer visits. While college classes are still in place, already gone are arts and crafts, the bonsai tree program that allowed prisoners to learn gardening, and most contracted social services like HIV support groups. "You're holding on by a string," she adds, "just like me."

"I'm sorry," I say, inept, wishing for words.

A guard beckons Dolly back to a line of women, all in jeans and faded workshirts, a far cry from the old days of bright red and orange print shirts, short skirts, and baseball caps. Reluctantly Dolly rejoins them.

"Come see me when you can," I call to her. Looking over her shoulder at me, she disappears into a sea of blue.

Dolly drops in on my classes sporadically that winter and spring. She is often loaded down with Kleenex, wheezing and hoarse. She complains about her asthma and how she can't get proper treatment in prison for her heart problems. She barely glances at the Zora Neale Hurston book that I am reading with my class, *Their Eyes Were*

Watching God, and doesn't ask about plans for the next play. Her hair is almost gray and her skin, leathery and colorless. "I'm afraid I will die in here," she says over and over. I wish I could tell her otherwise.

One spring evening Dolly arrives with a letter. "It's from my lawyer. She's trying to get my sentence commuted. Will you help me?"

I look at the envelope. It bears an official-looking stamp. "How did this happen?"

"There's no other way out for me, Jean. Vivian, that's my lawyer, says that I might not get the medical treatment I need unless the governor realizes prison is killing me and gives me a pardon."

"What do you want me to do?"

"Nothing illegal," Dolly jokes. And then, more seriously, as she pulls her chair closer to mine, "Just call her. She'll tell you what to do." She hands me the letter. "I would've had her send it to you, but I couldn't find your address at the college."

"Of course I'll write for you," I say stuffing the letter back in its envelope.

I hear about the results in the mail in 1996, a year after my last play at Framingham, a year after community college classes have gone the way of other programs that aren't "tough on crime." Dolly's lawyer writes: "As you most likely have already heard, the Advisory Board for Pardons has unanimously determined that Dolly's request for a hearing be denied at this time . . . Dolly thanks you from the bottom of her heart for caring enough about her to assist her in her petition by putting your feelings down on paper." I cry when I get that letter.

A year later a Christmas card arrives in the mail from Dolly. Under a night sky Santa and Rudolph kick up their legs and sing, to the surprise of the other reindeer, "There's NO business like SNOW business like NO business I KNOW. . . ." Inside, above the inscription, "Wishing you the sudden inspiration of the season," Dolly writes that she will finally see the parole board in 1999, and reminds me how often she thinks about the plays we put on behind bars. I know she must have jumped through hoops just to get that card to me.

In 1999, fifteen years after Dolly first came to Framingham, we sit in a room that looks like a miniature courtroom in a downtown office building—her brother; her son; Elizabeth, her daughter, all grown up; a nun who formerly worked at the prison; a friend from the ministry who's visited; and myself, her teacher—all waiting to testify for Dolly. The mood before she enters is tense, anxious. The family of the neighbor Frank killed sits on the other side of the aisle, presumably to say that Dolly does not deserve parole.

When Dolly enters, lumbering side to side, in handcuffs, her face is an ashen mask, almost as if the life has been tromped out of her. Her teeth are clenched and old—some look rotten—and her gray hair is pulled into a long simple braid that hangs down her back. She's done her best to be attractive. I can imagine her in her cottage, saying, "Jee-sus, is this all I have to wear?" and putting on the long-sleeved white over-blouse and pressed pants. She sits next to a prison official in a row of chairs along the side of the room, and immediately she asks about talking to her family. She sounds like herself, the same gravelly voice with the ends of her sentences going up, dropping the last *g* in words that end with -*ing*. The official tells her that she is unable to have any contact with her family today.

She watches the five members of the parole board—mostly ex-cops—file in, some with coffee or fruit punch in bottles, chatting among themselves. They are as detached and cool as I expected, and Dolly, too, seems to have little reaction when she sees them.

Dolly's handcuffs are removed, and she is told to sit with her back to us, facing the board. Her student lawyer, from a local university's free legal aid program, sits with her. The first part of the hearing is like another trial, in which Dolly answers question after question about her involvement in Frank's crime, question after question about her values and personal life. One of the men verbally pushes and prods Dolly, trying to trip her up. Another pursues her relationships before Frank (Mr. T): "You've had four husbands, is that correct Ms. H?. . . . And this Mr. T, he wasn't one of them, was he?" Even the black woman on the board, on whom I had put my money for compassion, doesn't give Dolly much of a break. "How did it come to be that Mr. T wrote a letter for your commutation hearing? Did he just happen to recant his trial testimony? . . . We don't hold much stake in his credibility, as you can imagine."

Dolly is strong and certain, repeating her story as she understands it, a battered woman who was afraid to call the police and report Frank; she is not the killer nor the advocate for murder. "Doesn't Dolly deserve to be one of the two percent who earn parole on their first time before the board?" her lawyer asks. Yes! I want to yell out.

A woman near me leans across the sister and whispers, "Men who commit murder sometimes get out in eight years."

The board members turn their attention to Dolly's conduct in prison. Her current lawyer tells how she's won a major humanitarian award this past year at Framingham, nominated by officers, and spells out her achievements in prison, from college to the battered women's group, from her involvement in religious activities and personal counseling to her artwork. In her prison career, the lawyer says, she has earned only four disciplinary reports. It seems that the board is not moved. One of the women questions Dolly about how she happened to yell at another inmate and wonders if this bespeaks an anger problem. The youngest member, a fresh-faced male, says, "Do you see yourself as a battered woman rather than a murderer?" When Dolly says yes, he says, "I have no more questions."

Finally her family testifies. "She's been my rock and my support," says Elizabeth, weeping. "Even in prison." Dolly's brother says that if she gets parole, she can live with him, and he holds back tears when he says that he owes her big-time—she took care of him when they were growing up. The woman from the ministry says Dolly has always been civic minded. I talk about her as a student, a talented writer, and an actress, and as someone who cares about others. The sister says that Dolly is one prisoner who has always "prayed for her enemies." We all offer to help her when she gets out.

The murdered man's father says that witnesses agreed that Dolly caused the attack, and that she stood by the tree and was there at the scene of the murder. Finally, at the end of the hearing, a board member asks Dolly, "Why should we release you?"

Dolly answers, "I have so much to give to my community. I have to make up what I owe my family. I'm a good person now. I deserve to go. Before I die I want to go home."

Three weeks after the hearing, I receive a postcard from Dolly.

> Dear Jean,
>
> Thank you so much for speaking at my Parole. You were wonderful. I wish we could've talked. Thank you. My hands are in pain. I hope to hear from the Parole Board soon.
>
> Love,
> Dolly
> P.S. God bless you and yours.

I read it in my study, sitting under a portrait Dolly created with pieces of colored paper, a picture that I bought at a prison art show years ago, when theatre flourished at Framingham. It shows a woman, half her face covered by bars, with a fractured vine growing out of the side of her head. Only one half of her seems to exist; the other part is hidden. It is a picture that reminds me that life behind bars is not what it seems.

Two weeks later I get the call. It is January 2000, and Dolly is going home.

Epilogue

The world we created at Framingham Prison was a world that felt free. Outside the classroom were officers, reprimands, demands from families, and all the constraints of prison. Inside we talked of books and told stories. The women laughed at their frailties and cheered each other's successes. It was a place where they came to feel safe and to be challenged creatively, a time when the prison did not intrude. For the hours that we gathered each evening, a space behind bars became, in a sense, sanctified.

In this space I felt the presence of an enormous generosity, a power that came from the women working together to create something larger than themselves. The women made room for each other, and they made room for ideas and for feelings. Whether in Program Room 2, the gym, outside in the yard, or even—as happened one year—in the chapel, the women came to class to get more deeply into themselves and more deeply outside themselves.

Art at Framingham was a catalyst for transformation. However, art does not produce the kind of metamorphosis that is easy to measure. Change happens when we read a book and a character sits inside us and becomes a role model. It is what occurs when we put aside our troubles, jump onstage to take part in an improvisation, and within moments find we are lost in the world we're creating. It is not always behavioral. Sometimes change is as small as an emotional half smile, the tilt of a head in response to a new idea. But in my prison classes, drama enabled the women to believe more deeply in their abilities, to use their risk-taking natures in ways that were productive and to create a community where they valued themselves and others.

The creation of art also allowed the women to take their sorrows and to transform them into something beautiful. Rhonda, plagued by loss and a sense that she could never regain her old self, kept her sadness at bay. But she had always wanted to be a lawyer, and onstage, she got to be one. She went back to her educated roots and, reintroduced to a world she had left behind, saw she could choose it again.

To step into the shoes of another, to take on another persona, also enables the actor to see a new way of being in the world. It is "such stuff that dreams are made on." When Dolly played Antonio and Lysistrata, she discovered that her dreams of being a hairdresser were only part of the picture. She was, onstage, the initiator, the powerhouse. The stage helped her to withstand what she felt were the prison's attempts to crush her at every turn. Now that Dolly is out, she plans for the apartment she will have someday and the car she wants to buy, and realizes that she deserves these things and doesn't have to hook up with a man to own them.

At Framingham I witnessed that getting inside a character can also create change in the human spirit. When Rose, whose life had little in common with that of an immigrant Jew, played Shylock, she found that she could feel his pain because she poured herself into the part. His words became a vehicle for her inner feelings, and portraying Shylock empowered her. I saw Rose go from being an outsider in the group to being accepted. She earned respect from other inmates and ultimately from prison officials as well, and in spite of the HIV that isolated her, she found a place for herself inside the prison. If she had not developed full-blown AIDS, who knows what Rose could have become.

When Bertie left Framingham, five plays after she entered and with a degree under her belt, she could speak English with more fluency. Through the discussion of great texts and of new ideas, she became less myopic in her view of the world. She stepped outside her daily life, not to deny her crimes but to reflect on them. She began to see herself as someone who could be educated and thus as someone who could lead a better life. Shakespeare has said that art is a mirror in which we see ourselves, but art is also a way to envision what we can become.

Sticking with something over a long period of time, not giving up on oneself, was a keystone to our theatre program. Over and over the inmates would write about what they had not completed—school, relationships, jobs. They never imagined getting through anything, much less a classical play, without backing out. Theatre gave them the chance both to study a part and then act it, to go through the many steps of fear and refusal along the way, and in the end, to overcome obstacles. They began to foster community, learning life skills such as cooperation, analysis, and perseverance, skills that many didn't have before incarceration. As Kit said, writing about what she gained by being involved in plays: "There is a different way of living other than the streets and I want to learn more about that kind of life." Exposure to great texts also allowed Kit access to a part of our culture that she had shunned and that she felt had shunned her. Now out of prison, Kit has not returned to crime.

Mamie could never go back to being a nurse after her horrific arson, but as a prison student, she was accepted. She was a caretaker too, certainly of greenery and sometimes of Bertie, and even before she got sick, of our intentions to do a play. Plus, Mamie was a good writer and her insights about literature affected others deeply. The inmates trusted her. Whatever these women had been in the outside world did not sentence them in our classroom.

Plays have potential to uplift the human spirit. Putting on spiffy clothes may not make the man, but wearing a billowy dress when you are used to prison blues or carrying a briefcase when you constantly are called by your last name does make a difference. Exit the dreary prison world when you are onstage in high heels, twirling a parasol and singing. Enter a world where you can be anyone you choose.

And so, with all this possibility for healing and growth, it struck me as a grievous mistake for the government to decide that higher education and ultimately the arts had no place in prison. When Representative Bart Gordon pushed through an amendment to a federal crime bill in 1994, most community college and public university classes behind bars were wiped out across the country. In spite of the fact that higher education was endorsed by correctional educators and by many prison officials, and in spite of the fact that education has been shown to significantly reduce recidivism, the Omnibus Crime Control Act eliminated Pell grants for prisoners, the funds that enabled incarcerated students to complete college classes.

After 1994 I hung on, as Dolly had foreshadowed, continuing my program at Framingham for another year. I hung on because I knew that women in my drama classes were affected just because they were able to take part in the classes. Even though each night they went back to a world that took away all individuality, and even though they struggled daily with their thoughts and feelings, their involvement in literature and learning changed something inside them.

I hung on because these women had come to be part of my life. When I walked across the compound, on my way to class, I always felt I was at home. I'd wave to women standing in line for meds and greet officers heading to do Count. I felt I belonged. On a personal level, I knew that if I didn't teach at the prison, I would miss the women and their sisterhood.

Under the auspices of Boston University, a private institution with funding that didn't depend on Pells, I directed my last play, *Arsenic and Old Lace*, in 1995. It was an experience unlike any I'd had before. Parts of the play were censored by the administration; every bobby pin I brought into the prison had to be counted. By then officers checked in on rehearsals. The prison did not allow families to see the play and inmates to fill playbills with their own words. The theatre project was now an afterthought.

I went back into the prison to teach the next year, advertised for students, and talked it up with the handful of inmates I knew from previous classes, but with no community college program, there were too few students eligible for a class in play production. Thus in 1996 my ten-year program ended.

It is a travesty that women behind bars remain the forgotten minority. Without programming that understands the needs of women, they will return to our society with no more skill or knowledge than they had before committing their crimes.

Many things should be done to improve conditions for women in prison. Certainly men guarding women can lead to sexual abuse;

health care for female offenders is still problematic; the lack of significant job training seems to promote recidivism; mandatory sentences for drug possession have put many women behind bars who would be better served by treatment programs; and the fact that only one prison for women exists in most states makes visiting always difficult, particularly for children. But my expertise is on what can be done in the classroom. My to-do list includes:

- Return higher education to prisons by reinstituting the Pell grant program.
- Institute arts-in-prison programs, following the successful model begun in California, where actors, writers, visual artists, and others go into the prison and create art alongside the inmates.
- Allow prison libraries to accept books from donors. Many do not.
- Return the system of "Good Time," which gives prisoners time off their sentence in exchange for being involved in programs that promote education.
- Support research on recidivism for those involved in education and arts programs.
- Offer college classes to correction officers in order to humanize the relationship between prisoners and guards and decrease tension around classes for inmates.
- Following England's lead, use theatre techniques in prison for anger management, self-esteem building, and job training, and allow potential employers to interview and hire women after viewing performances of plays.
- Decrease funds for building new prisons and increase funds for prison programming and for alternative sentencing.

Charles Ogletree, professor at Harvard University Law School and founder and director of the Harvard Criminal Justice Institute, once observed that we cannot make up our minds whether we want to rehabilitate or punish offenders. Today we seem to have cast our lot for punishment. But from my experience, punishment alone is a dead-end road.

The value of an arts program for female offenders is that it takes up where punishment leaves off. It enables real choice and real change and forces inmates to reckon with themselves and others. It is not sugar-coated; it is not an easy way out. It makes demands, values hard work, and celebrates challenge. The value of an arts program for female offenders is that it is good for the women because it allows them to grow, but it is also good for the rest of us. With education we can enable female offenders to leave prison with more assurance that they will be better citizens.

The world I want to live in does not lock up women and throw away the key. It does not make laws based on "an eye for an eye and a tooth for a tooth." It is a world where prisoners can transform their lives through the beauty of the written word, through the music of a line of poetry, and through an idea that soars through prison bars and endures forever.

Author's Note

In order to convey the world of women in prison, I decided to center *Shakespeare Behind Bars* on a core group of inmates. To disguise the prisoners I have changed their names, created several composite characters, reconstructed dialogue, and rearranged some incidents in terms of time. I've also changed the names and masked some of the details of the officials, officers, and other personnel I encountered during my years at Framingham Women's Prison.

Although I directed eight plays, including *Lysistrata*, *Waiting for Lefty*, *Rapshrew (The Taming of the Shrew)*, *The Scarlet Letter*, *Simply Maria*, *Madwomen of the Modular (The Madwoman of Chaillot)*, and *Arsenic and Old Lace*, I chose to focus on *The Merchant of Venice*. Work on that play most clearly revealed the Shakespearean drama of the inmates' lives and the prison themes I saw over my entire ten years.

This book does not necessarily express the views of Framingham. It is a story based on my experience teaching and directing plays with the women. All changes were made to tell the truth as I saw it.

Acknowledgments

Heartfelt thanks go to those who made this book possible: to my agent Anne Edelstein, who believed in the women almost as much as I did; to Diane Higgins, my inspiring editor, and Patricia Fernandez, wordsmith extraordinaire; to dear Sondra Upham, who nurtured every word of this book; to all the other careful readers who were with me at one stage or another: Pam Bernard, Judith Page Heitzman, Alan Breitbart, Marjorie Agosin, Connie Trounstine, Shela Pearl, Jacqueline Steiner, Fran Karp, Grady Hillman, Susan Llewellyn, copy editor, and mentor Pat Hoy; to my writers' group for putting up with endless rewrites; to David Huddle and my workshop peers at Stonecoast; to Middlesex Community College for its continued support over the years and specifically to audiovisual wizards Roger Miller, Nancy Curll, Matt Olsen, Noreen McGinness, and Rob Sakey.

Deepest appreciation goes to those who made my work in prison possible: to Larry Scott and Barbara Helfgott Hyett for getting me the job; to Kent Mitchell for backing me every step of the way; to

Gail Reimer and David Tebaldi at the Massachusetts Foundation for the Humanities for much more than grant funding, and to the MFH scholars who advised, Joyce Van Dyke, Larry Rosenwald and Marilyn Halter; to Duxbury and Nashoba Regional High Schools for grants and the Prison Issues Project; to Miriam Gilbert, Tony Hill, members of the Royal Shakespeare Company and the National Endowment for the Humanities for providing me with the opportunity to learn so much about Shakespeare; to people who took chances for me, including Amy Singer, Walter Silva, Judith Montminy, Massachusetts senator Daniel Leahy and state representatives Pat Jehlen and Barbara Gardner; to the administrators, educators, correction officers, recreation officers, and other personnel at Framingham Women's Prison, who not only helped with plays but believed in programming for female offenders; to the amazing Jeanne Kinney, the Boston Costume Company, and the goodhearted Priscilla Damon, Elaine Killea, Vicki Crocker, and Cathy Lubar, without whom I could not have succeeded behind bars; a special thanks to all the women in prison who allowed me to enter their lives and, ultimately, changed me.

Thanks and thanks and yet again more thanks go to those who offered me courage: to Mangiit Khalsa, my temple havarah and loyal friends; to my loving family, particularly my sister, Peggy, and my brother, Phil; and most especially, to my husband, Robert Wald, the man who grounded me and gave me wings.